THE GREATEST HUNT IN THE WORLD

Books by
George Allan England

ALIBI
CURSED
DARKNESS AND DAWN
KEEP OFF THE GRASS
POD, BENDER & CO.
THE AIR TRUST
THE FLYING LEGION
THE GIFT SUPREME
THE GOLDEN BLIGHT
THE STORY OF THE APPEAL
THE WHITE WILDERNESS
VIKINGS OF THE ICE

The Greatest Hunt in the World

by George Allan England

(originally published as VIKINGS OF THE ICE, being the log of a Tenderfoot on the Great Newfoundland Seal Hunt).

with an introduction by Ebbitt Cutler.

Tundra Books   Collins Publishers
Montreal   Toronto

Printing History

Vikings of the Ice   First Edition   1924
The Greatest Hunt in the World   Hardcover   1969
                                       1st Paperback   1969
                                       2nd Paperback   1975
                                       3rd Paperback   1981

ISBN 0-00-211616-2

Printed in Canada

To The
STRONGEST, HARDIEST AND BRAVEST
MEN I HAVE EVER KNOWN

THE SEALERS OF NEWFOUNDLAND

This Book is
Admiringly Dedicated.

INTRODUCTION

What role has seal hunting played in the subconscious of New-foundlanders? No one can read this book without wondering: is there a connection between the Newfoundlander who accepted meekly for centuries poverty, illiteracy, exploitation, irresponsible government, and almost-chronic economic depression and the sealer who each year immersed himself in a blood bath unequalled elsewhere in the world? Certainly, "not for mere gain do men endure such miseries as the hunt entails... it is their annual carnival", and the sealer who wears the hearts of baby seals in his belt like trophies and who drags a live seal back to ship on his gaff to amuse his shipmates is scarcely comparable to the abattoir worker in his detachment or the lab technician in his disinterest. The importance of England's work lies not, however, in the questions he causes us to ask about Newfoundlanders, but about man himself. For if the seal hunt has been little and inadequately written about, its significance has been studied even less. Historians, anthropologists and psychologists will find this work invaluable primary source material.

* * *

One searches vainly to find a parallel elsewhere to the Newfoundland seal hunt.

There are similarities to the buffalo hunt: the Eskimo resembling the Indian in the economical use of his prey, and the white seal hunter re-sembling the white buffalo hunter of the last century whose wanton slaughter left the western plains so strewn with carcasses that, it is said, the stench hung over them for decades. No similar evidence of waste remained to haunt the sealer, for the sea is an impeccable scavenger, it took its revenge otherwise, and one of the most poignant of outport sayings is: "The sea is made of mother's tears".

Like the buffalo, the seal herds have also been threatened with extinction, and although opinions differ on just how close to extinction the Atlantic seal is, measures have grown increasingly stringent in recent years to protect it, as both the time permitted and the limit to the catch are reduced.

But one must not force the comparison with buffalo hunting, for the Newfoundland seal hunt was unique. It was the largest hunt in the world, having involved as many as 14,000 men annually with kills ranging as high as 700,000 animals. Also, mainly because of the opening phase during which the whitecoats, or baby seals, are slaughtered, the strangest.

Largest, strangest, greatest! This account by an American journalist of the 1922 hunt aboard the Terra Nova under Captain Abraham Kean is the only detailed day-by-day eyewitness description of it ever written. George Allan England's purpose was quite simply to "tell it like it was" and his very avoidance of moral judgment stimulates the reader to ask the questions.

Cruelty and violence are the most widespread and difficult problems of our world at this moment in time. Admittedly, they have always been with us, but the urgency to understand them has never been more desperate. We need a Newton, a Darwin, a Freud to develop a new explanation of man's need to be violent, to provide a theory of cruelty that will assist us in managing, or redirecting, the drive.

Of the many disservices that Nazism did in its atavistic attempt to destroy the humanity in man, one of the most insidious has been the encouragement of the idea that cruel men and kind men are of two different species. Perhaps there are men who are only cruel and men who are only kind, pure devil and pure saint, but they are so rare as to be almost irrelevant. Most men are both cruel and kind, and the concept of the cruel monster as a creature apart is useless and diversionary, for it helps us avoid examining cruelty in ourselves.

We do not wish here to exaggerate the cruelty of the seal hunter, nor equate cruelty to animals with cruelty to fellow human beings. We are aware that sealers of the stature of a Captain Kean would consider nonsense the idea that seal hunters are cruel per se. And that is precisely why the evidence of this book is so valuable. The hunters we get to know here are so patently human, more courageous and more patient than most of us. to be sure, but nonetheless recognizably similar. And we get to know them very well, as we eavesdrop on their prayers, their stories, their songs, their jokes and even their dreams. In the hunt alone do they change, and by the hunt they are changed for brief moments. What do these moments of truth mean to them, and to the rest of us?

When the men first rush out onto the ice "mad with bloodlust", the hunt becomes a savagely primitive activity. No one reading England's description of the opening phase (his chapter Baptism of Blood surely ranks with great hunt passages in literature) can doubt the obsessiveness of it. From the beginning of the trip we—like England—have been waiting and watching for this moment and when the cry of "Whitecoats" at last electrifies the ship, we feel along with England that "even though I had no purpose to imbrue my hands in blood, my heart was drumming a bit, my temperature rising. For now the kill was close upon us." The contrast between the men, running, "like mad demons, yelling", and the white-coats looking like "great white or whitish-yellow pincushions" passively awaiting the attack, is extreme.

This is neither sport nor work in any accepted meaning of those terms. There is no challenge, no risk, except for the rare occasion when a mother seal turns to protect her young. Seal hunting is dangerous, but none of the danger comes from the baby victims. Nor does it have the discipline of work. Is this why we feel here something profoundly im-bedded in our subconscious is being released or enacted?

What do the baby seals represent: pure, white, helpless, innocent?

Two aspects of this kill are particularly interesting: one — and this applies more to seal hunting than to any other hunt — is the quantity of blood that flows, "a seal is so extremely bloody, and that blood so ex-traordinarily hot". Blood is everywhere, inescapably dramatic. "Spots of red dotted the ice-scape. Fwitt-fwitt-fwitt sounded the whetting of blades on steels, and rather horrifically the hunters wiped their dripping knives on their sleeves. Their clothing and the ice, alike, blossomed vividly. Their hands looked like gloves of red that dripped. All about pelted carcasses sprawled, twitched, steamed in crimson pools...... Over plaques of virgin white — white no longer when they had passed! — the hunters came labouring shipward. Long, wavering lines of colour formed; they joined to broader roads, all converging on the Terra Nova. Crimson trails, these, such as no otherwhere on earth exist". And later, on board, "the oppressive, sickly sweetish smell of fresh blood drifts up. Bright cascades flood the deck. Milk spurts, mingles with the blood, gutters away".

England writes in his prefatory note: "I have minimized a good deal of the hunt to make it at all acceptable to the reading public". If this is puzzling, since he seems to tell us quite, quite enough as it is, one example taken from his files indicates the nature of his "minimizing". It is a photograph, left out of the original book but included in this edition, of Joe Stirge with the caption: "Here he is standing on a pile of sculps of seals he has shot. The men grease their boots by wading in warm pelts".

The passages concerning blood are frequent and integral. Less obvious, but perhaps even more significant, are references to the hearts of the seals. How common the practice of cutting out seal hearts was, I cannot say. England has brought us one flabbergasting photograph of a young sealer — is the expression on his face prideful or sheepish? — wearing them in his belt like trophies.

In another passage, England writes: "Billy, our plump good-natured store-keeper, carries a dangling, blood-dripping carcass aft, to stow it in a barrel. His free hand holds a pulsing seal's heart. 'Look, dere's life in de heart, yet!' he smiles to me and passes on, to return in a couple of minutes with a pipe in fingers incarnadined. A fortnight ago, I could not possibly have dreamed anything like this; and now, at times, I ask myself: 'It is real? Or is it only, after all, an amazing dream?' "

Why this preoccupation with the heart? There is no reason to eviscerate a seal. We know that in primitive societies, warring tribes tore out the hearts of their conquered enemies to show their mastery. But why did the sealers do it?

I would not dwell on this did it not add further evidence to England's opinion that the economic factor was a minor attraction in seal hunting, at least so far as the individual sealer was concerned. If economics alone were involved, he writes, the seal hunters would nearly all have done better to stay home and not enter into violent competition for berths that "are as eagerly sought after as if some great prize were conferred instead of merely the chance for week after week of hardship and peril". He quotes an earlier writer: "The annual seal hunt of New-foundland is one great carnival of cruelty and bloodshed". The carnival idea is not inappropriate. After the drabness of the long Newfoundland winter, the spring hunt must have indeed seemed an escape to adventure. But boredom is no more satisfactory an explanation of the passion of the hunt than is economics.

When the first volume of THE BOOK OF NEWFOUNDLAND was compiled in the 1930's, its youthful editor speculated as to why Newfoundland has not produced creative writers. It is a question that has occurred to many visitors to Newfoundland, myself included, for here is a people much given to story-telling, warmly appreciative of song and verse, the turn of a phrase, the aptness of a saying; a sensitive people, re-sembling the Irish more than any other of their European forebears.

But to quote the young editor: "Perhaps the very nature of our struggle, of our methods of wresting a living from nature, has helped to unfit us for creative and constructive effort. It is a fact that for centuries we have lived by killing cod and other fish; by killing seals in the water or on ice, and animals on land; by killing birds, and cutting down trees. Has this developed in us a trait of destructiveness, or narcotized what ought naturally to be an instinct of creativeness?"

The writer of that passage was Joseph Smallwood, the New-foundlander who later led his people in the most extraordinary revolution of this century, and tried to change the nature of their economy so that it would no longer be dependent on destroying.

Killing — or cruelty — as a substitute for creativeness is certainly relevant. But there is more. For all his killing of animals, birds and fish, the Newfoundlander, if one judges from his history, would seem to be less violent than any other North American. Not that he did not have cause. For centuries, Newfoundland was one of the most outrageously exploited countries in the world, by both speculators from across the Atlantic (who arrived when times were not too bad — "good" is far too euphe-misitic a word ever to apply to Newfoundland's economic state — and left the Newfoundlander to survive alone when they were really bad) and by its own ruling classes, who acted as a perpetual drain by investing or spending their profits in London or New York and finally drove the country into bankruptcy in 1933. At that time the government was supported not from taxes on corporations or personal income, but from taxes on imported goods that were necessities for the poorest of its people: twine for fishermen and shoes for children. This preferential treatment, the Newfoundland establishment continued to confer upon itself right up to the time of Confederation (or revolution); I can recall visiting a lawyer's office on Water Street in 1948 where a sign inside the door announced that this was the world headquarters for some 30 firms, all registered there to take advantage of the convenient lack of corporation taxes — at a time when workers' wages were twenty dollars a week, while eggs cost ninety cents a dozen! Through all this the ordinary New- foundlander — the man you meet in all his variety in this book — saw his children die of malnutrition, ravished by beriberi and TB, educated — if at all — in shacks by teachers, the majority of whom as late as the 1940's had not themselves completed high school.

What people laugh at tells us as much about them as what they cry over, and one conversation England reports in the book stands out for the poignancy of both: it is also a superb example of England's ability to record dialogue.

" 'I'm a worn-lookin' man, sir, not in me time. I'm sixty-seven past; an' after a man passes farty, he'm coming down de odder way. I been on ice when it was man-murderin' wid snow. A murderin' time I had, ahl me life, an' I'm gettin' pretty well up wid it, now. I had fourteen little ones, and dem ahl die young cl'ar o' two...... Me hands is ahl crippled wid work, an' not a cent. If de fish fail, ye have to go cuttin' pit props. Here I been workin' ahl me life......an' I ain't got narry penny, sir. Not enough to babtize a fairy.' "

England comments: "Something of the anguish, of his toil-and- death-martyred race loomed in his face", then he continues to quote the old man: " 'De worst blow ever I got, dough, is now that me woman wants me to get her a set o' store teeth. Not as them costs so much, but 'cause if her has 'em, her'll eat a wonnerful lot more, an' I doubts if I can reach to feedin' she.' "

And all through these years of incredible hardship, no violent political protest ever seems to have occurred. While other western peoples were having revolutions, revolts, riots and strikes, Newfoundland- ers endured with unbelievable patience, keeping their kindliness and good- humour and dignity. Violence does enter the Newfoundland story in three ways, none of them political: in the religious strife that only very occasionally burst out between the varying Christian denominations of the island; in the fantastic enthusiasm and bravery with which Newfoundlanders fought Britain's wars; and, the strangest way of all, in the seal hunt. Even the revolution, when at last it came, was oddly gentle. At a time when peoples throughout the world were insisting on the right to self-determination, when new nations were emerging annually, Newfoundlanders followed the lonely voice of Smallwood and voted by a very slim margin to surrender their nationhood and join Canada, whose baby bonuses and old age pensions would at least assure a minimum family income.

The psychoanalyst Karl Menninger in his study of suicide and self-inflicted cruelty, MAN AGAINST HIMSELF, writes that "every suicide is a disguised murder". The reverse would seem to be equally true, that every murder is a disguised suicide. When we hate with vehemence, it is a part of ourselves we hate, and when we kill, we are trying to destroy an unwanted, also often unadmitted and unrecognized, part of ourselves. The sadism of the masochist and the masochism of the sadist are thus inseparably linked.

When we observe the sealers on the hunt, they are not attacking the seals as substitutes for those responsible for all the misery of their lives; they are attacking them as substitutes for themselves. It is their own helplessness, their own innocence, their own meekness that the newborn seals represent.

Would this explain the sudden upsurge of violence in the world at this particular moment in time? Do we not all feel helpless as the baby seals against governments that do not care, institutions that will not listen, and impersonal forces that seem calculated to dehumanize — and quite possibly — annihilate us?

Whatever the explanation (and perhaps the above, like the icebergs that figure so prominently in this book, are but a few visible peaks that announce presence but give no indication of the size or shape of the unseen threat), important clues to human behaviour are in this remarkable work by George Allan England, precisely because his objective in writing it was so unpretentious. He was not trying to write history for the ages, to collect evidence — such as most of the present-day journalists who observe the seal hunt do — to uphold a particular point of view. He neither opposed seal hunting nor favoured it; he was neither sportsman nor abolitionist. He had no axe to grind. Seal hunting involved thousands of human beings in activities beyond the imagination of men who had never participated. It was a great story and he wanted to describe it as faithfully as he could. The extraordinary literary achievement of the book is in this very balance of perspective he maintained between his horror at the blood, cruelty, filth, waste and hardship of the hunt and his awe at the incredible courage, endurance and spirit of the hunters. He does not even draw conclusions: It's as if he is so astounded, he can do no more than describe.

To that task he brought exceptional equipment: the care and respect for accuracy of the scholar, an ear remarkably sensitized to dialect and idiom, the "nose for news", or dramatic sense, of the first-rate reporter... and also, importantly, a camera.

Born in Nebraska in 1877, the son of a clergyman, he was educated at Harvard where as an undergraduate he already displayed writing talent by winning the Bowdoin Prize for a literary dissertation; he was graduated with an A.B. in 1902 and masters degree in English literature in 1903. Curious about the then-far-off places of the earth, he turned explorer-journalist, and from 1919 throughout the 20's his articles appeared in THE SATURDAY EVENING POST, then and up to its recent demise, one of America's leading magazines. Preparation for a series of articles on out-of-the way islands brought him to Anticosti and Newfoundland where he first learned of that fantastic annual rite: the seal hunt. Astonished that the outside world should know nothing about a hunt that had gone on for two centuries, involved thousands of men and hundreds of thousands of animals annually (even the encyclopedias he checked did not mention it), he began the long negotiations that finally resulted in permission to go out with the sealers in 1922.

In getting that opportunity, England knew he was a privileged person: "Observers and writers are not wanted by the seal hunters. Nobody is wanted among those men of blood and iron, in those far and frozen vacancies — nobody who cannot actively take part in the Saga of Slaughter". But he did not know that his account would remain the only detailed eyewitness description of day-by-day life aboard a wooden wall ever to be written. Other books on seal nunting exist, notably Major William Howe Green's THE WOODEN WALLS AMONG THE ICE FLOES that appeared in 1933, but none ever rise above the technical. Green's book actually sounds as if it was written as a kind of officially-sponsored reply to England's book, to change the image created by England's all too vivid and detailed report.

England's interest in dialect, idiom, folklore, songs and sayings adds enormously to the impact of the book. Never has the Newfoundland speech been so faithfully, so effortlessly and so quantitatively reproduced as here. The modern reader may be somewhat repelled at first sight of a page of dialogue where apostrophes indicating omitted letters proliferate, but anyone knowing the Newfoundland accent cannot fail to be impressed by how well it has been suggested without recourse to phonetics, and others will find initial patience more than recompensed by the way the dialogue illuminates the moods.

What indirect speech could ever evoke the following?

"Going swilin, is ye, sir? Me dear man! Ye'll be rale hearty. If y'r luck's in, ye'll take no harm. I was on de Florizel, time she an' ninty-four men was lost. 'Tis a wonnderful fine racket. I'd like to be goin' in collar meself, agin, wid me rope an' gaff an' sculpin' knife! I'd like to year de ole cry: 'Starboard over! ' an' year dem whitecoats bawlin.' I would, so."

Such passages, and the book abounds with them, are worthy of a Synge, a Conrad or a Kipling. When England died in New Hampshire in 1936, he had written ten books and translated two novels from the Spanish, but in his obituary, it was this book on seal hunting that THE NEW YORK TIMES singled out for special mention and compared to Kipling's CAPTAINS COURAGEOUS.

We have not had the opportunity to examine all of England's other books (among them is A DIALECT DICTIONARY OF NEWFOUND-LAND), but we rather suspect that his account of seal hunting is by far his best work. Great events not only make great men, it seems; they also make great writers.

Coming as he does from "a steam-heated apartment in Boston", he approached the hunt much as any other North American city dweller might. It is therefore very easy for us —even forty-five years later — to identify with him, and our initial reaction is likely to be astonishment, too. We share his squeamishness about not wanting to lend his comb, sympathize with his secretive attempts to brush his teeth, and recognize with him the hopelessness of trying to wash. Silly things, perhaps. Certainly of small import, compared with what is taking place around us. But they strike a responsive cord in us, inhibited as we are from childhood by taboos stronger against dirt than against hate. We accept to see it all through his eyes, watch the captain's collar get dirtier, burn our lips on the tea and smell the tobacco, the sweat, and all the other stenches, human and animal; we ride that ship with him until suddenly we are snapped back to reality as we come to the word "nigger". Nothing dates a writer like his prejudices, and the unexpected reference makes us realize that England is not the contemporary man he so often seems, but an upper middle class white American of half a century ago.

This must in fairness lead us to other questions: 1) how typical was this particular trip of seal hunting as it existed fifty years ago, and 2) how much similarity is there between seal hunting then and now?

The trip England took in 1922 under Captain Abraham Kean was not "typical"; it was "model". We are reading about the very best of sealing at the time. Captain Kean was then and remains the greatest sealing captain in history; he had come in more often than any other captain "high liner of the fleet" and this particular year he again takes the record. He also held the record for the biggest single catch ever made: in 1910, he had steered the Florizel into St.John's with 49,069 sculps after having been out only 17 days! He is the captain every sealer most wanted to hunt with, and those who succeeded in getting such a berth were aware of their enviable position. We can imagine that England's presence also encouraged the sealers to be on their best behavior, as they were observed, photographed, sketched and saw notes being taken of what they said and did. We can also further imagine, if this is the best of sealing, how bad it could get on other ships.

As we watch Captain Kean move through these pages, we are observing a champion, and his character as it emerges is a study in the nature of effective leadership. The secret of Kean's power over his men is not so much in his day-to-day behaviour (although the brass collar button and the carefully-folded, though filthy, table napkin become charming badges of authority, and his handling of a malingerer that turns a scared kid into the most ferocious of hunters is among the memorable vignettes); it is in his behaviour in a crisis during the desperate race against a gathering storm to find men lost on the ice at night. If ever I had to lecture on how a leader elicits loyalty, I would read them the chapter from this book on A Touch of Near-Tragedy.

England was impressed in 1922 that Kean had already been fifty springs to the ice and never lost a man; when the already-mentioned BOOK OF NEWFOUNDLAND was compiled in the 30's, The Honourable Captain Abraham Kean, OBE, had been sixty-seven springs to the ice, and wrote the article on what could be done to save the seal fishery in the face of declining herds. He had received his Order of the British Empire in 1934 when, at the age of seventy-nine, he had brought in his millionth seal.

How much has sealing changed in the past fifty years? Greatly.

True, as long as the killing of whitecoats goes on, seal hunting will seem different from all other hunts. But the "mystique" of the hunt is gone, the belief that there is always a single "main patch" of seals; and gone is the wild competitive search to find it. Today, air reconnaissance tells precisely the seals' location (we witness the first attempts at this in 1922). More baby seals are taken today by landsmen, dropped and picked up by helicopters, than by hunters from ships. This spring only one New-foundland-based ship took part in the baby seal hunt in the Gulf.

Much of the danger is gone, too. Where once the wooden walls were floating tinderboxes as the sculps ran to oil and one spark from the casually-handled gunpowder could turn them — as is suspected to have happened in the case of the Southern Cross which disappeared with all 173 men in 1914 — into funeral pyres, today the ships that take part in the hunt, whether in the Gulf or on the Front, are steel, radar-directed and with refrigeration that can keep the sculps intact for months.

Finally, the presence on the ice today of journalists, humane society observers and government officials inhibits some of the brash cruelty toward the baby seals that once existed; it even seems possible at this writing that world indignation over the slaughter of the whitecoats for use as fun furs may bring that phase of the hunt to a complete stop within a few years.

But in 1922, the hunt was challenging, dangerous, dirty and brutal, and this is the record we have before us.

In backgrounding the reader to appreciate it, we want to point up another character that dominates the story: the ship. The Terra Nova is the most romantic ship of this century because it is inseparably linked with the last heroic voyage of Robert Falcon Scott to the South Pole.

Built in Dundee, Scotland in 1884, she first came to Newfoundland the following year and was acquired by the Liverpool House of Bowring Brothers in 1898.* In 1903 The British Admiralty bought her for a very special mission. Scott had left on his first expedition to the Antarctic in 1901 aboard the Discovery, and when he failed to return on schedule, it was decided that the Terra Nova, as "the roughest and toughest icebreaker to be had", should be sent to rescue them. She so impressed Scott on the return trip that in 1909 when he was preparing for the crucial expedition where he would attempt to be the first man to reach the South Pole, he decided that the Terra Nova was the ship he wanted, and although by then she was back in Newfoundland sealing, he arranged to purchase her. On June 15, 1910, she sailed from Cardiff, carrying the polar expedition.

When she returned to that port three years later, almost to the day, she brought Scott's diary telling of his arrival at the Pole after four months of unbelievable hardship pulling sledges on foot only to find that the Norwegian explorer, Amundsen, had reached it by another route a month before, almost effortlessly, using dog teams. But it was a failure that impressed the world as few successes have done, for the diary entries during the next two terrible months, describing the futile struggle against starvation and cold and the courage and mutual kindness with which each of that little group faced death, were to make it a precious testament to the possibilities for greatness in the human spirit.

The following year, the Terra Nova was back sealing in New-foundland under Bowring ownership as we find her in this book, but the aura of Scott remained with her to the end of her days.

It is interesting that, just as England marvelled in 1922 that the force of the ice did not break the ship apart as it fought its way through the icefields, so exactly had Scott marvelled thirteen years before when he wrote: "The ship behaved splendidly – no other ship... could have come through as well... As a result I have grown strangely attached to the

---

* For details on the early career of the TERRA NOVA, I am indebted to M.S.E. Hope, director of Bowring Brothers of St. John's who transmitted information from the company's former secretary, Mr. B.H. Shears, and to the story of Scott's last trip by Apsley Cherry-Garrard in THE WORST JOURNEY IN THE WORLD, 1922.

Terra Nova. As she bumped the flows with mighty shocks, crushing and grinding a way through some, twisting and turning to avoid others, she seemed like a living thing fighting a great fight".

In 1922, she seems, except for her fight, fallen very far from her high estate as a ship of heroes. England describes her at the start of the hunt: "This veteran of the ice is dark, dingy, coal-dusty, and dirtier than anything I have ever seen; with snowy decks, rusty old hand pumps, a stuffy and filthy cabin, extremely cold; tiny hard bunks, a dwarf stove, a table covered with smeared oilcloth; everything inexpressibly dreary and repellant"; but that is comparative elegance to what she is to look like after four weeks of sealing.

Reading of how one could have kicked a hole in her boilers, how she was "condemned", that she "should have been broken up for junk years ago", readers should be appropriately impressed to learn that not only was she to go sealing again the following year, but for another twenty years. Then in 1943 she was chartered during World War II to carry supplies and equipment between Newfoundland and U.S. bases in Greenland.

I have an account of this last voyage of the Terra Nova in letters from Captain Llewellyn Lush of St. John's, the man who was her last master. He wrote me a few months ago:

"I left St. John's on May 28th, 1943, with a mixed cargo of cement and lumber. My crew were all from Newfoundland. I did not see land until I made Greenland, and discharged cargo on the southwest coast. I was ordered to go on the east coast with cargo for the weather stations. I had some American personnel on board, working men, and had American convoys between the ports. All along the coast there was ice and numerous icebergs of the largest kind and dense fog most of the time. Back again to the south west, I encountered heavy ice, and in order to keep her off the land and get the old ship through the heavy arctic ice, I twisted her stern out below the water line. She started to leak somewhat, but the pumps kept against the leak and I got the old ship back to a place called Julianehaab.

"Divers went down and reported the old stern was gone right to the main keel. The divers patched the stern as much as they could. There was no dock to put the ship on, and I was ordered to proceed to St. John's.

"I left Greenland at 8 a.m. September 13th. At that time in the morning there was a moderate breeze, but as the day increased, it kept freshing to a stiff breeze, and the Terra Nova commenced leaking badly. Sometime the same evening of the 13th, she was leaking so badly the pumps could not keep against the water coming through the damaged part that the divers had patched up. I sent out the SOS about 9 p.m. the same evening. The sea was getting rough at that time. Shortly after that the water got up to the fires, the dynamo went and the pumps got choked. We were finished with regards of trying to keep any water out of the old ship.

"There were some naval American ships around in that vicinity. About midnight I saw a ship blinking her dot and dashes. All we had was a flashlight to answer back. When the rescue ship got closer it was too rough, the sea too high, to be taken off. So I told the captain of the ship I would try and hang on until daylight. In the meantime the operator would keep in touch with him all night by flashlight.

"At daylight all the crew got off by dory; yours truly and the first mate were the last to leave. Her decks were awash. She went to the bottom shortly afterwards. I saw the old ship sink. The rescue ship stood by until she went down and my crew and I were taken back to Greenland again to await convoy... I would not like to be master of the old Terra Nova again at her age with a full load and a heavy sea running."

Captain Lush adds proudly of that final trip: "I sat in the same chair at the table that the late Capt.Scott sat in his last voyage to the Antarctic."

Apart from such memories, very little remains of the Terra Nova. When she returned to Cardiff in 1913, her figure-head, a draped female, was removed. It is today in the National Museum of Wales.

Ironically, a far different fate awaited the Discovery, the ship Scott had used on his first expedition. After periods of idleness and an extensive refit in 1923, she did research work in Antarctic whaling grounds until 1931 when she was laid up in honourable retirement in the East India dock in London. She now serves as a recruiting ship for the Royal Naval Reserve. Last summer I was one of the 300,000 who visit her annually. As I walked through the beautifully refurbished cabins, with the mahogany and brass shining from navy spit and polish, I thought of the Terra Nova disintegrating from old age and work in arctic waters, and I wondered which ending Scott would have the more admired.

Readers might also be interested in the fate of two other ships that appear in this account. The Viking burned at sea in 1931, with the loss of 28 men, plus another who died soon after being rescued from an ice floe. The Eagle — the boat on which England returns to St. John's at the end of the trip — was actually the last of the wooden walls to survive. About fifteen years ago, her owners took her outside St. John's harbour and set her afire with the sea-cocks open.

I would like here to make particular mention of Mrs. Blanche Porter England Churchill, the widow of the author, for her help in supplying us with the original photographs from her late husband's files. We hope her pleasure at seeing this work back in print equals our pride in presenting it.

Montreal, Canada,   Ebbitt Cutler
March, 1969.

PREFATORY NOTE

THIS book was written as the result of some six weeks' experience on two sealing steamers, the *Terra Nova* and the *Eagle*, out of St. John's, Newfoundland. Its purpose is to fill a gap which has persisted astonishingly long. For many years the Newfoundland seal hunt has been the greatest hunt in the world, and that so little has been written about it is a mystery. The world as a whole knows little of it. Even many Newfoundlanders of the "better" class remain comparatively ignorant of this gorgeous epic of violence, hardship, and bloodshed. In so far as personal observation can avail, I have tried to record and portray all the essential features of Newfoundland sealing.

So profound has been the neglect of the subject that the world's leading encyclopedia, in its article on the seal fishery (so-called), mentions Alaskan sealing and some trivial operations in the Arctic around Nova Zembla, but does not even speak of Newfoundland sealing! And yet the Newfoundland hunters each year kill vastly more seals than all others in the world combined. The conclusion is obvious that a book on the subject is badly needed.

Some who have read certain of my articles on sealing already published have accused me of exaggeration, of "not knowing what I was talking about." The fact is, I have minimized a good deal of the hunt to make it at all acceptable to the reading public. That none of my critics has ever been "to the ice," or so much as set foot on a sealing vessel, rates such objections at their true value.

23

I should like here to make the following acknowledgments and offer thanks to these Newfoundlanders: Mr. E. J. Penney, for having rendered my trip possible; Mr. Eric Bowring, for having granted me permission to sail on the *Terra Nova;* Captain Abraham Kean, of that ship, for his unfailing kindness and courtesy; Captain Edward Bishop for his goodness in bringing me back to port on the *Eagle;* P. K. Devine, H. F. Shortis, and the late James Vey for invaluable information on the dialect and traditions of Newfoundland; Levi F. Chafe, for his labours in supplying me with innumerable facts and statistics. Many other Newfoundlanders, including the crews of both vessels, have similarly laid me greatly in their debt for large-hearted willingness to enlighten me, a stranger. I also extend thanks to Blanche Porter England, my wife, for her help in arranging my materials and working on the manuscript of the book.

I acknowledge the kindness of the Boston *Globe* for having allowed me to use certain verses of mine which originally appeared in its pages; also that of the *Saturday Evening Post* for having given me permission to adapt to book form portions of my articles: "The Greatest Hunt in the World," "Vikings of the North," and "King Cod."

This book is, in a way, a composite work. Many hands and brains have been instrumental in bringing it to completion. To all of them my gratitude is profound. That the book may not unworthily convey their message is my sincerest wish.

GEORGE ALLAN ENGLAND.

CAMP SANS SOUCI,
BRADFORD, N. H.
September 28, 1923.

CHAPTER I

PRELUSIONS

St. John's, Nf.,
Feb. 9, 1922.

Sealing trip arranged on *Terra Nova* with famous sealing captain. No passenger accommodations. You will be quartered with three junior officers. Be prepared to rough it.

Edward J. Penney.

THIS telegram of good hap put a spur to my preparations and set me packing my warmest kit. It arrived as the climax to long negotiations, for this matter of getting permission to go out with the sealers of the Newfoundland fleet had been rather a business.

Observers and writers are not wanted by the seal hunters. Nobody is wanted among those men of blood and iron, in those far and frozen vacancies—nobody who cannot actively take part in the Saga of Slaughter.

"Three junior officers" sounded encouraging. The words seemed to couple with brass buttons and a smart little stateroom.

On my northward trek aboard the *Rosalind* I acquired a little advance information about seal hunting that just a trifle moderated my ideas concerning brass buttons and smart little staterooms.

"Not much real danger of your ship sinking in the ice a few hundred miles from land," a St. John's merchant explained, "though once in a way it does happen. The sealing ships are built of greenheart and oak, to meet the ice pressures. Of course," he sank the barb, "we've had some pretty appalling disasters. Sometimes sudden blizzards catch the men on ice, far from the ships, and wipe them out by the dozen and the score. I should advise you not to wander more than two or three miles from the *Terra Nova*, especially if the barometer's down."

"Oh, I don't think I will—not over three or four miles, anyhow," I hastened to reassure him.

"Well, then, the chances are you'll come through alive. That is, if your ship doesn't burn or blow up. Seal fat is enormously inflammable, and the men are wonderful careless with fire and blasting powder. As a fact, not one of our sealing ships is fit to go to the icefields. They're all worn out. The *Terra Nova* was condemned years ago. I've heard it said that a good strong man with a pair of stout boots could kick a hole in her boilers anywhere. Still, I don't want to make you worry."

"Certainly not!" I agreed, relighting my pipe, which had gone out.

"As for the men—oh, you'll get along with them all right. Rough? Well, rather! But treat them free and easy and call them 'Uncle,' and you'll have no trouble. A hard crowd, that! Most of them never wash or shave, on the sealing racket. They butcher all day and come in off the ice a reek of blood and grease; but you won't mind that. Dirt doesn't hurt them and neither does hardship. Why, they're half seals themselves! They'd die with decent treatment. The tough trip just fattens them. They come back with hides four inches thick—and so will you!"

Thus indeed it befell. I did!

The next Newfoundlander to encourage me—a carpenter—had been sealing many years.

"Goin' swilin', is ye, sir?" he asked. "Me dear man! Ye'll be rale hearty. If y'r luck's in, ye'll take no harm. I was on de *Florizel*, time she an' ninety-four men was lost. 'Tis a wonnerful fine racket. I'd like to be goin' in collar meself, agin, wid me rope an' gaff an' sculpin' knife! I'd like to year de ole cry: 'Starburd over!' an' year dem whitecoats bawlin'. I would, so."

The *Rosalind* ran into icefields soon after leaving Halifax and had heavy bucking nearly all the way to St. John's. As the ship advanced, long cracks fled away at lightning speed, like watery serpents. Shifting, grinding pans broke, slid, interlocked, smashing and slopping.

Weary as one presently becomes of ocean icefields, one's first impression is of majesty and beauty. This first ice that I saw ranged from luminous gray to blinding white. It looked like a brobdingnagian mosaic, interspersed with vast lakes and leads all wonderfully a-sparkle in the sun. Each pan was edged with a raised border of slush, making of it a vast Victoria Nyanza water-lily leaf of ice. And how the floes hissed, how they grumbled, as the ship—her steel plates booming—shouldered them aside!

The cry of "*Seals!*" in mid-afternoon of that day, February 25th, brought all hands on deck. Sure enough, there they were, six or seven huge, fat fellows resting on pans, off our port bow. The Captain called them "currier hoods," or scattered outscouts of the hood nation, and added that it was most unusual to find seals in this latitude. He comforted us by explaining that it harbingered tough ice conditions ahead.

Officers fired on the seals and made some brilliant hits —of ice pans. None of the seals paid the least heed either to ship or bullets, and very presently we left them all astern.

Gales and snowstorms soon swallowed us; ice blocked us; we had "de divil's own fruz" for some three lively days. But at the end, we found St. John's shivering along her curve of icebound harbour, behind her mighty cliffs.

One could write half a book about St. John's; but what we're after now is seals. So I shall record nothing but what bears directly thereon.

Very directly bearing thereon was Bowring Brothers' establishment; for Bowring Brothers is a famous firm of seal hunters, and the *Terra Nova*, on which I was to ship, belonged to them.

I found Bowring Brothers' place of business comfortably old-fashioned, quite in the British tradition, with open fires, ancient desks, a one-handed English 'phone, maps, samples of seal oil, pictures of steamers, lots of "clarks," and the general atmosphere of 1848. Eric Bowring extended a cordial hand and reaffirmed his permission for me to go "to the ice."

He introduced me to Cap'n Abraham Kean, scheduled to command the *Terra Nova*. The Cap'n looked a splendid type of seaman and a famous ice master: ruddy, hearty, hale, with shrewd blue eyes, a grizzle of snowy beard, a bluff manner, the vigour of a man of fifty, for all his seventy years, and a full half-century of seal killing to his credit.

"The Admiral of the Fleet," they call him in Newfoundland. And well he deserves the title, for he has come in "high-liner" more often than any other captain, and knows the icefields as other men know their palms. Many decades he has commanded ships plying into the Far North, "down the Labrador," and has never lost a passenger. A skipper in the Royal Naval Reserve, a former member of the House of Assembly, a writer and lecturer, he understands more about seals and sealing than any other man alive. I thought myself fortunate in being assigned to his ship, and so indeed the event proved.

My optimism faded somewhat as, in the bitter cold, transfixed by the slashing wind, I betook myself to the snow-sheeted wharf behind the Bowring establishment; penetrated narrow, white-washed runways already populated with sealers, and went aboard the *Terra Nova*.

There indeed for the first time I beheld her, one of the nine scarred, time-bitten old ships of the 1922 hunt. The harbour was grinding white with heavy ice. Beyond, snow-swept hills soared to a pitiless gray sky of storm. Gulls volplaned and screamed. Wharves swarmed with types of men unknown to me, strange men, ominous and wild, with never a friendly glance or word for the outlander. Winches cluttered and roared; steam drifted.

As I set foot on board rather horrific prospects dawned. Earlier visions of brass-buttoned officers and cozy cabins faded. My notebook records:

As far as being a slave ship is concerned, this one looks the part. The Australian convict ship *Success* is luxurious by contrast. This veteran of the ice is dark, dingy, coal-dusty, and dirtier than anything I have ever seen; with snowy decks, rusty old hand pumps; a stuffy and filthy cabin, extremely cold; tiny hard bunks, a dwarf stove, a table covered with smeared oilcloth; everything inexpressibly dreary and repellent.

A few minutes' exploration, with nobody offering me a word of welcome, showed me I had no sybaritic cruise ahead of me. Dejection gripped me on my way back to the hotel. Why not be frank about it all and say I had a bad case of cold feet?

Walking along Water Street, St. John's busiest thoroughfare, I had good opportunity to see the kind of men

I was to ship with. For already the town was filling up with "greasy-jackets," *i. e.*, seal hunters.

Along the soppy sidewalks they were clumping, girt with belts and sculping knives. The pavements clicked under the tread of their huge "skinny woppers," made of sealskin which had been tanned by Esquimau women—tanned in the primitive way, by being chewed. I marvelled at the thick soles of these waterproof boots: soles studded with "sparables," "chisels," or "frosters," as various kinds of nails are called. Open-coated, with rough trousers held up by "hippers," or nails doing duty for suspender buttons, groups of these hardy Vikings gathered at corners or stood peering in at shop windows that displayed sealers' outfits or stuffed whitecoats. By the men's glances at the city dwellers or "carner boys," no love seemed lost between them. The city folk looked equally disdainful of the "bay noddies," or outport men.

And here just a word of explanation and—if necessary —of apology to the reader. In the course of this narrative it will be necessary to dip heavily into dialect. The sealing gear, clothing, food, the hunt, the weather, all of life in fact, as named by sealers, will involve strange, unfamiliar words. The Newfoundland language is one unique and apart from any other. And without using it, no adequate picture of the seal hunt can be painted. Rest assured that I shall try to explain every term; and if you forget the meaning, you have but to turn to the glossary in the Appendix.

The seal hunters were having high jinks in an environment to me distressing. It makes a difference whether one has reached St. John's from the south or from the north; from a steam-heated apartment in Boston or from a tiny little "tilt" (hut) in some frozen outport jammed on stilts at the bottom of a fjord riven deep into a heaven-scraping cliff.

The hardships some of these men suffer even before they reach St. John's and "sign on" would kill the average American. For days before the sailing of the fleet, hundreds of them pile into St. John's. Some walk all the way from home and some travel on the partly snowed-in, irregular streak of rust that Newfoundland calls a railroad. Many of them walk forty or fifty miles to reach even this rust, braving blizzards that scourge and flay. They carry their pitiably meagre equipment in ditty bags. A lot of them, in the spring of 1922, got marooned at a place called Gambo, on the railroad. They had to sleep in cold empty cars there for two or three nights, till an engine could get through and pick them up—second-class cars; and if you have ever seen a second-class Newfoundland car, you know the worst. But none quit and none died. They came along eventually and all "signed on," and thought themselves lucky to get the chance.

For just as the sealing captains feel the most bitter rivalry about the size of their kill, and are consumed with anger and jealousy if they fail to get a ship, so the "common hands," too, enter into violent competition for berths —all to the benefit of the firms, which get the big end of the stick.

The captains "give out tickets" and so do the officers; and these tickets, entitling men to berths, are as eagerly sought as if some great prize were being conferred instead of merely the chance for week after week of unbelievable hardship and peril, with only a few dollars' reward at the end. "Room berths" are berths given out by the firms. These are greatly desired; firms and captains alike keep their retainers in true feudal style by judicious distribution of the privilege of toiling and perhaps dying, quite as in the good old mediæval days.

In "The Tenth Island," by Beckles Willson, you can read: "The annual seal hunt of Newfoundland is one great carnival of cruelty and bloodshed." This explains why the seal hunt every spring grips the city and the whole island with excitement. The carnival spirit, indeed! Not for mere gain do men endure such miseries as the hunt entails. No; it is the annual carnival. And greatly do they revel therein. What dazzling tales the hunters have to tell back home of the wonders in St. John's; of the tumult and fury of the hunt!

Now their rough and high-pitched voices were loudly sounding through the town. Many of them were sucking unseemly pipes. All seemed "up in chair" (cheer), at the wondrous sights of the metropolis.

Powerful, great fellows, with frost-reddened faces cracked and seamed by gales and unthinkable cold, they paraded through dingy streets, half-awed by the splendour and immensity of St. John's. Raw laughter echoed. Some looked "half-slopped," or worse. For though Newfoundland is a dry island, there seems to be a leak somewhere.

We shall soon put out to sea, I promise you, but as we shall never have another chance to take a peep at typical old sealing cap'ns, let us not ignore the opportunity.

There they sat, two of them, and a good "mate" (pair) they looked. Side by side in the hotel office, in armchairs, they took their ease for one day more. They had walked part of the way to St. John's, and driven part, over frozen bays and snowdrifted headlands, facing black squalls that howled with screaming fury. And now they rested, those ironclad sons of the ice, "chawing" and indulging in very defective target practice at the brass cuspidor, the while they held counsel together in a language strange to hear.

Ill at ease they seemed amid such luxury, all bedizened in their best bibs and tuckers, even unto knitted mufflers and violently crimson and purple silk kerchiefs sticking from the breast pockets of their decent Sunday suits.

One was a little chubby round man, round faced, round headed, and bald, who, when he walked, had a round, rolling gait. He had a round belly and round short legs encased in wide trousers that hung and wrinkled like the hide of a once fat elephant, now grown thin. Very short, his feet were, and his boots shone as brightly as boots can be made to shine, which is very brightly indeed.

The other, who over his black suit wore a tremendous greatcoat with a heavy astrakhan collar, had been built on huge, rough lines; massively blocked out, partly hewn from the oak and then left unfinished. Both were huge-shouldered and hard-fisted sealing cap'ns. And clean, painfully clean. Cleaner than they were destined to be again, for many a long week.

In raw voices they talked of their entertainment at Government House, where His Excellency the Governor had graciously received all the cap'ns and had wished them a bumper trip and a safe return.

Next day I bought a ditty bag, plenty of tobacco, ice-goggles, some first-aid equipment, raisins, peppermints, limejuice, and smallwares. I also acquired, after due medical formalities, a quart of medicine to fend me against the arctic winds when icebound out yonder in the Unknown.

More sealers kept piling into town, with bags and battered blue sea chests. Some, having no tickets, were coming "on prospect," with the hope of picking up a berth at the last moment. The wharves were crowded with expectant hunters and supplies going aboard. Humble as dirt were the jobless. One felt sad that fine types of men like these should so entreat for labour.

Some of them were now "cropping," which is to say, getting their equipment. At a bare little shed, the sign: "CROP HERE" directed them where to get their tobacco, knives, boots, or whatsoever they most desired. The sealing companies allow each man $9 worth of goods. If no seals are taken, the companies stand this as a dead loss. If seals are taken, each man is charged $12 for his "crop." The chances of no seals being taken are about those of one's not seeing stars on a clear night.

I pushed aboard the *Terra Nova* once more. Everything was a gorgeous confusion of screaming winches, of shouts and orders, of coal in deck pounds; of inverted and nested dories that bespoke possibilities of a quick getaway in case of trouble at the icefields; of flat wicker baskets, gaffs, and crudely hewn oars and long iron-shod "stabber poles."

Men were shouldering boxes of biscuit, stacks of pails, barrels of flour, birch brooms, granite-like slabs of cod, and ominous green corrugated-iron canisters of powder. It gives one a turn to see men handling powder while smoking pipes, but Newfoundlanders don't mind. Many rifles and boxes of cartridges were also going aboard, eloquent of grim business.

From the forward galley a brown-faced man with a huge coffeepot was peering. Later I came to know him as "De Blacksmith" or "De Standin' Man," alias "Ole Glass-eye." Behind him on a rusty range bubbled a "copper" of some gray and greasy concoction, with blobs of something in it. I penetrated the fo'c's'le, or "top house," and found a V-shaped, whitewashed space; a tiny cracked bogey, or stove; low beams; narrow, dark, and dirty bunks in tiers; dim lamps gleaming.

Everybody viewed me, "de quare fish of a 'Merikin," with curiosity as lively as my own. Nobody seemed at all

Old Glass-eye, alias de Blacksmith, one of our cooks.

unhappy at the prospect of weeks aboard such a ship. On the contrary, an air of pleased expectancy permeated all groups of these whiskered, wrinkled fellows, whether lounging on the wet decks all a muck of coal and water, rolling

casks, slopping about the stenchful wharves, or sitting on snowdrifted barrels and boxes. Some were drawing water at an icicled faucet near the cropping shed, bringing "sluts" (kettles) aboard, and brewing tea. Smoke from funnel and stovepipes began to look like business. And all this hard, chill, barren misery seemed a treat to these expectant men!

Presently I saw the *Viking* sail. The wharf was jammed with those departing and those come to say farewell. A sprinkling of wives and sweethearts coloured the scene, and more than a sprinkling of men who had been too liberally prescribed for and who were making things noisy. Little boys and big dogs threaded the throng. Adventurous younglings larked about, or climbed high up the ratlines of a neighbouring ship. Some of these young hopefuls excited cheers and laughter by shouts of:

"Whitecoats to starburd! Patch o' swiles to port!"

The *Viking's* whistle blared. A tug fussed and broke ice at the stern. Exultant yells sounded from the topmast barrels of other ships. Ice pans crashed and thudded. Jumbled phrases filled the frozen air:

"Us'll soon be gadderin' de pans now, b'ys! Soon 'aulin' 'em aburd o' dis un!"

"I'll bring ye a gad [string] o' fippers, Liza!"

"Hello, me son! First I t'ought it was y'rself, an' den I t'ought it was y'r brudder, an' now I see 'tis needer one o' ye!"

"Well, b'y, I hopes ye get a whippin' good bill [pay]!"

"Dis un'll soon be burnin' down in de patch, now!"

"Her'm 'aulin' off, now! Dere she go!"

Last tag ends of gossip flew back and forth and affectionate abuse therewith, such as Anglo-Saxons use the wide world over.

"G'wan, ye flamin' scut o' hell! Y'r forepeak's full o' water!"

"G'wan, y'rself! Ye got a face on ye like a smoke-box door—like de back of a crab!"

"If I 'ad a face like you, be God, I'd walk back'ards!"

A couple of stowaways were routed out from under dories and summarily fired ashore. It's the worst of bad luck for a sealing vessel to get away without at least one stowaway—it is "jinked" or "hoodooed" from the start; yet when such are found, they are always heaved off the vessel, if possible.

Cap'n Bartlett bawled lively orders from the bridge.

The screw thrashed, the hawsers were cast off; and away into the harbour ice backed the stout old *Viking* amid shouts and yells of "Good luck!"

Packed from stem to stern—for every sealing steamer goes out cruelly overcrowded—she swarmed with weather-beaten, patched, excited, greasy men. Along the rails they crowded, up the ratlines, in the rig, atop the dories. Hands, hats, caps waved, but few handkerchiefs. I don't suppose sealers carry handkerchiefs. I never saw one use such a thing.

The *Viking* turned, pointed her jib at the Narrows, and heaved slowly under way. One of the fleet, the first, was gone.

And to-morrow would be the *Terra Nova's* turn—and mine!

CHAPTER II

THE WORLD'S GREATEST HUNT

BEFORE we venture out into the ice, it would be well, I think, to form some general idea of just what the seal hunt is and where it takes place, and what the Atlantic herds are and how they live and migrate.

The Atlantic seals are very different from their Pacific cousins. The latter have long, curving flippers and commercially valuable fur. They maintain breeding colonies on St. George and St. Paul, and on some of the other islands of the Pribilof group, and seem more distinctly land mammals than their eastern congeners. The seals in our aquariums and parks, and those that in vaudeville acts bounce rubber balls from their noses and perform diabolical music on drums, are usually Pacific ones. No self-respecting Atlantic seal could be induced to enter an orchestra.

Wise men have classified about fifteen species of seals; but for our present purpose we are concerned only with the "harps" and the "hoods." Let us get the Latin out of our systems at once, and name them respectively the *Phoca groenlandica* and the *Cystophora cristata*.

Their pelts, save in the case of the "cat" or still-born harp seal, are usually valueless as fur, the hair not being "fast." The great value of the sculps, or pelts, is due to the thick layer of pure white fat, and to the extremely high grade of leather manufactured from the skin.

The Esquimaux first discovered the worth of this skin.

They make skin boots, tobacco pouches, bags of various kinds, and many another useful article out of this excellent leather. The Newfoundland seal hunters bring their skins to St. John's every spring, hundreds of thousands of them; and there the skins are peeled from the fat. The skins are sent to England to be worked up into leather. The fat—much pleasanter to read about than actually to smell—is ground, steam cooked, refined, sunned in glass-roofed tanks till it becomes a pure, white, tasteless and odourless oil. And that's a miracle, no less; for if anything in this world doesn't remind one of the roses of Gulistan, it's seal fat.

A good sculp will often have three inches of solid white fat adhering to it. Many are the uses of the seal oil derived therefrom. My Lady Dainty's costliest soaps and perfumes often contain seal oil; and by chance her purest Italian olive oil holds a good percentage that came from the frozen North. The finest of illuminating and lubricating oil, too, is a seal product. Perhaps the same Lady Dainty oils her sewing machine with the product of the icefields. She may wear fine boots made of seal leather, or carry a handbag of the same. Purses, bicycle saddles, cigar cases, harness, bindings for books are all made from seal leather. The Chinese at St. John's, I am told, pluck out the seals' whiskers to make brushes of them. Then there are other uses; but enough! Next to codfish and its products, seal oil and skins give Newfoundland her greatest source of marine revenue. The value of oil and skins exported in 1921 came to $248,422 and $147,935, a total of $396,357—a very considerable amount in a country as poor as that.

The Colony's prosperity hangs largely on the annual hunt. A bumper "fishery," as they call it—for Newfoundlanders insist that seals are fish!—feeds thousands of hungry mouths ashore. A failure brings misery in its train. The price of fat fluctuates sharply. During the war it went up to $12 per cwt. for young seals, $9.40 for "bedlamers," and $9 for old seals. It is now down to about $4 for "whitecoats," or young seals, and perhaps $3 for bedlamers and other older seals.

An average old bitch harp will weigh from 135 to 150 pounds. The old dog harps will go from 200 to 280. The hoods bulk much larger. Big, stupid creatures, some of the old dog hoods will on occasion crowd the scales close to 900. The hunting season begins soon after the young are born, for the reason that the pups are easy to catch and kill, and also because the "young fat" brings higher prices than the old. The pups can be gaffed or batted. In many cases the wary old ones have to be shot, and ammunition costs money.

The open season is from March 15th to May 1st, or till some weeks after the young have rolled and "scrobbed off" their protective white covering, and have "dipped"— that is, plunged into the sea.

The sealing steamers are owned by a number of firms, and all aim to hit the young fat as early as possible and to keep killing young seals till these have disappeared, after which they must needs go after the older ones. One or two ships usually go "to the back," which means into the Gulf of St. Lawrence. The others all go "to the front," or northeast, into the Atlantic ice pack drifting down on the Labrador current. A few thousand seals are sometimes killed by adventurous men working offshore on the drift ice. In 1922, for example, as one old sealer told me: "De landsmen made a scrabble from shore, an' got about of ten t'ousand, w'iles dey was passin' alang." Some are taken in shore nets, while migrating. But the vast bulk of the hunt is carried on by the regular St. John's fleet.

Old-time wooden ships they all are, using both sail and steam, and often carrying 160 or even 180 men apiece. Some crews are smaller; but 150 is a fair average. Built of greenheart and oak, massively timbered and with iron-sheathed bows, these dauntless ships in charge of ice masters incredibly bold and skillful, slog out into the icefields. They operate for five or six weeks between the Newfoundland and Greenland coasts.

An enormous area is worked over. Day after day, week after week, the ships—sometimes close together, more often out of sight of one another—grind, crash, shudder through the ice; blast their way through it with bombs; drift with it when nipped; free themselves and struggle on against every possible obstacle and hardship that Nature can fling against them.

And ever they are killing, ever icing-down the precious pelts. The only limit to the kill is determined by luck, skill, and the capacity of the ships to carry fat both below and on deck. Coal, living space, everything is sacrificed to the fat; sometimes even life itself, as Newfoundland only too well knows.

The seal hunt is without any question the greatest in the world, not only in number of mammals slaughtered but also in point of perils from ice, blizzards, fire, explosion, drowning—a whole catalogue of hardships that only Newfoundlanders, and of these only men from the northern bays, can possibly endure. The ice will nip and sink a ship as easily as a nutcracker smashes a walnut, if pressures develop just right. Then there is to be considered the breaking of shafts and propellers and of labouring, outworn engines, as has so often happened. Add to these the possible explosion of boilers long since condemned. It may have been an explosion that caused the *Southern Cross* to vanish without a trace. Never was there anything like the bland indifference of the sealers to the fire menace. Their methods of handling fuses and blasting powder are, to say the least, startling. Also, seal oil is about as inflammable as gasoline, and is almost impossible to extinguish, once it gets a fair start. It not only burns like mad, but it chokes and strangles its victims with thick black smoke. And it is everywhere, above, below, on a sealing steamer. Such a ship well on fire becomes a hopeless case.

The place of the hunt depends on how and where the vast annual migration of the harps and hoods happens to run. In a general way the herds are slaughtered on and among the icefields that drift down from Greenland and the Labrador, finally to melt on the Banks or thereabout. Get the idea clearly in mind that the harp and hood are migratory animals. They pass their entire lives in enormous cycles of flux and flow, extending perhaps 2,000 miles north and south each year. The Pacific seals may have a wider swing; I do not know. The Atlantic seals at all events range fully 2,000. Their northern terminus seems to be Baffin Bay or even farther up, in Smith Sound; their southern is about 44°. Thus they live almost always in arctic waters, for their migration is so timed that only for a little while are they ever away from that beloved element. Seals have to live on ice or in cold water. Even a mild winter distresses them greatly.

The details of the migration are hotly debated, and to some extent unsettled, but its general outlines are pretty well established.

Two great Eastern seal-nations are known to exist: the Hudson Bay herd and that of Baffin Bay. Whether both harps and hoods live in Hudson Bay I cannot tell; but certainly the Baffin Bay herd is rich enough in both.

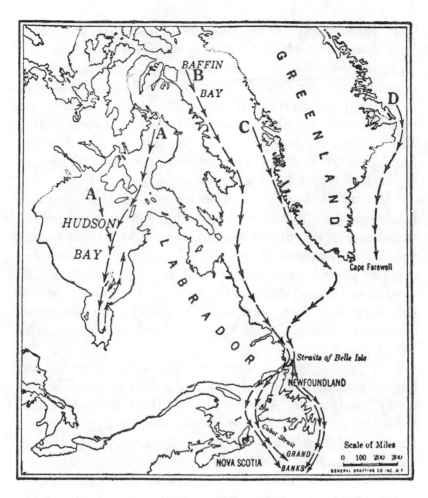

A. Hudson Bay herd, not hunted commercially. The migration is north and south up and down the Bay.

B. Harps. Summer home in Baffin Bay. Winter fishing found on the banks. Migration divides at Straits of Belle Isle, part passing down to the coast of Newfoundland and part through Gulf of St. Lawrence and Cabot Strait.

C. Hoods. Summer home in western coast of Greenland. Winter fishing found on banks. Migration divides same as B. But hoods are always to seaward of harps. This entails a crossing over of the "strings" of seals, in Straits of Belle Isle.

D. Comparatively unknown body of seals on eastern coast of Greenland.

43

The two species, though they never mix, are motivated
by the same wandering instinct, which drives them in a
vast, never-ceasing ambit of travel; the largest movement
of animal life, by far, of any in the world.

In the case of the Hudson Bay seals, the migration
swings—so I am told—back and forth between James
Bay and rather indeterminate regions up around Baffin
Land, Cockburn Land, and Lancaster Sound. The trek
of the Baffin Bay herd is better known.

"Herds," perhaps we had better say, for the harps and
hoods occupy different quarters and even when migrating
together rarely come to close quarters. Both these species
are strictly pelagic. Very little if any at all of their life
cycle is passed on land. They have reverted from the
condition of land mammals very much more to life in
the open sea than their cousins on the Pacific coast,
which establish rookeries and have their young on rocky
islands.

In a general way of speaking, the headquarters of the
harps lies along the western side of Baffin Bay, while that
of the hoods is on the eastern, along the Greenland shore.
Only the young of the two species occasionally associate
together; the old ones are mutually exclusive. Here is
a rough outline of how the herds spend their year:

As autumn begins to nip the seas to ice in Baffin Bay,
the gigantic herds heave into motion. The "making" of
the young ice is their dispossess notice, evicting them
from their summer home. Let us conceive of the migration as beginning with the southward move, anywhere
from September 20th to the 1st of October. The herds
migrate at night, taking it easy; swimming ten to twenty
miles a day. Remember, seals are air-breathing mammals,
and for them to be caught in solid pack ice is fatal.
Twenty minutes is about the limit of time that they can

remain under the ice without coming up to breathe. True, the Church in Newfoundland has ruled that seals are fish, so that even the most pious Newfoundlander can eat seal meat on Friday or during Lent; but in this case, as in so many others, clerical rulings and the facts of nature run counter to each other.

To resume the migration: the harps keep on down the Labrador coast. "Up" the Labrador, Newfoundlanders call it, "up" meaning south, and "down" signifying north in their speech. They pass Quiripon, Labrador, about November 1st, coming down in a long string—millions of individuals, probably—while at the same time, away off to eastward, the hoods are moving down the Greenland coast. About the 20th of December, the hoods turn southwest from Cape Farewell and cross over to join the harps. One of the most curious facts in nature is this almost symbiotic association of the two species in migration. No other mixture takes place; the two species never interbreed. They seem to be biologically true species, not varieties. The hoods' sense of location must be marvellously developed; for without fail, in about three months, they will turn again toward Cape Farewell, shedding their coats on the way and resting after their exhausting travels. Some sealers claim that part of the hoods are scattered and do not migrate with the harps, but of this I know nothing.

The harps cling to land as much as possible, if they can manage to escape heavy ice during the early part of their voyaging. They keep a quarter to half a mile at sea, and are called "inshore" seals; but if any danger or obstacle threatens, they beat away promptly from land. At this stage they are lazy and love to bask. But the ice is always at their heels—their "scutters," rather. On the southern way they hunt and fish, till ousted by the "slob" or new ice. They are thin at this time of year; later they fatten for the return trip.

From the end of November till the 1st of January when they are passing Battle Harbour, the ice relentlessly comes along after them. A good index of their rate is furnished by the fact that from Cape Walsingham to Belle Isle is 840 miles, and that the herd takes about sixty days to make the distance. Note this fact, too, that although heavy ice would destroy them, they must always keep near ice of some sort. Seals cannot drink salt water. They must have ice to suck—or so the wise ones say. How they manage in the summer when away from it a while is one of the still unexplained mysteries.

At the Straits of Belle Isle a curious movement takes place. Part of the harps and hoods pass through the Straits and down the Gulf of St. Lawrence. Oddly enough, the hoods that go into the Gulf are usually shorter and stouter than those that keep to the Atlantic.

Here the two species must for a while be pretty closely associated. No one understands the reason of what happens now; but in the Straits the "skeins" of harps and hoods cross each other. By "skein" is meant the long string in which the herds migrate. Thus, though the land now lies to the eastward of the Gulf herds, the harps are still closer to shore than the hoods. It almost seems as if the hoods had elected themselves guards for their cousins, always keeping two or three miles to seaward of them. It cannot be that the hoods stay farther at sea because of greater timidity. On the contrary, the hood is rough, surly, pugnacious, very different from the peaceful and confiding harp.

Some of the Gulf seals apparently go no farther south, and whelp near the Magdalene Islands. Others, seldom hunted, whelp around Anticosti. But the major portion seem to keep on down, passing through Cabot Strait, where again the relative positions of the hoods and harps are reversed. These eventually reach the Grand Banks, the St. Pierre Bank, the Banquereaux, and even Sable Island— probably the farthest southern limit of the migration.

Here they join the Atlantic group which all this time has been working down the "Front." The two nations live and feed together on these fishing grounds for a while, playing havoc with various food fishes, especially the cod. Anybody who knows the voracity of a seal can imagine what a million or two of them will do to our fish supply. Levi G. Chafe, the world's greatest sealing authority, estimates that the seals dispose of *three million codfish a day*, to say nothing of other kinds.

As spring draws near and the pack ice begins to be riven loose, the inescapable call of instinct summons the mighty herds to turn back and once more make their northing. Part of the seals return up the Front; others go north via the Gulf. They start north in the latter part of January and the first of February.

Working north, they meet the ice, necessary for them to whelp on. They mount the ice, and about the end of February give birth to their young, the pups or "white-coats" so eagerly desired by the hunters. February 28th is called "the seals' birthday," and the accuracy with which practically all the young harps are born within a day or two of that date is one of the most amazing phenomena of nature.

All over the ocean, then, to the northeastward of Newfoundland, as well as "on the Back," young seals will be lying about the first of March. The total area covered by them amounts to thousands of square miles of icefields, anywhere from close ashore to hundreds of miles away, depending on the urge of winds and currents.

Some of the seals are scattered; some lie in immense patches. These patches, especially "the main patch," form the seal hunters' goal. There is supposed to be a "northern patch" and a "southern patch," but discussion about this is endless and sterile. The main fact of importance is that whitecoats and young hoods—which shed their white jacket in the whelping bag and are not white at birth—are swarming by the hundreds of thousands some two weeks before the legal date for the open season on seals—March 15th.

The young Atlantic seals have to be born on ice and, moreover, on a special kind of ice, called "whelping ice." They are helpless as kittens; and for about a month have to be nursed and cared for like any other young mammal. Thus the young and their mothers—truly devoted mothers—with the dog seals more or less in attendance, "ride the ice" for a month or so. And this proves their undoing as we shall most abundantly see.

I have read that young Atlantic seals can take to the water and fend for themselves the very day of their birth. Nothing could be more absurd. Perhaps the Pacific seal babies are thus gifted. I have never hobnobbed with them; but I have made the personal acquaintance of Atlantic seals aplenty, and more feckless infants than whitecoats and young hoods never drew the breath of life. Many a young seal I have seen fall into the water, only to scramble out in hot haste, and as for feeding themselves, they simply can't do it.

The whelping ice has to be low and more or less open, preferably with plenty of "leads" through it—leads or bays, of course, being stretches of free water. The old seals cannot dig or maintain their "bobbing holes" through heavy ice. Each female has only one pup a year. Twins are extremely rare. Even so, and with the "young fat" as the chief object of the hunters' zeal, the herds seem to be increasing; though Doctor Grenfell thinks otherwise. The hood pups are considerably larger than the harps and show a dark slatey blue colour. In a fœtal condition they also have a white coat; but they lose this before birth. A whitish belly is all the trace they bear of the protective covering which would be of incalculable value.

The young harps, better outfitted for life, keep their snowy dress for about a month, till nearly ready to "dip" and go on their own. Just why the hoods, born on ice like the harps, are not similarly protected makes a very baffling speculation. Perhaps in some remote age the young hoods were born with the white coat; but later the hoods took to bearing their young on land; later still they reverted to the ice and evolution has not yet fully readjusted them. All this time, both harps and hoods maintain a real family life, though the hoods keep in single families while the harps are given to congregating in masses. But once the pups are able to look out for themselves—say about the 1st of April—it's good-bye for ever. The old seals abandon them and go away to ride the ice, grow a new coat, and have a general jollification as they swim north. During the month on the whelping ice the whole seal nation has been drifting about in a predominatingly southern direction; but now the northward journey begins again.

The hoods leave the ice during the first week in April, and swim so vigorously that they get back to Cape Farewell in June. Both they and the harps, after abandoning their pups, strike for land, they take "the inside water" and work north as rapidly as possible. By the middle to the end of May, the harps are once more moving up the Labrador coast, catching capelin and other fish in the

bays and fjords. The water is open in Baffin Bay by
June 15th, when the great body of seals return from their
nine months' excursion to the Banks.

And the abandoned youngsters, what of them?

They have unerring instinct to guide them. Off
the pans of ice they slide and, like homing pigeons,
head for the northwest, if harps; for the northeast, if
hoods.

Greenland calls the latter; Baffin Bay, the former.
Fifteen hundred or 2,000 miles of icebound, stormy seas
intervene. That matters nothing. Small, weak, un-
tried, and facing unknown enemies of shark, fox, polar
bear, and, worst of all, man, the young "beaters" none
the less "bow the current" for home. No longer suckled
by tender mothers, they have to hustle for themselves.
Just how the young hoods live and feed till they reach
shoal water in Greenland, no one seems to know. The
young harps—"rusty-jackets" now that they have
"rolled off" the white coat—make for land, get into shallow water, go to the bottom, and probably supplement
their diet of such fish as they can catch with clams and
mussels.

If the weather holds fine, they delay their starting, as if
unwilling to undertake the long and perilous hegira.
But, as Newfoundlanders say, "come a drap o' rain on
deir tails, an' dem away."

The harp beaters are of a pearl-gray colour with brown-
ish spots: engaging little creatures, able to do their fifteen
miles or so a day among the ice floes or under them. For
the most part they travel in herds. Unfortunately for
themselves, they like to rest on pans and bask in the spring
sunshine; and there thousands meet death.

Eventually, however, the majority, showing a truly
marvellous courage, enterprise, and strength, reach their

chilly home in the north. They arrive in Baffin Bay about the end of May or the first week in June.

But once there, no rest awaits them. The brief summer of open water soon passes; and with the coming down of the ice away they must all fare again, for the Banks. And so on and so on, *da capo*, world without end.

In addition to the harps and hoods, a few "square flipper" seals are sometimes sighted by the Newfoundland hunters. These are larger, but so few in numbers as to have no commercial importance. They also migrate from the north, and whelp near Newfoundland; but apparently the young are not born until well into April. These young square-flippers weigh from 160 to 180 pounds when only a week or two old. The old ones are solitary in their habits, and are rarely seen in pairs or groups. *Phoca barbata* is the wise ones' name for the square flipper; but as he can't be profitably turned into fat or leather, who cares? The same applies to the rarely found ring seal. *Phoca nispida*. Year after year, harps and hoods are the sealers' standby.

I have heard rumours of other seal migrations not yet accurately determined. A seal nation has been reported on the east coast of Greenland; but its movements are not known. For this let us be thankful. At least one branch of the family is safe—for the present. Some old sealing captains say there are big "patches" that whelp away up along the Labrador and Greenland coasts without ever coming south. Such seals are rumoured to go back into the remote north, before Baffin Bay opens for navigation.

The experience of the American exploration ship, *Polaris*, in 1873, seems to bear out this report. Heavy ice threatening to crush the *Polaris* about 1,200 miles north of Newfoundland, the crew unloaded her stores and abandoned her. Part of the crew was drifted away by the Labrador current, and for some weeks—until picked up by the sealing ship *Tigress*—lived on young seals. As this was in March, certainly these youngsters could not have belonged to any part of the herd making the usual southern migration.

CHAPTER III

NORTHWARD HO!

THE day arrived on which Cap'n Kean bade me go aboard—March 8, 1922—and with my ditty bag, a battered suitcase, and no few misgivings, I embarked.

In the cabin I found men lying, smoking, sleeping in unlikely places. The steward—a thin, worried-looking chap with a sandy moustache—stretched out on a hard bench beside the table, was snoring like the Seven Sleepers of Ephesus. The cabin looked a bit more cheery than erstwhile. A coal fire roared in the glowing bogey, and a certain warmth had begun to dispel the clammy cold. Nobody had much to say, but everybody stared. Who and what was I, anyhow, and what did I want? A writer, eh? "My glorianna, dat'm a quare t'ing, dough!" It passed comprehension—was "fair beyend ahl." Why the devil should anybody want to write—or read—anything about "de hard rowt o' swilin'?"

So I was heavily handicapped from the start, and found myself accepted only under suspicion.

Doctor Hollands arrived, a Kentish man who was to have charge of the health of a full 160 men; heavy responsibility in the far icefields where no hospital facilities exist. Arrived, too, Cap'n Kean, something of a fashion plate in a fine felt hat, well-cut overcoat, and white collar. A fine old sea dog: proud, virile, dominant. One of the real "fore-now" men, which is to say, the genuine old heart-of-oak breed of mariners, now, alas, dying out.

Gloomily the old *Terra Nova* lies at her snow-muffled wharf as night comes on [says my notebook].   On deck, sealers are carrying shovels of live coals to start a fire somewhere, in preparation for a "scoff," as a feed is called.   Sparks are eddying from the aft-galley funnel. A stockish man, lumped down on a bench in the galley, is intoning a *come-all-ye*.   No sleeping accommodations, or any of whatso kind, have been made for me.   I have just dumped my "fit-out" and my-self into a kind of little hellhole aft of the main cabin.   This hellhole is partly occupied by the rudder trunk, partly by several rough black bunks.   A tiny place it is, with a sign branded into a beam: "Cer-tified to Accommodate One Seaman."   Here I am awaiting devel-opments.   Everything is dim, dark, smoky, glum.

I waited, and continued to wait, while snores reverber-ated through the cabin, but after awhile one came in who was to prove my guide, philospher, and friend indeed.

"Ain't got narr bunk, is it?" he kindly asked.   "Well, sir, I'm ondly too proud to gi' ye mine!"   And this he at once proceeded to do.

He lighted the hellhole lamp, dim and without a chim-ney.   Its vague illumination revealed a disconcertingly black berth of hard boards, wherein lay ragged, tattered quilts of ebon hue.

"But dirt 'm a good t'ing on curvies [quilts]," he philos-ophized.   "'Cause when dem dirty, don't narr bit coal dust ner grase [grease] show on dey.   T'ings is ahl in a fruz, now," he added, "but you'm soon goin' to like dis racket.   I been farty springs to de ice, sir, an' twenty of 'em wid dis same Cap'n Kean.   He'm a gert man, sir; I loves dat man.   An' I t'ink me an' you'm goin' to be good shipmates, ain't it?"

I showed him my quart of medicine which I unpacked from my ditty bag.

This produced an immediate effect.   He told me his name, adding:

"Dat'm an azy name to mind, sir, an' I hopes you

won't ferget un, whatever. To-day's de proper day fer
de whiskey. Dough I don't go on no t'ree-days' square-
benders [drunks], I belang to de breed to drink everlastin',
sir. 'Gard o' baccy, baccy don't 'larm me none; but whiskey—I never wants to be cl'ar of it!"

I did the honours, and he rapped down a stiff drink,
neat, with a mighty smacking of the lips, a smearing with
the hand.

"Ah, sir, you'm de white b'y!" he approved me. "A
glutch [swallow] o' dat's as good as a fire; good as five
dollars, sir. I'm charmed wid it! Cl'ar o' pickles an'
cayenne an' whiskey, nothin' seem to wahrm dis man."

Of course, he had to have another.

Then he went away somewhere; and presently one of
the "master watches" showed up. You know how ants,
when they find a grasshopper's leg, go and tell other ants.
Well—anyhow, this master watch came into the hellhole,
murmuring:

"I don't want to intrude, sir, but——"

Presently another husky showed up, with an ingratiat-
ing trend of conversation. He too received spirituous
consolation, holding his quid in his hand while tossing off
his medicine, then popping the quid back into his mouth
again. Not content with this, he produced a flask—
empty—and begged for a little medicine to carry away.
"Hayve it in dis odder bottle, sir, an' I'll call ye a complete gintleman!" I acceded, and *he* went away, and
another arrived. Almost at once I found myself in the
rôle of a full-fledged bartender, and rapidly acquiring
merit, as the Buddhists say. My being a writer was
forgotten and forgiven. But my medicine—alas, poor
medicine!

The social ice having now been shattered I learned that
men of this type were some of the "junior officers" with

whom I was to bunk. My erstwhile visions of brass buttons took wing, never to return. But though there wasn't a brass button on board, I soon found that even the raggedest, greasiest jacket covered a heart of gold. Splendid fellows, those Newfoundlanders, once you get to know them; the very best. Men, white men, clear through and through. What I had at first thought surliness soon turned out to be only shy reticence. Odd that such huge-fisted six-footers should be often downright bashful.

Water kept steadily leaking down through the deck into the cabin with "the stupid persistence of inanimate things," and somebody shouted: "Carpenter, y're wanted 'ere, b'y!" So "Chips" came—Uncle Edgar Tucker, his name was—and rigged a tin trough to catch it. The cabin grew cozier. I plucked up heart. As evening deepened, the steward, George Yetman, cleared a pair of trousers off the sticky oilcloth of the cabin table where they had been lying, and began grooming the place a bit. A ruddy-faced chap, this "Gearge" as everybody called him; the type of red-head that Newfoundland always nick-

George, our inimitable steward.

names "Foxy" or "Ginger." He was distinguished from the others by wearing a real collar. True, it kept getting a little dirtier, as time passed; but it still remained a collar. After it rotted off, he still kept wearing the collar button as a mark of elegance. His shirt band was fastened with an ordinary button, the brass collar button being inserted in a hole cut somewhat at one side of "dead centre." Much of his authority and prestige in the cabin seemed to depend on that brass button. He wouldn't have lost it for worlds.

The *Terra Nova*, her owners decided, would not sail till morning, so there was nothing more to wait up for, and greatly I longed for sleep. A pilot friend of mine, Mr. Penney, dropped in with a frosted cake which I was kept busily doling out to all and sundry. The cabin swarmed with visitors; but they gradually dwindled away, and snores took possession. My new shipmate who had given me his bunk lay down on a bare board and presently slept.

I had at first some vague notion of trying to undress and wash my hands, though of course I abandoned every thought of my toothbrush. The best I could do was turn in all standing; that is, just take my shoes off and tumble into the ragged black bunk. "Certified to accommodate one seaman" proved a merry jest, for three others also bunked there. The lamp burned all night. Predilections for oxygen seem, after all, to be purely academic.

Early morning found me (singularly enough) well-rested and fresh as any daisy need be. No time was lost in dressing, because there I was, all dressed, just except for pulling on my shoes. I stole an unfair advantage by getting my toothbrush out quickly, before anybody else woke up. To have been caught using it would have irreparably damaged such slight reputation as my bartending activities had built up. In that pallid hour I commandeered a little boiling water from the kettle on the bogey and managed something like a rudimentary wash in the communal basin.

One of the master watches woke up in time to reprove me for throwing away this water after I'd washed in it.

"Yare [there], now, sir, ye wasted good water! Dat wasn't dirty enough to hayve away yet. Us covey fellers don't mind water like dat, whatever. 'Twould of done fine fer me! Ain't got a rack, is you?"

"What, Uncle?"

"A rack, fer y'r hair, o' course." He seemed astonished at my ignorance.

I fished out my comb, broke it in two and gave him half. That half comb did yeoman service for many during the long weeks. Better by far to give away half one's comb than have everybody using all of it.

Cap'n Kean came shouldering out of his cabin singing "The Man Behind," and brimming with expectation. All hands in the cabin tumbled out—a frowsy, rough-haired, bewhiskered crowd indeed—and Gearge poked up the fire to white heat. Tea simmered. Scuffy tramplings echoed on deck, above, with sounds of cordage being dragged about. I drank a huge, life-saving mug of tea, lighted my pipe—ah, what a friend and comforter tobacco was destined to be in the long, tough weeks ahead!—and clambered up the cabin companion ladder.

The "Old Man," already on the bridge, invited me up beside him. In his gigantic fur coat and cap he looked even a finer figure of an ice master than the day before; of a "jowler," which is to say "a prosperous man wid de swiles." His vigorous tugs at the siren lanyard sent screeching bellows, like all the brazen-lunged bulls of Chalcis, to rip echoes from snow-coiffed hills and sleeping town.

"Ah, he'm de b'y can puff de whistle," a sealer admiringly nodded. "A very knowledgeable man, dat!" The black decks filled with a jostle of hunters impatient to be gone. A few sightseers and friends spotted the wharf, but only a few. Ours was to be no such send-off as the *Viking* had received.

The fact now developed that one of our firemen was missing, locked up in the local bastille, sequent to excessive medication the night before. A swift Marathon runner was dispatched hot-foot, various parasangs, to pay his fine and get him free from the law's clutch.

Fogs blent with smoke from the galleys and from the red-cross-barred funnel. Gulls swung high, against a sky drifted with mottles of ominous black and cloudy purple. Long files of shipping blurred into the chilling vapours. And now arrived a reporter with news that a steamer, the *Grontoft*, had just sunk near Newfoundland with all hands. Encouraging, for a send-off!

"Four hands to the wheel!" the Cap'n shouted; for the *Terra Nova* was no luxurious, steam-geared vessel. No, she steered by human muscle applied to twin wheels, in regular old-time style. Later, how intimately was I to know the heft, the drag and kick of those wheels! Four men ran aft, up over the coal pounds built alongside the housing topped by the skylight that served to make darkness visible in the cabin far below.

On deck the jostle of men thickened. Powerful hands shoved off the gangplank. Cap'n Kean wrenched the telegraph. The *Terra Nova's* engine—only 120 h. p., or less than some racing cars, and yet pitted against the arctic ice!—thrashed astern. With a slopping, weltering grind of pans, at 6:30 on the morning of March 9th, we craunched backward into the harbour.

Scant was our godspeed as we drew away. In chill, drab loneliness we slipped from contacts with the world.

"Hard aport!" vociferated the Cap'n. Strange, but the four hands all jammed their weight to starboard—an ill omen. Even though by mistake, the first order issued from the bridge had been disobeyed. "Hard aport, hard!" the Old Man indignantly bellowed. "*That's* not aport!" Disconcerted, the steersmen wrenched their wheels the other way; and turning, the old black ship slowly jiggled her bowsprit toward the Notch.[1]

---

[1]Exit from St. John's Harbour, between gigantic cliffs.

The telegraph spun and whacked: "Ahead." Then, "Steady!" cried the Cap'n; and from the wheels rang a four-throated antiphony of "Steeeee-ay!" as the four huge sealers hauled them back with mighty paws.

Our actual getting-away awoke a bit of interest. From a wharf the *Eagle's* whistle blatted salutation which our own shrieked back. And now a scatter of other whistles, even at this gray-misted, frozen hour, joined in. From schooners, as we thrashed churning down the harbour, and from black, ice-coated steeps, men yelled and waved caps. Along our rails the "greasy-jackets" jammed, roaring back messages and cheers. Sirens whooped as through the Notch we blustered, brazenly saluted by the foghorn. The headlands shattered uproarious echoes.

We were away, to the ice!

The *Terra Nova* swung nor'-nor'east against a cold, strong wind ruffling frigid gray open waters to a sharp display of fangs, and almost immediately slid into the wet wool of a fog that blotted away the towering headlands. Thus the world faded.

Bits of speech won to me—"She's two p'ints inside her course." "Keep 'er as 'andy to it as ye can." "Us got a good start at darn." "Dis un can 'op over de ground, she can." "Wind's nor'-be-east; 'andy 'bout dat." Voices murmured things unintelligible as yet to me, greenest of greenhorns. Half-bemused, I stood on the bridge, peered over the weather-cloth and watched something of the stark old vessel's life, now so strange to me but destined to become—how familiar!

Atop the cabin housing lay frozen beef wrapped in dirty "brin-bags," which we call gunnysacks. A cook bore off some of this and began chopping off hunks of it with a "tomahawk." That, in Newfoundland, means a hatchet. The word "hatchet," up there, means our "axe."

Men on deck began carrying coal in the flat wicker baskets. At a primitive little grindstone, a couple of hunters were already putting a keen edge to their sculping knives. The Cap'n sent someone to have a look at the aft binnacle, near the wheel; perhaps to verify that compass with the one on the bridge. In this new, strange world where now I found myself, all seemed a gray-veiled mystery of confusion.

Between steering orders, each order lustily shouted back at him from aft, the Old Man told me of a ship being wrecked hard by in just such a fog as this—another cheering bit of information.

"Not a very good glass to-day," he concluded, "but no real sign of a starm. And once we reach the ice, we can let her blow, and heed nothin' to it. For the ice, y'see, is the finest o' harbours!"

It sounded comforting. . . .

"Ye'll have a wonnerful time, Mr. 'Merikin, goin' shipmates wid we rale ole Newf'un'lan' dogs," a rheumy, whiskery, spare-ribbed ancient assured me. "Dem whiteycoats is wonnerful azy to kill, sir, but ye'll have to look out fer de ole dogs an' bitches. Ye don't need to hit de whitejackets very hard. Deir skulls is ondly a kind of a cristle; an' if ye hit 'em too hard, ye'll smash up de bones an' den de bones 'll dull y'r knife."

I told him I wasn't going to hunt seals except with notebook and camera, but it didn't sink in.

"Look out fer de ole siles," he repeated. "I see a feller stoopin' over, killin' a whitecoat once, when de ole bitch rosen up out o' de bobbin' hole an' ketched un by de pants, an' tore 'em 'most off o' he. Dat feller 'd of been pulled down an' drownded, sarnly, widout de odder men sove he. But to see dat feller runnin' fer de ship widout hardly narr pick o' pants on, was good as arr nickel!" (movie).

Up on the "barricade," or fo'c's'le head, where groups of men stood hands in pockets, smoking and spitting, I penetrated to the very forepeak and for a while lost thought of all the griminess and dirt by watching the creamy rush of the seas. But the heart-piercing chill presently drove me below. Newfoundlanders can stand around bare-armed in zero weather with their coats un-buttoned and flapping; but we softer folk, not so. I therefore slopped away aft again, to the cabin companion. A steep, ladder-like stair, this, in a kind of alley that housed the carpenter's chest, a clock, lamps, gaffs, skinny woppers, tow ropes, and pigeonholed signal flags. At the bottom of the ladder opened a fetid little hole with a couple of dark bunks—the ship's hospital. Close by swung the door of the cabin proper. And right in front of the cabin door, darker than Erebus, lay the lazaret hatch. Billy Richardson, the storekeeper, a stout, smil-ing, silent, but humorous man, warned me to keep a sharp eye out for this hatch.

If it happened to be open, with dim figures toiling below among boxes of supplies or slabs of cod, one had a splendid chance of doing a high dive down into regions profound and black as Egypt's night. Billy told me of a man who last year fell down the hatch, "an' druv de two legs o' he nigh up troo un, an' was in bunk de 'ole spring." Metal bars were theoretically slung across the cabin door and the ladder when the hatch was open, and sometimes a warning cry of "'*Atch!*" would greet one from hidden depths. But for the most part it was all distinctly a case of every man for himself and hatchway take the careless.

The men seem to have no prescience of perils. At the beginning I got used to seeing them sit on powder cans and calmly smoke their pipes. Later I observed them filling bombs, still smoking. That was a mere commonplace. They handled cartridges with a magnificent familiarity. One time a "dog," or gunner's attendant, dropped a bag of them and a lot went off; but as nobody happened to get shot, "what odds?"

Coming back to St. John's, aboard the *Eagle*, I saw seal oil leaking through into the engine room, trickling down a wooden bulkhead. One touch of fire, and the steamer would have gone up like tinder. The men told me about a sealing vessel once catching fire that way, but they didn't seem to mind their own leak. *Laisser-aller* is the sealers' motto.

They're a hardy breed. Cap'n Kean once went into St. Anthony Harbour with his hand on the engine-room telegraph of his steamer and with a sailor holding snow to his "burned" (frozen) cheeks to keep them from freezing more.

I have seen Newfoundlanders working on the *Terra Nova* with one hand while the other was so cruelly lacerated that any American with such an injury would go to bed and send for a doctor. Men hardly able to stand up will go on ice and haul tows. Men stab through their feet with gaffs, and still go right on working. Some of these wounds, on account (it is said) of the seal fat, develop terrific infections. "Seal fingers" are such infections of the hands. In spite of all, the men continue their labours. They work even with pneumonia. And rarely have they any serious "complaint," as they call a disease; they very rarely die in the ice.

"If a man die," the carpenter informed me, "us builds un a coffin out o' pound boards, an' salt un down [ice him],

an' putt un de Marconi house or the fo'c's'le 'eed." He
said it as if mentioning a side of beef.

And now—as we have no seals to slaughter yet, and
as we must dwell for several weeks aboard a sealer—it
seems apposite to give some general idea of the cabin
which is to be our home.

It lay wholly below-decks, far aft, and was pallidly
illuminated by a skylight with round bull's-eyes. At the
forward end opened the entrance door and that of the
pantry. Along both sides extended doors of the tiny
cubicles that berthed the Old Man, the doctor, Marconi
operator, engineers, master watches, mate, and others.
Aft was a storeroom where slept the after cooks and
storekeeper; also the hellhole that bunked the carpenter,
bosun, a bridge master, a scunner, the pantry steward and
—for a while—myself.

One feature of great interest in the cabin was that all
the rum was kept there. The doctor had charge of some
of it, and some lurked in an immense, osier-covered
demijohn in the Old Man's cubicle. The doctor's ability
to dispense rum, in case of need, made him something of a
magnifico. Gearge, too, I soon discovered, used to hand
out a few nips from the Old Man's demijohn; used to
bestow it on the needy, with odd, gallinaceous jerks and
twitches.

The private quarters of a sealing captain are worth
glancing at. In addition to the main object of interest,
the "gert, hoi dimmyjohn," as the men called it, it contained a polished brass lamp; carven bunk, really clean at
first; shelf of books; rack of telescopes and binoculars; the
ship's chronometer and what the Old Man called his
"sexton"; also other navigating instruments, settee, lot
of drawers with maps; more maps and charts rolled up in

racks overhead; oilcloth and a coarse-woven "runner" on the floor—a palatial apartment, truly, by comparison with aught else on board. Before long it became the only near-clean spot on the whole ship; and a little later than that, I wouldn't have vouched for even the Old Man's cabin itself. But let us return to the main cabin.

There, between the entrance door and the pantry door one beheld—of all things!—a handsome tryptich mirror of bevelled glass, some of it still retaining the quicksilver. This glass had a carven gilt frame and in the middle a gilt clock. Below it extended a mantelshelf with a brass rail, right over the bogey. The rail kept back a few oddments of books, and usually held a lot of "cuffs" and "mitts." The former are mittens with only the thumb detached; the latter have the forefinger also in a separate compartment.

In the middle of the cabin stood a table, flanked by a swivel chair with a leather cushion, for the Cap'n, and by three benches. A barometer with a cap usually draped over its dial, and a year-old calendar, hung at the aft end. Over the table swung a bronze lamp. The cabin walls and doors were painted white, and white they remained for a few days; whereafter coal dust, grease, and blood maculated them with grotesque patterns. Mouldings and little gilt figures of seals done in metal ornamented the tops of the walls.

A mat at the entrance; linoleum flooring; a perpetual teapot and coffeepot simmering on the bogey, completed our elegancies. Such was the place destined for a good many weeks to be my floating, icebound, snow-lashed, and tempest-harried home.

Now, on the table, indubitable signs of breakfast were appearing. Breakfast was brought aft from the galley by the pantry steward, Uncle Absalom Gaulton, in kit-pans with cloths (still clean) over them.

The violent *clang-a-lang-a-lang* of a bell brazened as a welcome summons.

"Braffus, sir," Uncle Absalom nodded to me. "First mess goin' now. Putt a good wahrm mug-up into y'r body, alang o' y'r sowl, an' it'll be wonnerful fine fer ye!"

I needed no second invitation. In those hibernal regions, one eats all one can get and tries for more. Break-fast proved a happy surprise—beefsteak, if you please; potatoes, bread and butter, and jam; hard-tack and tea. My place was honourable—at the Old Man's left. Mr. McGettigan, Chief Engineer, had his right. Of course, our Chief was a Scotsman, and naturally he was called "Mac." You know the old saying that if you shout: "Oh, Mac!" into any steamship engine room in the world, you'll always get the answer: "Here!"

Our mess included engineers, doctor, carpenter, "Sparks"—as the Marconi man was dubbed—bosun, scunner, and a master watch or two, also a bridge master. Master watches, usually four, are petty officers in charge of "goes," or gangs, for work both aboard ship and on the ice. The duty of the scunners is going aloft to spy out ways through the ice, leads and ways; bridge masters transmit orders from the scunners to the men at the wheel. No introductions were in order. I just got acquainted, hit-or-miss. By way of luxury we had a white tablecloth. That lasted about a week. It gradu-ally became a white cloth with black spots, and then a black cloth with white spots; and eventually all the white disappeared and the cloth was junked.

The Old Man had a napkin, too; the only one on board. That napkin certainly lasted well. Every meal the Old Man would invariably wrinkle it up and throw it into his chair, when he left the table, and Gearge would always fold it carefully and put it away. And the Old Man would always call: "Gearge, my napkin, b'y!" Then Gearge would produce it from the pantry. That became a real ceremony; the napkin was one of several badges of aristocracy that set the Old Man apart from and above us common proletarians. Toward the end of the weeks it became a trifle fallen from its high estate; but to the very last an indubitable napkin it remained.

Meek-mannered and gentle-spoken Uncle Absalom officiated in the pantry. Gearge waited on table with a nervous, preoccupied air. Conversation, blent with the steady thrash of the engine, remained fragmentary. I noticed then, and till the finish, that these people seemed to have some difficulty in understanding each other. Their speech was constantly broken by: "Huh?" and "What say?" Perhaps their astonishing dialect is hard even to their own ears; or it may be that their thick-tongued, sloven pronunciation does not carry well. I seemed to catch their meaning almost as well as they themselves could. The most trying factor of it all was that, if questioned, a speaker would invariably begin his whole sentence from the very beginning, and repeat it word for word as at first. This sort of thing got badly on my nerves after a while; but none of the sealers appeared to mind it, perhaps because sealers are not troubled with nerves.

CHAPTER IV

SHAKING DOWN

WE GOT into loose ice almost at once, and there began that quivering and cruel battering which for long weeks was to companion all my days and nights.

The work of the ship fell into routines. The "ash-cat" gang laboured at their ventilator hoist, windlassing long steel buckets of ashes up from the glory hole and sluicing them into the sea; then letting the buckets racket down again with a clatter.

Some fell to work seizing cruel points on gaff sticks with a kind of tarred cord known as "spun yarn." Others shovelled snow and miscellaneous filth overside. Still others hoisted coal out of a bunker below, with huge bucket and rope run over a pulley slung to a boom. Tailed on in a long line, they gave way with a will, to the rough-chanted strains of "Johnny Boker," led by a "shanty man":

> We'll do our Johnny Boker,
> We will 'aul an' 'eave togedder,
> An' we'll do our Johnny Boker,
> *Do !*

> We will do my Johnny Boker,
> Oh, we'll 'aul dis 'eavy bugger,
> An' it's do my Johnny Boker,
> *Do !*

Our "'levener" came none too soon—a 'levener being an eleven-o'clock mug-up of toast and tea. Even thus early in the sealing game it was evident that tea and buttered toast formed a vital part of the grim business of seal hunting. Odd, eh? One would as soon expect a pirate expedition to indulge in perpetual cocoa and lady-fingers. But the sealers are Britons all and have their tea before breakfast, at eleven, in the middle of the after-noon, and at night, as well as at every meal. They take it straight. "Milky tea" is rare, though some use a dash of condensed milk. The main point is that the tea must be powerful. Both in the fo'c's'le and cabin, tea and buttered toast are staples—good toast, too, made of fresh white bread, baked every day on board.

One reason why tea is so popular aboard the sealing vessels is because the water can't be tolerated. For the most part, unless one has a dash of limejuice to add thereto, the water—made of melted ice—is not only "brachey" but also provokes distressing thirst. Tea masks the salty tang, and quenches drought; and what's more, it scalds the germs to death.

Hearty food, the regular old stalwart provender, is another essential to the seal hunt. Our first dinner aboard the *Terra Nova* came to me as a heaven-sent blessing. A brace of meats, white bread, lobscouse, turnips, potatoes, and hard-tack made a regal banquet. 'Twas a spectacle worth seeing, those Viking sons of the North slopping Worcestershire and divers ardent sauces into the 'scouse or over their other tucker. A spectacle, to behold them spooning huge pickles out of the dish into their mouths and slapping the spoon back; then gulping pints of tea. Anything to "get a wahrm"!

Privately, after this Lucullian repast, I devoured raisins from my own store—but not unscathed. Ah, no; a sealer discovered me in the very act, and I promptly went into the dried-fruit-distributing business. And a little later they discovered my limejuice and peppermints.

A passage in my notebook, somewhat later still:

They borrow my spy glasses, scissors, knife, tobacco, talcum powder, strop, and everything borrowable; and no doubt they'd borrow my toothbrush, if they used toothbrushes. *Meum* and *tuum* are conspicuous by their absence. Some of the men, with engaging frankness, have asked me for the gift of my fur gloves, cap, overcoat, arctics —"when I get troo up wid 'em." It's only fair to say, though, that their hospitality equals their annexing proclivities. All that they have they'll share with you, and welcome. They have got away with all but one of my pipes, by the very direct expedient of smoking them; after which, somehow, I just sort of let the pipes go. These hardy hunters smoke freely in communistic fashion; even a cigar is passed round.

On deck again, I found the fog fanning away under the urge of an ever more biting wind. The dim sun ball was beginning to flick bronzed lights across ice pans; to gleam on far pinnacles of ivory. Hues of jade and emerald glowed vaguely in fantastic carvings of the ice edges.

"Now we're gettin' into her!" declared the Old Man, and so indeed it seemed. He sent the scunner up to the "parlour," or barrel on the foretopmast, clambering aloft up the shrouds to the trapdoor in the bottom of the barrel. A dizzy height!

"Go aloft, skipper," the Cap'n commanded, "an' see how the leads are." (Everybody aboard a sealing vessel is "skipper.")

The man in the scunner's barrel is said to "take charge." And only the captain's word can overrule his. The progress and often the safety and very life of the ship depend upon his judgment. A good scunner can do miracles in worming the ship through seemingly impossible obstructions. A bad one "will jam 'er in pea soup!"

Strings of ice now checking the ship, and a fair wind serving, the Cap'n gave orders to set a bit of canvas.

"We'll putt up three stays'ls! An' how about y'r spanker, b'ys?" he called from the bridge. "That help a lot, that do. That make this one two knots smarter in the water!"

Wondrous gymnastics were those of the gang that sweated up the booming, slapping canvas with a:

"'Aul away! Ee-yah! Sheet 'er, b'ys! Yay! Steeee-ay!"

At a better clip the *Terra Nova* thrust the ice aside. Water and ice churned to milky absinthe as huge blocks leaped up and over. The brine gleamed full of ice, vivid with wondrous blue. The ship heeled with shivering impacts, but rode down the ice and vanquished it. And the Old Man himself clambered aloft, despite all his seventy years, agile and surefooted as a boy.

"I'd just as soon go up into the barr'l," he later told me, "as eat me dinner. Ice on the ratlines? Shah! I don't mind that, whatever!" And I, never venturing beyond the main-top, felt properly abashed.

Heavy ice flew, pans whirled and ground. The ship quivered as if rent asunder, but her stout oaken beams heaved aside the floes with sovereign contempt. When she struck the ice full tilt, water flew higher than the barricade rail. Immense jagged rifts darted ahead; ice masses reared and crumbled. Whole acres of ice ground, wheeled, shifted. The ship seemed a giant hand summarily rearranging the pieces of a Titans' picture puzzle.

"We got a grand shot on us now," cried the Cap'n. "We'll be into the fat afore lang, me sons!"

Three stowaways were reported—"sprats o' b'ys" that somehow or other had managed to "stole away."

As usual in such cases, they got a "tongue-banging," and were then turned over to be serfs for the firemen; to clean the firemen's quarters in the to'gal'n' house and bring them food. Suspicion is usually directed against the firemen, that they connive at stowaways' getting aboard so that such services may be rendered. As for the boys, they are never allowed on ice to kill seals; for should they kill, they might claim a share of the ship's "bill." At most they get odds and ends of coarse food, a dark hole to sleep in, and perhaps a few cents of pay. "A stowaway's life is not a happy one." And yet each year the beggars manage to go. I heard of one stowaway who was so afraid he'd be put ashore that he didn't come out of hiding for three days after the ship had left port. When found, starving, the first thing he asked for was a chew of tobacco!

Wandering about the deck, a stranger in a strange land, while the ship thunderously butted ice, I saw one fellow in his shirtsleeves, with bare arms exposed to the freezing clutches of the wind. On one arm he had joined hearts tattooed, with the motto: "In Remembrance of Jennie." One can imagine such a motto producing complications in case of a change of sweethearts.

Crouching down a ladder-like flight of amazingly filthy steps, I found the 'tweendecks—where most of the common-hands bunked and ate—a place not easily to be forgotten. Its rough floor was strewn with coal, ashes, and mud from melting snow. Masses of black shadow, grids of wavering firelight checkered the stenchful place. In double tiers of bunks with dirty quilts ("midnight glories")—some not innocent of vermin—men with soot-blurred faces were lying, smoking, snoring, talking, even laughing.

Confusion and crowding surpassed belief. In a sealer's

'tween decks, two men share a bunk. Four usually eat
together, one of their number going to the forward galley
with dirty pannikins and kettles. The food tins are
rarely if ever washed. *I* never saw one washed, at all
events, in my weeks aboard.

Let this not shock the sensitive. I am suppressing
much. Some of the sealers' habits are altogether un-
printable, and I shall let them pass.

The day of my first visit below, some of the men seemed
sunk into a dull torpescence. Others eyed me with
suspicion. Many were crouching on their battered chests;
a few were cobbling their skinny woppers, tapping soles,
driving in sparables.

"Doze skinnies so bad," one was grumbling, "de vog
[fog] leak troo 'em. If it rain to-morrer, dem be wet inside, de day!"

The stanchions of this truly penitential place may
once have shown whitewash, but that was many a weary
year agone. On those stanchions, and on steampipes that
overhead extended to the winches, oilskins, tow ropes,
sou'westers, jackets, gaffs, jumpers, boots, and caps were
swaying with the slow roll of the ship. Lanterns pendu-
lumed. Wicker baskets, shovels, a grindstone, and a
wheelbarrow added to the confusion, half visible in a
pallid glimmer down the hatchway or in the smoky lamp
blur. A couple of cracked bogies stood in pans of ashes,
with socks and mittens hung over them to dry.

Through cracks in these bogies, vagrom fire gleams
flickered over black, unshaven faces and picked glints of
eye gleam from the dark. And at these bogeys men were
squatted, making toast. Others were lighting pipes there
with paper spills, then pinching out the flame with fingers
of horn. Still others were chipping tobacco with their
"shayth-knives" from plugs harder than a nigger's head.

Only a short man could stand erect down there. I had to crouch. I stifled, gasped.

Near by sat an ancient, splicing a rope and crooning a dull singsong. Some were devouring beans and salt meat; others, gulping tea that steamed. "Switchel," this tea was; that is, boiled-over tea whereto now and again fresh leaves are added.

Some of the men wore jackets made of old bags, with printing still visible. Many were ragged and extensively bepatched. Poverty! Lord, what poverty! All was rough, dark, dirty—incredibly dirty, gorgeously and grotesquely dirty. And this at the beginning of the trip. Later, when the men had really "grased deyselfs to de helbows in de fat," and when everything had become tainted with grease and blood, and the sculps were stowed at the aft end of the 'tweendecks and many others were dragged through it to be flung below, forward, conditions there beggared description. Oh, dignity of Labour!

And now the weather began to worsen, coming on ruthlessly cold. The brief, watery sunshine faded to a blur; an arctic gloom strode over the ice; and in thickening mist drives, the wireless began to whine. With a crisp ringing like steel, the ice sundered. It closed again behind us. Already I felt a million miles—and years—from the real world.

Back in the cabin I thanked whatever gods there be for the enheartening bogey, and with interest watched the setting of the watches. Until you understand the organization of the crew, you cannot properly grasp the seal hunt. Therefore, be patient with a word of explanation.

The Old Man sat with Olympian dignity at the table, with the ship's register before him, while many of the aft crowd admiringly looked on. With the aid of the four master watches he apportioned the gangs. Some argument arose concerning what to do with Levi Butts, the ship's preacher; but this was soon settled with:

"Well, clear o' Levi, ye got thirty an' thirty-one apiece. Can't get it nigher 'n that!"

Now then for the ship and her personnel.

The *Terra Nova* is a carvel-built, bark-rigged, three masted steamer of 400 tons, carrying 160 men for a sealing crew. She was built at Dundee, Scotland, in 1884 (and should have been broken up for junk, long ago!); she is 187 feet long by 31 beam; carries 90 pounds of steam (by the grace of God); and—with luck—makes eight knots.

At first she used to come out from England in January, prosecute the seal fishery in March, then in May go whaling. Her first trip to the Antarctic was in 1904. Scott and Shackleton, who had gone thither in the *Discovery*, were a year overdue. The British Admiralty fitted out a relief expedition, and chartered the *Terra Nova* as the roughest and toughest ice breaker to be had. The *Terra Nova* brought Scott and Shackleton back in 1905. In 1909, Scott went on his successful expedition to the pole which, however, ended fatally for him. He took the *Terra Nova* in preference to the *Discovery*. In 1914 Bowring Brothers bought her from the Admiralty, and ever since then she has been a Newfoundland sealer.

Her 1922 complement, exclusive of my own superfluous self, comprised: Captain, second hand, barrel men (or spy masters), scunners; engineers, firemen, and oilers; bosun, carpenter, doctor, storekeeper, stewards, bakers and cooks; four bridge masters, Marconi man, master watches and second master watches (four of each), preacher, government inspector, and common hands; a total of 160.

The barrel men keep watch in the main-topmast barrel,

spying for seals. Duties of the scunners and bridge masters I have already explained. The storekeeper, because he has charge of the butter, rejoices in the euphonious title of "butter bitch." The master watches are in charge of gangs both on the ship and when the men "go away," on ice, and have to be responsible for the lives and safety of the hunters. In case a master watch is killed or disabled, his second master watch, or "deck-router," (pronounced "rowter") replaces him. The preacher exhorts, and butchers seals. The government inspector must see that sanitary conditions are satisfactory, on deck and in the men's quarters. (Judging by what I observed on the *Terra Nova* he must have been a total paralytic, blind, deaf, and otherwise disabled.) He must also enforce the law against killing seals on Sunday.

The bosun is a kind of deck captain, and is known as ship keeper or owners' man. He looks after the gaffs, compasses, ropes, lamps, candles, torches, and so on; keeps the deck clean (theoretically!); and whenever he has nothing to do, invents something. Never was there so "yary" (energetic) a man as our bosun.

As for the common hands, they have nothing much to do except steer, shift ballast and coal, hunt seals, kill them, skin them and drag the sculps aboard, load sculps and tally them down, and do a lot of other painful, dangerous and laborious tasks.

Each man seems jealous of his job, and resents having another intrude on it. I have heard of a "manus" (mutiny) almost being caused by men insisting on going on ice when they ought not to have gone.

It is very difficult to get exact information about the manner of sharing the proceeds. But roughly speaking, the proceeds of the trip are divided into three parts.

One goes to the shipowners; one to the officers; one to the common hands. It would take too long to delve into the exact division of the profits, but the general one third principle holds. In other words, out of every three seals killed, one belongs to the hunters.

The common hands' share, divided among 100 to 120 men, gives each man for five or six weeks of incredible toil only the merest pittance. And out of this, the $12 "crop" has to be paid. Such a disparity between labour and pay cannot be found elsewhere among white men. The men, of course, are simple fellows, easily befooled. Sometimes the owners

Bosun Mike Donovan, always worried.

have offered a case of oranges as a prize to the ship bringing in the biggest load! Sometimes a seal hunter, after his travelling expenses are paid, will clear only $15 or $20 for his "spring"; and I have heard some of the men growl that more than once they had "got home wid not'in' but a bundle o' dirty clo'es an' a gad o' smatchy [tainted] fippers!"

The men's pay, for the 1922 hunt, according to figures compiled by Levi G. Chafe, was as follows: *Sagona*, $27.62; *Ranger*, $18.13; *Thetis*, $45.36; *Seal*, $27.22; *Viking*, $74.68; *Eagle*, $49.22; *Neptune*, $73.54; *Terra Nova*, $74.90. On second trips, *Seal*, $15.57; *Ranger*, $30.54; *Thetis*, $29.63. The average pay was $42.40. The total net value of the catch was $197,837.91.

If a hunter makes $50 or $60, he's doing well. That comes to $10 to $12 a week, and board—God save the mark!—for hardships, perils, and toil beyond anything we know here at home. I have never known a country where employers enjoyed such a sinecure as in New-

foundland. Labour, there, has hardly begun to dream
that it has any rights. And the game of exploitation goes
merrily on.

Talk presently turned on perils and disasters.

"Sometimes when de snow come t'ick, sir," bridge
master Joe Stirge explained, "ye won't year de ship's
whistle, if you'm to winnard. Got to watch out fer dat!
Ye won't be in much danger, dough, fallin' troo a rint
[rent] in de ice. Ye'll 'ardly go more 'an halfway in,
'cause de salt water 'm wonnerful strong, an' bear ye up.
An' de odders 'll haul ye out wid dey gaves [gaffs]—if ye
don't get too far away from de gang."

"An' even if ye falls troo," added Uncle Tucker, the
carpenter, "dat don't matter. Ye can go on workin' ahl
day, an' no harm. Y'r clothes soon freezes, an' kipps ye
wahrm on de inside of 'em. An' at night ye thaw out by de
bogey, till de steam comes out, an' ye're ahl rate. I know
lots o' fellers fall in on purpose, to get a glutch o' rum."

"An' de laysses' [least] little piece o' sish [thin ice] is
enough to copy [jump] on," Stirge assured me. "Dat
is, sir, if you'm annyways spry!"

"If you'm caught in a starm on de ice," said bridge
master Llewellen White, "an' a lake breaks between you
an' de ship so you can't get aburd, you build up a barricade o' clumpers an' make a fire. Yes, sir, when it come
t'ick, when it come wedder, you'm able to be wonnerful
fine on de ice, if you'm knowin' to what to do. You ahl
tries to huddle togedder, den. De ropes gets grasey-like
[greasy], draggin' swiles, an' you make shavin's off y'r gaff
sticks, an' cut strips o' swile-fat an' let 'em drip on de
shavin's. Dem burns like de hobs o' hell. But you got
to be careful, not let de dirty smoke blow in y'r eyes, or
you'm liable to get blind from dat."

"Yes, an' look out fer de ice blind, too," warned master-watch Roberts. We were all sitting on the hellhole bunks, having a cozy little time. "De sun on de icc 'm enough to scald de bloody eyes out o' y'r 'id. An' travellin' fer de day's len'th, you'm liable to get a dose o' ice blind, even if you'm got smoked glasses. Dat feel like sand in y'r eyes. I've had wonnerful eyes meself, sir. De steam out o' de salt ice make dat, sir, an' tarmentin' it be's, too. I've seen a good many few gangs helpless wid it. I wouldn't be ice blind not fer de whole load o' fat—not fer a farm up sout', Mr. 'Merikin. Nothin' like dat to take de puddick out of a man. When you'm ice blind, you'm in a gert garricky [trouble], sure!"

The talk turned on disasters, whereof the seal fishery has had its appalling profusion, and my new shipmates gave me some details of the *Greenland* tragedy in 1898. Captain George Barbour was in command; the date was March 21st. The day seemed fine; but about six o'clock in the evening a "livin' starm" shrieked out of the north. Only one master watch succeeded in getting his men aboard. Forty-eight sealers, of those caught on the floes far away, died the blanched death of the arctic. They were found with frozen froth on their lips, distorted, huddled under clumpers, sprawling grotesquely. Some had died while crawling; others still clutched hard bread in their frozen hands. Some of the survivors, when rescued, had gone mad and had to be run down and dragged to the rescuing steamer by force. Some had "just enough life into 'em, sir, to blow on," but managed to pull through. It was a dark day for Newfoundland when the crippled survivors and the stark dead were brought to St. John's; a day never to be forgotten! That day was March 27th. Nearly a whole week elapsed from the disaster to the landing of the survivors and the frozen bodies.

At the first sign of fog or snow, when the men are on ice, up goes the signal flag and out shrieks the siren; but alas, sometimes too late. The North strikes with swift fury.

So it struck the sealing steamer *Newfoundland*, on the last day of March, 1914. On that ship, Captain Westbury Kean had 119 men caught on ice by an immense blind whiteness that raged for two days. Seventy-seven men died. Sixty-nine frozen bodies were brought in on April 4th, by the *Bellaventure*. Forty-two survivors remained mutilated and crippled, after treatment at the General Hospital in St. John's. Eight men, alive when found, later succumbed. Again the Colony was plunged in woe.

Some gruesome tales, starkly dramatic, lie in the finding of the bodies on ice. Men were discovered huddled in groups, frozen solidly together as if they had tried in vain to warm each other, all shrouded under the same palls of snow that inwrapped the dead seals, victims of their fruitless butchery. Some were frozen to ivory, crouching or kneeling as if in prayer.

Some few had mistaken the blackness of "rifters" (cracks) for that of the ship, had fought toward that blackness, plunged in, and struggling out, had swiftly frozen to death. Still others had floated away on wallowing pans, out into "the blue drop," and had died there under the blizzard's lash.

Some were found crouched dead behind ice pinnacles, while a few had tried to build rude shelters of ice. One father and his son were brought in, the stiffened arms of the father still clinging to his boy, trying to the very end to shield him. They had to be winched up on the *Bellaventure's* deck, fast-frozen together.

Oddly enough, some of those who escaped death were

the weakest and most thinly clad. Survivors told terrific stories of suffering and delirium; of men, gone stark crazy, mistaking open water for houses and rushing to death in the black rifters. Some of the men were on ice, without food or fire, for *fifty-six hours !*

The frozen corpses were brought in on the rescue ship's hatches covered with tarpaulin. They were unloaded on the wharf in presence of a stricken multitude. Some of the Newfoundland women "went off deir 'eed entire," that day, as toilers "winch dem bodies on de w'arf." The corpses were carried to Doctor Grenfell's King George V Institute, where they were thawed out in the swimming pool and in bathtubs before they could be identified and made ready for burial. Oddly enough, I later met a man who had helped in that work; and can you imagine what he complained of?

"Dat work was so damn cold, I 'ad to go get a glutch o' whiskey after thawin' every five bodies, an' nobody paid me fer dem drinks, needer! Ahl come out o' me own pocket, my dear man!"

Close-treading on the heels of this disaster came another and even a more terrific one. For that same spring, the *Southern Cross,* commanded by Captain George Clarke and with 177 men aboard, went down with all hands. Incidentally, she carried down 18,000 sealskins. She was last seen in open water off Cape Pine, not far from St. Pierre, Miquelon. The *Portia* spoke her there on March 31st. Nothing more was ever seen of her, nor was any wreckage found, save a lifebelt picked up, months later, on the coast of Ireland. And the Colony of Newfoundland bowed her head a second time in one same spring, and cried aloud in anguish.

Next year, however, the sealing armada went to the ice no less courageously. It put out into the floes once more, fully manned. Nothing, short of complete annihilation, checks the indomitable spirit of these supermen.

And "take a chance" is still their motto. In the *Terra Nova's* cabin the stovepipe, without any asbestos covering or insulation, extended right up beside a beam deep-charred by the heat. Directly above was the Marconi room. Below, the lazarette contained enough blasting powder to have blown the ship clean off the ocean.

If we ever had any fire-fighting apparatus, I was never able to discover it. The situation was almost unimaginable. Yet nobody minded. Nobody thought of lining the charred beam with tin or sheet iron. When I called Uncle Absalom's attention to the pleasant state of affairs, he smiled and nodded and in a prideful voice murmured:

"Dat pipe, now, sir, don't us kipp un rid hot, dough?"

CHAPTER V

INTO THE ICE

NIGHT [says my notebook]. We are up against an impassable field of ice, at which the iron-sheathed prow gnashes in vain. The world a pallor of milky, misty, phantom gray. The lifeboats hang, black blots, from davits blacker still; and masts—inordinately tall—spars, ropes, are etched against the spectral vagueness.

Incessantly, futilely, the engine labours its heart out; bells jangle; the screw thrashes in reverse, hauling the ship back for another butt and thrust at the enemy here in this unthinkably vast solitude.

The wireless snarls like a trapped wolf. Men are hauling coal from below; and the shouted order: "Go a'eed, *gently !*" strikes me as amazing. What a word to use here! Some rough skylarking is under way in the galley. Shouts, raw laughter echo; and laughter too from the 'tweendecks, even from the "dungeon," or under-fo'c's'le, vastly filthier than the 'tweendecks. How can men laugh in such places?

With a rattle of chains, with lusty yells from stern and bridge, the wheel flings over. Joyful and savage shouts sound as we smash through the ice barrier and shatter down the pans.

Down in the cabin again. Old Uncle Absalom was puttering among his precious cups and plates in the pantry, wiping dishes with a long towel draped over his shoulder, then drinking tea and putting the cup back into the rack again without even rinsing it.

"God bless my soul!" he murmured—almost his only oath—as irregular gusts of tumult from ice-ramming shuddered the cabin. "Gettin' pretty knobbly in de water, dat time. Heavy buttin'. Us gettin' into de hard, now; into de pinnackly ice. An' I see de glass goin' down, too. But we'm goin' on still!"

The Cap'n was slowly pacing up, down, his shadow black-crinkling along walls and doors; pacing, singing in a cracked underbreath:

"Carry me back to ole Virginny,
  Dat's where de cotton an' de common 'taters grow!"

His frequent changes of key compensated any verbal errata. As he paced and sang, he smoked cigarettes— strange, for so husky an old seal killer! Stranger still, he used an amber cigarette holder, wore a white collar, a fancy green waistcoat, a gold watch chain, and gold-rimmed pince-nez. The Cap'n's cravat always sagged down, revealing his brass collar button; but it was an indubitable cravat, none the less—the only Newfoundland one on board—and as such conferred distinction.

"Get me my blue chart an' my things, Gearge!" the Cap'n called. Gearge hastened to bring the chart, dividers, parallel rulers, Brown's Nautical Almanac and scribbling-diary from the holy of holies—the Old Man's cabin itself—and Cap'n Kean settled down on the bench to work out the ship's position.

This evening function, which bore almost the solemnity of a religious rite, was always watched with a respectful attention. Lamplight streamed on deep-lined faces, reddened and purpled by cold, wind, and sleet while the Cap'n manipulated his instruments with pontifical dignity. Next to receiving wireless messages, this evening calculation expanded his ego more than aught else. The veneration his simple folk showed for his ability to read, write, figure, unravel the mysteries of latitude and longitude, and understand the close-packed columns of figures, degrees, minutes, and seconds, was the breath of life to him.

Cigarette smouldering in elegant amber, there he sat and hummed, "Under the Anheuser Busch" and magically located a tiny dot on the icebound Atlantic; "stepping off" parallel lines with the ruler, and making wizardly measurement with the dividers—to what purpose I landlubberly knew not. With an artistic joy I studied the Old Man. I privately sketched his healthy, rubicund face, weather-bitten like a ripe apple all ruddy and full of sap; his thin white hair meticulously parted in the middle; his famous collar destined gradually to darken, darken. I admired the ornate buttons of that startling waistcoat, the heavy gold ring, the poise of the pince-nez halfway down to the tip of the nose; the neatly trimmed white beard. By all these things, as also by right prescriptive, Cap'n Kean ruled his men, his ship.

As he plotted our route through what seemed a perfectly routeless fog and ice, the murmur of voices sounded thickly in the hellhole, and jets of tobacco juice came squirting out into the main cabin.

Now the door opened, and Sam Ballam, alias "Marky" or "Sparks," our wireless man—a slim, good-looking young fellow, a veteran of the World War—came in with a blue envelope carefully sealed and superscribed: "Captain, S.S. *Terra Nova*." True enough, Ballam had just that moment sealed the message before bringing it down to the cabin; and true again, all the message said was: "Jacob Kean in big ice," but every propriety had been observed. Had this been a crack liner and the wireless announcing a world's record, it couldn't have been more formal.

"Message for you, sir."

"Thank you, sir!" And the Cap'n condescended, quite in the grand manner, to bend his gaze on it. Then the ceremonial opening of the blue envelope, the decoding of the message, the poring over the code book to frame out an innocuous, "Making slow progress. No sign of fat." Send it without the code? Never! Etiquette and pride demanded that secrets be kept when so vital as these.

The evening droned along with Cap'n Kean working and various men—their expressions piratical, their hearts the hearts of children—watching in awe.

" 'E got a gert appetite fer figgers," said one.

"I loves dat man, I do," judged another. "Him a gert man, my son!"

"Ain't narr nudder man like dat un," murmured a third. "Wind ner ice ner wedder can't douse [fool] *he!* Kipps on high-linin', year after year, an' never lose a ship. We'm safe as a hitch, wid he; safe as if in God's pocket, an' bound to bore up wid a big jag o' fat!"

Fortunate Cap'n thus to enlist the hearts as well as the hands of your men!

Humming, whistling, smoking, he finished his calculations and announced:

"Well, me sons, I'm goin' to hold this cut [course] a while."

Early next morning—March 10th, still five days before the open season on seals began—I found the *Terra Nova* once more engaged in her uproarious dance with the ice. I awoke to discover that most of the night coal-dusty water had been leaking down on me. An umbrella would have helped, but the ship carried none.

Out in the main cabin, men were already having a good before-breakfast smoke. Master-watch Roberts, ruddy, stout, and genial, with prominent eyes, blue as cornflowers, was chipping tobacco from a plug with his skinning knife. The fire burned bright, mug-ups were in order—ah, the delights of tea and buttered "toasses"

at 4:30 A.M. in the ice!—and shouts of "*Starburd!*
. . . *Steeeeay!* . . . *Port!* . . . " rang
cheerily from above. My tea excited the amazed in-
credulity of both Gearge and Uncle Absalom. That
anybody could drink it less strong than boiling lye surpassed imagination.

"De like o' dat I never see," murmured Absalom.
"Oh, mercy, oh, my!"

And Gearge, with nods and becks and wreathed smiles:
"You'm de divil's quare 'and, ain't ye now? De
quarest fish in de sea! Ye make me laugh me hinsides
out, Mr. 'Merikin. You'm de comicalest feller!"

"T'ink of a feller layvin' a fine placc like de States
an' goin' to de ice to write books about dat, just!" put
in another, huge-shouldered in a blue "gansey" (jersey),
as he squatted down before the bogey and toasted bread
on a knife point. "Ain't such a feller hoffy [crazy], now?
An' to sketch off pitchers [take photographs]! I niver de
divil iver!"

"Proper time fer de whiskey, doze days [now]," suggested a third. They wheedled the rest of my precious
medicine all away. After that, they didn't talk any more
about my being such a quare fish.

Warmed by my matutinal bartending, master watch
Abram Best made dazzling promises:

"I'll get ye a rope an' gaff, me son, an ye can go on ice
alang o' me, killin' swiles. I'll get ye some good offers
[chances] as 'll putt ye up in glee. Ye mightn't like dat,
first-alang, an' it might putt ye in a fluster, but after ye
tracks round a spill [while] wid we an' gets de how of it,
I 'lows ye'll get shockin' fond of it. Yere," and he drew
his knife, "yere'm a knife ye can have, b'y. A wonnerful knife, dat. Two jags on de steel wid dat, an' ye can
rip a swile rate out!"

My popularity had now risen to a point where Gearge assigned me to downright luxurious quarters, in a tiny cubbyhole with the second hand, Nathan Kean—the Cap'n's son—and with young Cyril Kean—his grandson.

Uncle Edgar Tucker—he who had lain on a hard board to give me his "pew" (bunk)—now busied himself with hammer and nails and tinkered up for me a berth in the cubbyhole mentioned. Gearge gave me a mattress; and after I had rooted out of it a few unexplained and stony junks of hard-tack, it proved not too distressful.

Outside, ice crashed and bellowed along our hull, sliding, interlocking, slopping over, smashing, as the stout old veteran of the floes shoved her way through. Water continued to drip into the cabin, but nobody cared. Came now a message by the wireless: "The *Ranger* is into a patch of rusties." (Rusties are second-year seals.) Even though the close season was still on, this thrilled the ship with excitement and vast discussion. I noticed then, as ever, that comparatively few oaths interlarded the speech of these people. They are little given to blaspheming, perhaps because they still actually believe in hell. Nor, for another thing, do they indulge in the gaulois. Let me bear witness that, rough-and-tumble though they be, these Vikings are clean-mouthed men. Between the current talk among "better-class" men in an average passenger steamer's smokeroom and that aboard a sealer, the comparison lies all to the sealers' advantage.

On deck, before dawn, I found the gallant old ship bucking her way into the gray North, crashing floes with shocks that made her leap and shudder. She was rolling a bit, too, so the heavy ice must have been feeling a little swell.

We sighted the *Thetis* miles astern, crashing after us; and on far, jagged ice horizons, scarves of smoke from other steamers of the fleet. The sun swam slowly up into an ineffable morning glow and the evanescent pallor gave place to lurid gleams piercing mists of vivid crimson—storm breeders, as every sailor knows. "Red in the morning, sailors take warning!" An arch of fire blazed above the slow-breathing ice swell; shot long, level shafts across the ivory plain; flecked burnished glints athwart the mirrors of open bays, and ever the thunder of ship and ice reverberated with hollow rumours.

Still on, ever on, the stout ship hammered. On, into the waiting North.

Black clouds of ill augury began to stream across the sky. The wind grew "coarse"; presently deluges of rain drowned the world; and the glass fell and fell. A heavy blow set in, but the ice proved a fine harbour, indeed. A gale at sea, in a steady ship, was something of a novelty to me.

That night, after tea (they never have "supper" aboard a sealer), the Doctor entertained us with some natural history. An ingenious man, this Doctor; an ex-Tommy Atkins who had spent much of his time "in the cava'ry hout in Hinja." His "h's" rattled around like birdshot, popping out in the most unexpected places. Proudly he informed me he had been Sir Edgar Bowring's valet. His uniform was blue dungarees and a brown sweater; he kept his brave mustachios neatly twirled; rolled innumerable cigarettes; always by some amazing shift managed to appear neat; was about the only man on board who could hold the Cap'n at checkers.

In consonance with the "wedderish" barometer, and with the men's opinion that "de kind of a moil [mild spell] is over now," a roaring blizzard that night screamed furiously out of the northern dark and gathered the

Terra Nova into its stinging drive. Squalls of sleet, of hail like rattling volleys of shot, of needle-pointed snow whirls scourged down. So withering grew the cold that the ventilators down into the stokehole had to be plugged with brin bags. The night clamoured with exultant fury. Shrieks of storm devils shook the masts and a ravening madness smudged out the universe.

"Dirty wedder" was about all the sealers would admit. "A bit airsome, sir." Airsome, indeed!

The tired old ship, unable to advance in the teeth of such frenzy, "burned down" for the night; which is to say, stopped and reduced steam. Her boilers needed cleaning, too, and behold the opportunity. To have seen that the boilers were in trim before having left port would have been too much to expect of people who—in Kipling's phrase—are used to "doin' things rather more or less."

I am lying on a vile quilt in a foul hole [my notes record].

I am fairly warm, with two suits of heavy underwear, a sweater, and coat on, and sheepskin-lined slippers. To me this night is bodeful, but no one else seems to mind. The men here in the hellhole lie in their bunks, smoking and murmuring together:

"Wouldn't dis be a big night to year a whitecoat bawl!" "I wish't we was pickin' up fat, b'ys! Pickin' up pans!" "My glorianna, brud, I'd like to be battin' ole swiles!" "Yes, even so!" "But de steam's wonnerful bad. Dis-one go troo de ice like smoke, like a buzz, when her goin' ahl rate!"

Out in the main cabin, despite blizzard and all, the Chief is laughing; the Old Man is chuckling. . . .

Morning again, the eleventh of "de lang, hungry March month." Morning, after a night spent in fitfully trying to keep the "curvey" and my rug over me. My first sight was of Joe Stirge sleeping on his face. Later he told me why he always slept that way:

"So de 'baccy juice won't run down me t'roat in de night." That explained the bulge in his cheek.

Portholes this morning were deep-furred with frost. In the main cabin, Gearge, now minus his celluloid collar was adjusting the maculated tablecloth. Master watch Roberts, jerking his head at the barometer, ominously remarked:

"De glass'm bottom up, sir. Her'm down to 29, an' havin' awful works!" His manner was bodeful. Evidently he had just come down from deck; his face looked parboiled and his brows hung beaded with ice.

I agreed that the situation looked dubious, though "29" meant nothing to me.

"If us gets nipped out yere, we'm 'll be in a shoutin' tangle," he continued. "Mabbe de Man Above knows what us'd do!"

Oddly enough, I felt keen and well. I hadn't undressed for three nights—I never *did* undress, out there, for nearly six weeks!—and I had slept without any ventilation whatever. But nothing seemed to matter.

Tea, toast, and a good smoke before the boistering fire made the world brighter. One by one the aft-crew dragged out of their cubicles, yawning, stretching, spitting, lighting pipes, and jostling into the pantry where poor Uncle Absalom timorously sought to defend his condensed milk, sugar, cups, and hot water against vandal raids. Privately he whispered to me, as he showed me a whole drawer full of clean cups:

"I ondly lets 'em 'ave a few cups, sir. Dem can drink after one nudder. If I putt out twenty, dem ahl be dirty!"

The engine now began to thud but proved unable to force the ship against the ice pack and the gale. On deck I found everything a howl and rattle; a few minutes in that furious tumult quite sufficed.

Down in the cabin again:

"Makin' any wayhead?" asked the Old Man from the berth where he had calmly slept on his back, one arm across his breast—slept peacefully as if at home.

"Eh? What say?" characteristically demanded "Skipper Nat," his son. The Cap'n repeated his question.

"Yes, sir," Skipper Nat informed him. "A little, but not much if we don't get the canvas on 'er. She's just drawin'. Better crack on sail, sir."

"It'd wet the canvas," judged Cap'n Abraham. "But we'll get the stays'ls on her, 'rectly. Don't want to putt 'em on too soon, though, fear they'll tear to pieces."

"Dat canvas 'm a gert 'elp, sir," said another, thick of speech. "Better'n a hengine."

"H'ist up y'r mainstays'l on a lang tayckle, an' fore-stays'l," ordered the Cap'n, still from his berth. "Tell the bosun to putt the lang tayckle out."

"Can't jam this-un," declared Skipper Nat.

"Goin' troo, ahl rate," said the other—a master watch. "It'm a hup-an'-down game, sir, but us goin' troo."

"She's too much by the starn, sir," declared Skipper Nat. "Ain't ballasted rate. An' weepin' [leaking] a bit, too."

"We got to shift some ballast rate a-forrard," judged the master watch. "Rate to de forrard end o' she. Den us'll be goin' a'eed fer fun; yes, sir!"

"Four hands to the wheel!" at length the Cap'n ordered; and presently we were in for a determined try at ice-breaking.

Fiercely the gale smote. The frozen canvas up (after God knows what labour!), banged and slatted as if the very robands would rip loose or the sails' bellies split. They all drew stiff as metal.

"De nippin' fros' barns ye up a bit," admitted bridge master Jonas Hillier. "But we'm goin' on. Dis-un 'ull rattle it fer fun, once us gets troo de jam. A gert ship to buzz round, dis-un is. Dey swiles is a good bit from we, sir, but 'twon't be lang, praise God, afore us gets a rig'lar surge o' fat! If dere'm anodder p'int abaft, dis-un 'll travel good!"

Men with barrows were shifting rock ballast forward, shoving along the snowy deck—an incredibly hard job. Bosun Mike Donovan was flinging salt on the runways from deck to break of the poop to melt the snow and ice there. The barrelman had gone aloft, careless of the "glitter" on shrouds and ratlines, indifferent to the shrieking zero gale. The four steersmen were shouting their *"Port, Steeeeay! Starburd, Steeeeay!"* in answer to commands from the barrel and from the bridge; but that morning the shouts rang less loudly. A couple of them had no warm coats—just a canvas jacket or an outworn sweater.

Toward noon, though "de wedder didn't get no better fast, an' it'd nip ye to pieces," the Old Man—in his vast fur coat and black fur cap a most delectable figure—took his "sexton" and tried to get a shot at the sun.

"I'll try if I can see the 'orizon, an' get a sight," said he. "Then I'll know if we're on the right jife." And somehow or other he did manage it and came down again "wid de sun under 'is arm," as Uncle Edgar declared.

The *Sagona* now lay astern of us as we ground slowly northward "wid a little better stick [speed] on us," under steam and sail; the *Eagle* was racing us, off our starboard bow. Farther off, the *Ranger* came struggling. Who would first "strike de fat"?

I began to share the nervous tension of the ship. It gets you, inevitably.

That afternoon the glass took a decided upward turn and the sky cleared. The ice began to "go abroad" a bit. Cap'n Kean went aloft to look for some trace of the patch, spry as any boy—"damn catty," as one of the cooks expressed it.

He came down, well pleased, though vexed at the other ships so closely tagging.

"They ahl want to dog in the same road!" he grumbled, his face like raw beef with frost and gale. He hated to admit the Newfoundland icefields were free for all. "But anyhow," he added, "we made the field ice, now; got down to the reg'lar sheet ice, now, an' no more slob. You'll see somethin' like seal runnin' afore lang!" He was radiant. "We got great goin', now. Got a fine click on 'er. A good tune on this one; she's shakin' her tail some, now!"

Chief "Mac" beamed with equal satisfaction. He worried over his engine as if it had been a child; and now he revelled as she began to shove through the ice, grinding it to "pummy."

A steel ship would have crumpled and split in a moment; but the *Terra Nova*, staunch veteran of nearly forty winters never even cracked.

The long afternoon flogged on, and night at last enfolded us. A jewelled night; for now all the cloud battalions fled away and more stars came out than ever I had imagined. Pitilessly hard and clear, a full moon swung aloft over ragged ice horizons and laid broad-shimmering ribbons of silver across the bays of ink. Everywhere the ice shimmered with a hard glaze; near and far, the heaped-up pressure ridges glinted, slashed by black shadows. The wizardry of that moon-silver spilled across that plain, like the dead moon's own surface, none shall tell. Death looked on death; moon and ice, all dead.

In the moonlight, spars and rig glittered, ice-crusted. Moonlight clung to the top hamper, froze there, in a fair tracery of ice. Stars shimmered in pools as the ship surged through them. Obscure gushes of phosphorescent green flashed up, then vanished, virescent stars of the sea, in jetty waters, so that the ship rode in stars. The barrelman, still dizzily aloft, dropped his echoing cries through the white emptiness.

Our first bit of news, early next morning—Sunday— was the sighting of two huge seals off the starboard bow. Out on deck in haste, I beheld the immense old dog and bitch a couple of hundred feet away; and lively was the babel they raised. But, on account of the day, their lives were safe.

The bitch lay quiet on a gleaming pan; but the old dog as the ship crashed by, kept turning round and round, then toddling forward with a sinuous, slithering and un-gainly motion. I felt an odd sensation, lost in a frozen, insensate world, thus suddenly to come on life; and on such very warm-blooded, vertebrate, highly evolved life.

I wanted silence. But no one else saw anything there but just two fat seals; and what a pity the day was Sunday! Men shouted gleefully:

"Dem de outscouts o' de patch, by's! Dis-un goin' rate di-rect fer de patch, jonnick [I swear]!"

"Power o' swiles a'eed, I'm t'inkin'. Good sign! Us got more luck 'an a cut cat!"

"Us goin' to bore up wid a full trip o' fat, a logger load. Us 'andy to de fat now, me sons! Dis de rale ole-hood ice, now."

"Ain't it hell, dough, dis got to be Sunday? Dat'm ahl as sove 'em. If 'twasn't Sunday, us wouldn't bide

yere aburd o' dis-un. 'Twould be a bloody garagee [free-
for-all scramble]!"

All hands grew jubilant; but all execrated the other
ships "dogging" us. These were the *Neptune, Sagona,*
and *Thetis;* though how the men could identify them by
the smudges of smoke on the skyline passed my comprehension. They even knew that the *Ranger* had stopped
to take ice!

"Braffus" over, Sabbath hymns began drifting from
the top house. "Nearer, My God, to Thee!" came first;
and then a livelier one, lustily roared forth:

> "Will y'r anchor hold in de starms o' life,
> When de clouds unfold deir-uh wings o' strife?
> When de strong tides lift an' de cables strain,
> Will y'r anchor drift, or firm reeeemain?

> "*We* 'ave an anchor dat kipps de soul,
> Steadfast an' sure, while de billows roll!
> Fastened to de Rock which cannot move,
> Grounded firm an' deep in de Saviour's love! . . ."

As morning wore on and gleaming pinnacles marched
past, all a-glitter in the sun, more and more seals became
visible and excitement grew ever more taut. Men packed
the rails of waist and barricade to watch them at play,
innocent of death so nigh. My first impressions of seals
at close range:

Their habit is to swim forward three or four lunges, or undulations,
then to dive. They are playing, as certainly as a gang of children in
the water. As we skirt a vast field dotted all over with leads, I can
see the splash and fling of water jewels in the sunshine. We pass a
hood "family," thus showing that the harps are probably off somewhere to westward. The family consists of the dog, bitch, and pup
all on one pan, as usual with this species. The dog looks a huge, fat,

lazy creature, stupid enough. As the ship fights her way past, he keeps raising and lowering his head, but does not budge from the pan, even though we are close enough to see his very whiskers. The bitch disports herself gaily in the water of a nearby rifter, lashing up foam. She seems the life of the party, not her logy husband. As for the pup, that is just a blobby blue-gray creature, indifferent to fate.

That afternoon the numbers of seals kept steadily increasing. Excitement ran ever higher. Alas for its having been the Sabbath!

CHAPTER VI

WORSHIP 'TWEENDECKS

SUNDAY night the ship lay idly rolling in embayed, slow-heaving waters. For now was church-time, and she must halt an hour while her men "got a mouthful o' prayers."

Services were held below in the 'tweendecks, whither I repaired with my good friend Uncle Edgar Tucker. I made no very elaborate preparations, nor did any.

"Wash y'r 'ands, an' you'm fit fer church," Uncle Edgar bade me. "Just fruz up y'r hair, an' dat'm well enough!"

An unforgettable experience it was, to crouch down in the hold, to watch these Vikings at worship. To-morrow they will be gory butchers. This night they bow, with a sincerity that thrills you, to the Power they feel very near; while not far off deep surges thunder all along a drifting berg.

A good deal of coughing sounds, but no one talks. Every man pays devout heed. Some wear belts with the buckles of religious organizations. I can see on such buckles mottoes of: "Christian Lads," and "Methodist Brigade."

The vigour of their song is tremendous. Familiar old hymns, all. The preacher—Levi Butts, baldish, in spectacles and a brown sweater—"lines out" the hymns, stanza by stanza. Deadly in earnest is he, for the salvation of souls. You can see that by the mighty shouts of his singing. He is doing his best to make a glad noise before the Lord. Later, I am to see Levi crimson-handed as the rest; but on that night he is a Peter the Hermit, preaching his crusade against the sin of unbelief. No, hardly that. Unbelief has not yet entered the periphery of these men's lives. To them, God is as real, as personal as their own friends. The preacher's appeal for faith is rather that faith shall be revivified, that its white flame shall ever burn and burn!

The preacher talks to them and once again they sing. None venture into the bass; all, alike, sing treble. The very timbers shiver under their intensity. At the last stanza all sit and bow their heads, cover their eyes, and make a prayer of the hymn. Then the leader prays. Though the critical might have smiled at his grammar, none could have failed to yield homage to his burning sincerity. On Protestant and Catholic alike he invokes God's blessing—and Newfoundland is more than one third Catholic, so that many of that faith must have been present there.

After another hymn he reads the Lord's Prayer, which all repeat. He preaches an odd little sermon about the vine and the branches thereof; and then all sing, "I Need Thee Every Hour." Comes, then, his own testimony and that of many others. Haltingly, roughly, the men stand forth and tell what Christ has done for them, and how they love him.

The baker, Hubert Warfield—ruddy-faced, thin, shy-appearing, and in a clean blue sweater—tells how great has been his saving from sin. Several offer prayers. How their voices quiver with earnestness!

Now they sing: "If ever I loved thee, My Jesus, 'tis now!" and loudly they proclaim their love. The preacher reminds them that they are only a little lower than the angels. Privately I ponder that this is a slander on angels, but I hold my peace. As others pray or testify, the preacher keeps exclaiming: "Amen! Yes, yes! Amen, yes, Lard!" or "No, no! Praise de Lard, amen!" From dark corners and bunks unseen echo "Amens!"

One giant Viking, in enormous boots, stumbles to his feet and with deep earnestness, simplicity, and child-like faith proclaims:

"God an' Christ is me best frien's. Dem'll stan' by me. I'll stan' by dey, so when I nade 'em, dem'll stan' by me! I was plunged in de pit o' sin—" ("Amen! Praise de Lard!") "—but now I'm sove. I ain't ashamed fer to testify fer you, Lard. I praise thy dear name an'—" ("Yes, yes, brudder! Amen!") "—an' I knows in de hour o' deat' you'll stan' by me! Amen!"

A chorus of "Amens" follows and the Viking sits down.

In all these prayers and testimonies, *thou* and *you* are wondrously jumbled in addressing God; and another thing, there seems ever to be a canny sense of *quid pro quo*, of payment for worship rendered. Many references crop up to families at home and to prayers there being said for the far wanderers in the ice. Many appeals are made for "dis ship's company, w'iles on de boosum of de deep."

They refer to Dear Jesus in the most startlingly familiar way and get him badly confused with God the Father. They mention casually that Christ "made heaven an' yearth," and discuss him as if he might be merely Tom, Dick, or Harry, living in some hard-by cove—a very rich and powerful friend, ready to help them in exchange for a kind of feudal homage.

"All nations is brudders, an' ahl worship God to-gedder!" the preacher cries. "Come on, let's praise Him on de face o' de great waters, an' let's do it 'earty, b'ys! Rate from de 'eart!"

In all their religion, as in all their lives, death ever obtrudes. These men think often of death. To them it is an ever-present contingency, not something far-off and problematical, for every Newfoundland family has met sea losses. Death is no rare visitor as with us more sheltered folk. Not that they fear it. A braver, more heroic breed never lived. But—death is always there, just crouching.

That night we heard the whitecoats bawl and knew the kill was near. Now here, then yonder rose the tremulous thin cry—ma-ma-ma-ma-a-a-a-a-a—the faint, quivering mew of the young harps, plaintive and penetrant. It drifted down wind, swelled, vanished to a stillness that mocked and waited. Then again it came, and always from some different quarter.

Early next morning whitejackets still were bawling not far off; not enough, perhaps, for a "rally," but harbingers of "de t'ick patch." And there were mother seals, too, out fishing in the ocean depths, bobbing up and suckling their babies as they lay in ice nurseries.

Feet of steersmen going aft clattered in crisp air. Breath hung like steam. Rig and deck gleamed frozen white. At the "top tanks," otherwise called "pinnacle tanks," grimy sealers were drawing rusty red and very dirty water into their slut kettles for matutinal tea. In those tanks ice blocks were melted by steam coils; and once one grew accustomed to rust, dirt, and brackish taste, one didn't mind the water—much.

Smoke from funnel drifted far and low; lazy smoke that hugged the ice, seemingly loath to leave the *Terra Nova*. At the stern, a master watch adjusted his pocket compass by the binnacle; a sign of impending far excursions from the ship.

The cold grew keener as we fronted a building breeze. Huge lakes opened out. Long, steely lines of "slob," or fresh ice, scintillated. Circles of ice like giants' dollars wallowed in the wash of the screw. Off to westward the ice grew pale gold and milky silver as level sun rays struck across. A sight for gods!

More and more seals kept "braychin'," or playing, in the slob ice as we advanced.

Men brought "chisel bars," inspected them on deck, in preparation for possible blasting. If we jam, 'twill be bombs! Uncle Edgar told me sometimes the cold is so intense up here that solid steel bars snap short. Thank heaven, not yet. But even to-day burns the face. And this is "a moild"!

A message buzzed in and was duly delivered by Marky with all ceremony, that the *Eagle* had picked up a "cat," or stillborn seal. This was taken as a good omen.

The clangour of the breakfast bell was welcome. A moderate little breakfast of beans, huge slices of half-cooked bacon, bread, jam, potatoes, and tea. Water, for such as condescended to such, was warm and rusty.

"Dat'm what us got to drink, sir, from dis out," explained Tom Fillyards, cook. The name, for a sailorman, seems too good to be true, but true it is. A saturnine, lean, dark, mustachio'd man, this Tom; shrewdly good-natured and the most obliging of mortals.

"Wonnerful 'ummocky ice, Cap'n," judged a master watch.

"But not too 'ard," averred the Old Man, putting his gold-rimmed glasses into their case and the case into a pocket of his famous green waistcoat. "The very instant we broke that last key pan, it ahl raftered together, but we got through. An' now she's whippin' it on the two sides. Looks like good whelpin' ice, me dear b'ys. We'll soon be into the blood of 'em, now!"

"If don't come wedderish agin," judged Uncle Edgar.

"De humours [traces] of 'em is ahl round evverywheres, now."

"Look like we'm handy to young fat," said Kelloway. "Look like de first spurt comin', 'treckly. But dey'm wonnerful spilled [scattered]."

"In 'gard of runnin' in arr patch," declared Joe Stirge, picking his teeth with a fork, "pap say dis an' pap say dat, but *I* says we'm too far suddren, yet. Got to get down a good bit more nothren, afore——"

"How dis-un bear from Bonavista Cape?" asked Arthur Roberts. "Nar-east-be-east, eh? By de Law Harry, we'm dravin' some! We'll give 'em a cobbin', now, in no time. But if I was you, Cap'n, I'd 'aul dis-un in to de west'ard, some. Us got too much room out yere to kipp cl'ar o' de swiles!"

Marky, our wireless man.

"Safer out nigh the selvage, me son," the Cap'n declared. "A no'd-east wind 'd full evvery bay on the Front an' might jam us." The Cap'n, as was proper, talked a rather better English than his men; though when betimes excited, it broadened. "The seals may be gone to the straight edge. I'd give a wonderful lot to find where them to! We're givin' this one a good shake!"

"But I don't like de way evvery pan go rate unner our tuck!" the carpenter affirmed. "Can't dem foolies to de wheel kipp us cl'ar when us gocs 'starn? If it's 'pend on *dey* to putt us in de fat, us'll get dere on Tib's eve [never], I'm t'inkin'!"

"Not enough yere to bodder wid," said Joe, lighting a black pipe. "Can't see how dey tracks, but look to me

like dey'm ondly a little string of 'em. An' de ice is wonnerful tight, in spots. Dat was skinny, las' night, 'bout
two o'clock. Us was pretty nigh an' handy to a poor
fix!"

"I think dem odders is, too," opined Kelloway, massive
of frame, blue of eye. "Dem can't get out o' where dem
to!"

"Ahl de better fer us, brud," rejoiced Gearge, crossing
his thin, freckled arms. "We'm bound to be 'eed. Oh,
tapers, yes!"

A shift of the wind began driving smoke down the
bogey stovepipe into the cabin. In some infernal way
the spankers forced that smoke to flood the cabin with
strangling fumes. I had to retreat up on deck. The cold
was sharpening, new "sish" forming. Turrs flapped
heavily away—ungainly black-and-white birds, fat-
bodied and heavy of flight, with legs wide-sprangling as
they laboured to rise from open leads or took fearful
slides as they tried to land on new ice.

The ice grew formidable, "nippin' to de land," a sealer
told me. Our two rivals gradually drew near and crossed
our stern so close that we could hear their helmsmen
shout.

"Her light, *Diana* is!" a common hand rejoiced. "Got
no coals—her'll be burned out an' done in a fartnight!"
And greatly he rejoiced. More truly he predicted than he
knew! Never was she destined to reach any port again.

The *Thetis* and *Diana* dogged our every "jife" and
"cut." They spied on us. Not if they could help it
should Cap'n Kean steal a march on them. He, "admiral
of the fleet," should not be allowed to strike the fat and
leave them out of it.

"An' if they make a blank, I'll be blamed," the Old Man
complained. "Whatever happens, I'm blamed. I mind

one spring they *all* tagged me, an' it was an off spring. Nobody got into the main patch at all. An' what d'you think, sir? They blamed me for leadin' 'em 'stray!"

So close *Thetis* pressed that collision threatened. It came to collision, too; not serious, but at all events we carried off one of her boats—whereat, indignant yells from her, derisive laughter from us. Well, good luck, anyhow; *Thetis* to some small extent was crippled!

The interminable afternoon began to fag on, with naught to do save cough in the smoke-rank cabin, and yawn, drink tea, watch endless checker games; when all at once——

A yell!

From the masthead flung, it electrified our labouring ship:

"*Whitecoats !*"

CHAPTER VII

BAPTISM OF BLOOD

AN INSTANT, breathlessness held us all in its vise. Then confusion burst like a shell.

Cap'n, bosun, carpenter, master watches, all jumped up. The checkerboard was overturned; pieces rolled to the floor; no matter. On deck, louder yells summoned. Keen with the blood lust, all who could go on ice began heaving on their gear. Such a shouting, such a leaping to arms, such a buckling-on of sheath knives, steels, belts; such a grabbing of tow ropes and murderous gaffs you never could imagine.

Young Cyril, the Cap'n's grandson, with flying leaps shot through the cabin, ducked into the cubicle I shared with him and Skipper Nat, snatched his gaff and nearly impaled me as I ran for my "oppers" (spyglasses) and camera.

Even though I had no purpose to imbrue my hands in blood, my heart was drumming a bit, my temperature rising. For now the kill was close upon us.

Up tumbled all hands and out upon the coal-blackened decks. Spiked boots ground the planking. Forward, streams of hunters came milling from the to'gal'n' house, the 'tweendecks, the dungeon. A rapid spate of cries, questions, cheers, troubled the frozen air. Grimed faces appeared at galleys, at engine-room scuttle. Sealers lined the broad rails gesticulating out toward the illimitable plain of arctic ice that blazed, dazzling white, under the March sun.

The thrill that comes but once a voyage had arrived. For now we were to have "a rally at de young fat." We, first of all the fleet, had struck the longed-for whitecoats.

Already Cap'n Kean had gained the bridge. He seemed more like a "gert, bear-lookin' stick of a man" than ever, as, bear-like, his furry arms waved over the weather-cloth.

"Overboard, me sons!" he shouted. "Make a pier-head jump [a quick start], an' get into 'em! Over, me darlin' b'ys!"

But the men needed no urging. Even before the ship had bucked and ground, rearing, into the edge of the groaning floe they had escaladed the rail—dozens, scores of them.

They seemed now to have no organization. There was no gathering of "goes," or gangs, under command of master watches, as later in the old-fat kill. . This was just a free-for-all scramble.

First of all actually to make the ice was Cyril. Not more than sixteen, he; but boys are daring in those hardy latitudes. He led the leaping, yelling crowd that jumped to the loose-broken pans; that scrambled with goat-like agility to solid floes, and in heavily spiked skinny woppers ran like mad demons, yelling, across that fantastic confusion.

At the rail, meantime, I watched; I, who by the grace of Bowring Brothers had been permitted to go "to the ice." My first interest was less with the hunters than the hunted. At the beginning of it all, the whitecoats looked to me like great white or whitish-yellow pincushions, woggling along, lying still, taking their blobby and full-fed ease, heaving around, blatting with a sort of puppy-like, kitten-like, lamb-like bawl, mew, bark, or what you choose to call it.

As the whitecoats passively awaited the attack, some of the old seals raised inquiring heads, began to get under way with a peculiarly sinuous motion. The dogs, to their shame be it said, were first to make for rifters and bobbing holes; for these were harps, and not the fighting hoods. Open waters thrashed with escaping seals. Up, down, and up again the old ones surged, with a startled and anxious air; glorious, sleek, brown-eyed creatures, gleaming and glistening. They seemed inquisitive, willing enough to find out what manner of thing this swift, two-legged animal might be that ran and laughed and yelled.

Some of the females lingered, but not long. They had to go, one way or the other—into the sea or under the sculping knife. I was astonished at the mother seals' lack of maternal devotion. Perhaps half fled. With a farewell wave of the scutters, scores of them vanished. But the young, the coveted whitecoats, still remained.

"Dere'm de fat, sir!" a grizzled old Notre Dame Bay man exulted to me. "Ondly a little larry string, but dat'm a beginnin'!"

The kill was in full cry. Swiftly the men ran and leaped over rough ice. They caught seals, struck with their heavy, cruelly pointed and hooked gaffs. Cyril later boasted that he had slaughtered the first seal.

I beheld Cyril's feat. A fat dog was his prey. The dog faced round at him, raised its head, flashed sharp teeth—the sort of teeth that sometimes work havoc on incautious hunters. It flung a throaty "*Rrrrr-r-r-r-r-r !*"

Whack!

The seal's head dropped. Far from dead the seal was; still thrashing; but never mind about that! Cyril jammed his gaff into the ice, flung off his coil of tow rope, jerked out his flensing knife and whetted it, all with the correct technique of a finished sealer. He rolled the seal over; with a long gash split it from throat to scutters, and, amid perfectly incredible floods of crimson, began skinning it. Colour? The ice glowed with it!

Everywhere men were going into action. Everywhere the gaffs were rising, falling; tow ropes being cast off; sealers bending over their fat booty of both young seals and old. Everywhere the seals were being rolled over and sculped.

Almost invariably the seals met death head-on. They might flee at man's approach, but once he was upon them, they would stand and show fight. Nearly always they would rear up, fling their growl, make show of biting. But one or two slashes with the long-handled gaff usually fractured the skull; the seal dropped, dying; and the knife expedited his departure to some world where perhaps polar bears, sharks, and men were not.

The actual work of blood at first—though later I grew used enough to it!—was rather shuddering to me. A seal is so extremely bloody, and that blood so extraordinarily hot. The fleshy *whack-whack-whack*, dully drifting in over the ice, isn't an agreeable sound, either. Nor is it pretty to watch seals die.

All over the ice, near, far, among clumpers and pinnacles and in sheltered seal nurseries, the hunters were shucking seals out of their sculps as deftly and almost as quickly as you would shell a peanut. Every sculp—the sculp is the skin with the fat adherent—had one flipper cut out, one retained. Spots of red dotted the ice-scape. *Fwitt-fwitt-fwitt* sounded the whetting of blades on steels; and rather horrifically the hunters wiped their dripping knives on their sleeves. Their clothing and the ice, alike, blossomed vividly. Their hands looked like gloves of red that dripped. All about pelted carcasses sprawled, twitched, steamed in crimson pools.

Afar off men were still running. From distances beyond leads dusked by catspaws, where seals were leaping, echoed shouts of the kill. Along the rail, those who had borne no hand in the exploit were gathered and tumult arose. Men clung in rig and ratlines. Officers peered from the bridge. Gibes, cheers, laughter rang into the thin and shining air.

Somebody yelled that this was the southeast "carner" of the main patch; but in this wilderness, how could anybody know?

Now some of the hunters, having slain all they could make shift to get aboard, were returning. Open came the loops of the lines; swiftly the nimrods laced their "tows." They cut holes in the edges of the sculps, passed the ropes back and forth through these, and made a peculiar, complicated knot. A turn of rope served as a grip for the left hand. The long end was passed over the right shoulder, wrapped round the arm, and firmly held by the right hand. Lacing a tow is something of a trick in itself.

Through ice defiles and around pinnacles they toiled, each "scotin' his tow," bending far forward with the weight of the load. From every man's shoulder, thus toiling, swayed and swung his gaff. Over plaques of virgin white—white no longer when they had passed! —the hunters came labouring shipward. Long, wavering lines of colour formed; they joined to broader roads, all converging on the *Terra Nova*. Crimson trails, these, such as no otherwhere on earth exist. Man's mark and sign and signal in the North.

On and on, over the glazed, shining surface the red trails lengthened. A few whitecoats were still bawling, wopsing their puffy, furry bodies about, but now only a few. And even those would very presently be attended to.

The whole world lay beaten by a drenching surf of wind that paralyzed; but still I stood and watched—as who would not? In came the sculps, fur side to the ice, flesh side quivering like currant jelly—quivering and smoking. The thin steams of life departing, not yet quite gone, hung tenuously. And on those sculps the flippers wagged and waved like little hands, bidding farewell for ever to the world of ice. No longer white, the whitecoat sculps had become redcoats. Red indeed! Here, there, a "round-swile," which is to say one as yet unskinned, was trailing at the end of a gaff.

Some of the seals, appallingly vital creatures, are not at all dead as they are hauled in on gaffs. They writhe, fling, struggle. Here comes a baby with a gaff point jammed through its jaw. Here, a mother seal, bleeding in slow and thick runnels. Both, at the ship's side, are rolled belly up and slit. They gush.

On the bridge Cap'n Kean jubilantly makes oration:

"Out with them straps, now! Look alive an' throw out them straps. You, there, come on aburd now, b'ys. John, kill y'r seal—*don't* sculp 'em alive. Now, 'aul out y'r whipline! Stand by with that whipline, you—over with it. Take 'em on the after winch. Lots of 'em there, to winnard, now. Jump overboard, some o' you fellers! There you are, me sons; there's a great lead. Turn to y'r left, you two! An' you, there, don't putt y'r gaff p'int down! Remember, arr hole in a skin, aft o' the fippers, is ten cents out o' y'r pocket. Now then, aburd with 'em. Look yary!"

Out go the straps, ropes with the ends spliced together. The gory-handed fellows on ice haul the tow lines from the sculps and run the straps through the hole in each sculp where the flipper has been cut out. Bitter cold means nothing to them. Hard work and the wine of excitement warm them; I, meanwhile, shiver in heavy overcoat and cap of fur.

The straps passed through a bunch of sculps, and the "wire" or rope from the winch dragged out from its pulley on a spar, by the whip-line, eager men hook the strap of seals to the wire.

"Go 'eed de winch!" shouts a huge-booted, thin-faced man standing precariously on top of the rail. With a

"Go 'eed de winch!"

roar and rattle, a hissing of steam, the winch snakes up its quivering load. Shouting men tug at the whip-line, holding back the sculps as best they can from catching on the side-sticks. Up, up the ship's side the sculps drag and then swing free, a heavy, dripping pendulum of hair, fat, skin, blood.

"Walk back on de winch!"

Swiftly the sculps swoop, and *plop!* they fall on deck. Joyous hands grab, unhook, twitch out the now bright-red whip-line and fling it all a-sprawl once more far over the rail. The ship's first bit of wealth is "aburd o' dis-un."

Again the same process. Exultation runs high. The rail reddens; so, too, the coaly deck. Lusty toilers are meantime, with "seal-dog" hooks and ropes, hauling the round-seals up and in. Once on board, the men pelt these in a jiffy.

"More in the scoppers, me sons," warns the Cap'n. "Take 'em down in the scoppers more. Don't get blood ahl over the deck!"

A comfortable pile of fat accumulates, smoking. Meantime, work is still under way on ice, alongside. Men are sculping there, bent double. The oppressive, sickly sweetish smell of fresh blood drifts up. Bright cascades flood the deck. Milk spurts, mingles with the blood; gutters away.

One round-seal is so big they have to winch it up; and thereat they cheer. Men on ice are jabbing their gaffs into pans, winding up their tow ropes around foot and knee; making the ends fast; heaving them, still a-drip over their shoulders. Every carcass, I see, has the scutters left on it. This gives each skinned body the appearance of wearing fur boots.

A few more round-seals come dragging on gaffs. The ice grows spotted with *disjecta membra*. Some of these twitch and quiver. One can see the ripple of muscles in carcasses that, dead, still protest death.

Men jostle and crowd along the rails, flecked with red snow. On the rails, blood freezes.

Those who have had no hand in the slaughter envy their more fortunate brethren. Alas, that there are not seals enough to go round; enough to warrant everybody "goin' away!" The disappointed ones grip their gaffs, adjust their tow lines. Next time, perhaps——?

Lest anything be left alive, the Old Man looks abroad; with loud and joyful shouting directs the tag-ends of slaughter. From high up on a step at the end of the bridge, he gesticulates, bellows:

"Go get evverythin' with hair on it, me sons! Here, Skipper Tom, can't you cross that lead? Jump on that piece o' slob, man—it'll hold—it's broad as Paddy's blanket! I'd like to putt on skin boots, meself, an' try me luck! You two men, there's a scattered one off to winnard. Get 'em! Rate behind that wad of ice—there, there! Jump out there, Moores, an' bat that one! There, now," as someone falls *ker-splash!* into the waters of an open lead, "what ye mean, makin' a hole in the ocean that way? Look where y're at, man! Wait, now," as the unfortunate scrambles out on a drifting pan, "bide where y're to. Don't jump, yet. Now, *now*—ah, knew y'd make it! Go on; more seals! Go on, me lucky b'ys!"

Along the rail:

"Dey ahl deed, now, cl'ar o' one young un, a-dere. Deed as a dick."

"An' *dat* un deed, now. Picco, 'e bat un, ahl rate."

"What was they, mostly, brud? Ole harps or beddamers?"

"A wonnerful fine rally, sarnly, fer de first-off!"

From the bridge I hear the Old Man again:

"I hate to kill these seal, I do, indeed. It fair pains me!"

Astonishment! Has the Cap'n gone mad or turned tenderhearted? Neither. For now he adds:

"They're so wonderful small; some of 'em 'ardly worth the bother. If they could only have been let grow another week——"

I understand and mentally apologize to the excellent Cap'n for having misjudged him.

The kill draws to its close for lack of killable material. Odd bits and random observations: Three men running for a pan with a trio of whitecoats thereon, and one bitch. She escapes, hunching herself along with a speed truly amazing. All three whitecoats are killed and sculped in a minute. The swiftness of it amazes.

Yet the technique is perfect. Two or three very swift cuts open the whole body, exposing the rich white fat. Niagaras of blood cascade. A seal appears to be merely a bag of blood and fat. The head of the skin is rapidly but perfectly dissected off. How the enormous eyeballs stare!

The body itself looks surprisingly small and thin; a mere muscular core to all that huge obesity. Yet I am told that a seal, hard put, can for limited distances swim at the rate of 100 miles an hour; and this, too, using only the scutters.

One very small whitecoat is stabbed, dying; but, after all, is overlooked. Too small, perhaps. The men leave him. Not worth bothering with, after all. He welters and dies. Wasted. Somehow this saddens one. Not so bad when used!

The cook issues from his galley with a sharp knife and begins cutting flippers from sculps.

"Fipper f'r tea," he smiles at me. "An' wonnerful fine meat dat is too, sir, widout ye l'ave a bit o' fat on it. Evvery laysses' little bit 've got to be skun off. De Ole Man got to 'ave fipper. Ah, ain't 'e de b'y to eat un, dough?"

I wonder if I, too, am going to eat flipper? Probably. Nothing astonishes one, here.

Now "Marky" is bidden to his labours, and the wireless begins to whine. It shoots the glad news to others, that the *Terra Nova* is "into the young fat."

Men bring a "jig," or steelyard, up on deck, and weigh four of the old-fat sculps. One tips the yard at ninety pounds. At this, all rejoice. Such heavy fat augurs a big bill.

A pandemonium of jubilation bursts forth as now the hated *Thetis* (she whose boat we carried off) comes crashing through ice on our port hand, and rams into the now depleted seal nursery. Too late! Dejectedly she ploughs on and away, without getting so much as a smell of young fat. Howls of derision, catcalls, gibes pursue her. Our own spirits soar in unison with the depression of those aboard the rival.

"Come ashore now, ahl hands!" orders the Cap'n; the word "ashore" in Newfoundland ship talk meaning "aboard." "We're goin' on, now. Maybe goin' to get another rally 'fore night!"

Night is approaching. The west is beginning to flame with gold and scarlet. But still enough light may endure for a bit more slaughter. The men cheer and laugh as they swarm in. Up ropes and over side-sticks, red-painted now, they escalade with the agility of apes. They catch the rail with gaffs, haul themselves to the rail, leap over to the reeking deck.

"Easy 'starn!" from the Old Man. The engine-room bell jangles. Out backs the *Terra Nova* from the bottom of the "bay" where she has lain. The archaic engines begin to thud and thump again, like a tired heart. Away the ship surges, away from that red-blotched place of desolation where, save for some few frightened survivors still surging in sunset-glinted waters, all seal life has vanished. The first "whitecoat cut" has been made. Man has passed.

Away the ship grinds, crushes, shudders through the floes, but now with how exultant a spirit! Her men are different men. For the first honours of the spring are the *Terra Nova's*. She is now, as till the end she remains, "high-liner" of the fleet.

CHAPTER VIII

THE LIFE OF THE SEAL

IF YOU want to study animal instincts in all their wonder, wholly uninfluenced by man, go up into the North and watch the seal herds. There you shall see the mother infallibly recognizing her own precious, among whole acres' of moon-eyed white pincushions, all exactly alike. The mother slithers about on ice, nuzzling at one whitecoat after another until she finds her own beloved. Snappishly she repels all others that try to hump themselves near the maternal fount. Scent is probably the determining factor in the recognition of the young. Levi G. Chafe says, in a letter to me:

Seals are governed more by scent than sight. Whether in the water or on ice, they are sure to scent a man to windward, at least 500 yards away. They can at times apparently detect the presence of men, miles distant, and if the smoke of a steamer drifts down on them from a distance of five or ten miles, they may take to the water.

Another amazing fact in the seals' life is their sense of location, their power to return to the same bay, lead, rifter, or bobbing hole where they have left the young. This has been tested by tying leather tickets to seals' scutters and releasing the animals; watching on the drift ice, and timing their return. They go away fishing, stay all day, and infallibly return—unless killed by bears, sharks, narwals, men, or other predatory animals.

This is an almost incredible feat. The seals not only swim away under ice, coming up now and then to breathe,

117

and go ten, twenty miles; but all the time the ice is wheeling, grinding, turning. No fixed landmarks exist.

Seals usually travel perhaps twenty miles an hour, though they can "bolt," with flippers close to sides, at the rate of one hundred. They can live about twenty minutes without breathing. Now, in some mysterious way they are able to gauge the width of a strip of ice they mean to swim under, so as to avoid getting caught and smothered. They won't attempt too wide a strip. Even a man, up on a pinnacle, would find it practically impossible to be sure of finding open water two or three miles off unless the lead were very large. Yet the seals, which probably cannot see anything like that distance, make no mistake. They never venture under ice more than two or three miles wide and too heavy to be broken with their heads. Drowned seals are never found. No human intelligence can cope with the problem of how seals estimate width and thickness of ice. A "spot o' swiles," close beset by enemies and caught in nipped ice where the bobbing holes and rifters have been closed up, will sometimes gather in a bunch, by their combined weight break the ice, and escape.

The young are born on "whelping ice," which Chafe in a letter describes as:

A particular form of ice, in extensive sheets seldom more than three or four inches thick; that is to say, freshly made ice, soft and easy to bore. The harp is a gregarious animal, and the mothers all like to be close to one another. There may be one or two hundred thousand in the patch of seals on one sheet several miles in length and breadth.

I suppose Chafe is right; but I have certainly seen whitecoats on thick ice. Perhaps it thickened after they were born. Some of it looked to me as if one could build a brick block on it.

Seals have a good many stillborn pups. These are the "cats," whereof the fur is fast. This "cat" fur is apparently the only Atlantic seal fur that will not shed its hair. The cats make an excellent white or very pale yellowish fur, immensely thick and warm. All whitecoat fur is of a peculiar woolly texture, impervious to cold, a very different fur from the hair of the old seals—like swansdown, perhaps, as much as anything.

The young harps weigh seven to nine pounds at birth and put on fat at an amazing rate, which some estimate as high as three or four pounds a day. Others claim it is not more than two. They average about two feet long to two-six, at first, and rapidly lengthen. The young hoods weigh eight to twelve pounds, and seem to fatten and enlarge even faster than their cousins. Nature apparently knows that their ice-riding stage, unprotected by any white coat, is especially dangerous, and rushes them to the swimming stage.

The young seals usually sleep on their sides or backs. You'll hardly find a prettier sight than the pups asleep, flippers in air, now and then twitching their little hands. Old Atlantic seals sleep on ice or in the water; never, like their Pacific cousins, on land. When asleep in the water, they lie on their backs, fold their flippers, expand their scutters, and throw their heads back, pillowing them on the waves.

The hood pups suffer from their lack of protective colouration. Their gray to blue-slate backs, fading into white below, with brown spots, make them very much more conspicuous than the young harps. Nothing could be better hidden than these latter on snowy ice; and if they only had brains enough to keep their mouths shut, thousands would escape that are yearly slaughtered. The poor simpletons insist on calling "mamma," even when the hunters are nigh; and this is their undoing. Herein seal instinct seems imperfect. Many another young animal knows enough to "freeze" and keep mum in danger. Perhaps young seals instinctively trust so fully to their white coats, that they forget other factors.

Oddly enough, the whitecoats need rough, hard, cold weather to develop properly. They love to be buried in snow, and eat a great deal of it. A bitter, stormy spring with lots of snow and rain—this is their choice. They fatten more on snow and milk than on milk alone; and fine, quiet, warm weather greatly retards their growth. For about a fortnight after birth they lie in one place, sheltered among the pinnacles and clumpers of the seal nursery. Their enemies, during this whole time on ice, are sharks, swordfish, bears, arctic foxes, and men.

Nature works a kind of poetic justice on a good many of the bears and foxes that go out riding the ice and looking for young seals. Floes go adrift, pans break away, the southern-setting current carries them into warmer waters where the ice all "goes abroad," and they have to swim for it. The foxes obviously find short shrift. Consider the thousands of dollars' worth of magnificent furs that miserably vanish!

The bears, I understand, put up a game fight, and some are said to swim upward of a hundred miles to land. Even so, a good many must get drowned when the berg or growler they take refuge on finally melts.

Instinct, for these animals, seems faulty. Nature obviously does not warn them of the dangers of venturing out beyond the "ballycatters," or shore ice. Probably the reason is this: the animals which safely return are not afraid; those which do not, never live to breed caution in any offspring.

The young hoods shed their white coat in what the

Newfoundlanders call the "wop bag," which seems to be a kind of afterbirth, and which—for both species—one finds scattered all over whelping ice. Gulls and other sea fowl relish these "whelping bags," and spots of seal are sometimes located by flocks of birds. Wild ducks are said to fatten on seal milk they find on ice; and after seals have been killed, the carcasses feed birds, sharks, and— eventually sinking as the ice melts—doubtless some of the same finny tribes that the seals themselves have earlier devastated.

Only a few hours after birth, the young hoods can fend for themselves and swim. Seal hunters have told me that sometimes, when a hood family is hard pressed, the bitch will take the young in her flippers and go into the water with it. This I have never seen; but I have seen attacked bitch harps nose their whitecoats into the water; and sequently the young idiots clamber back on ice and get killed there. The whitecoats stop bawling the minute they get into water. Can it be that the mothers shove their babies into it to keep them quiet?

Independent as the young hoods are, they usually stay on ice for about twenty-five days with their parents. As the hoods pup anywhere from the 10th to the 20th of March, or two to three weeks later than the harps, dipping time for them is later than for the harps. In both species the family work is all done by the mother. The dogs just amuse themselves, disporting in open leads; though, truth to tell, they seem to enjoy basking and idling more than swimming. A surly, ill-tempered race of "ice-riding pinnipeds," the hoods. They refuse to associate even with one another, and keep in scattered families, widely dispersed on the eastern edge of the ice. Lazy, too; they choose thinner ice than the harps, where boring is easier— or so the Newfoundlanders say.

If you want to start an argument, ask sealers just how the whitecoats are fed. There's no end to this discussion. Aboardship, I asked Uncle Edgar. He said: "De whitecoats butts an' butts, an' fulls up like an egg. Dey sucks till de mudder's gone."

I inquired of another. He insisted: "No, sir, dem don't suck, 'tall. Look-see de sculps, y'self. Ain't narr sign o' narr nipples, on dey." I looked, and there was none; at least, none that I could see. Also, the sculps showed no perforations such as mammary glands might be expected to make.

After I was ashore again, I referred the matter to E. J. Penney, a St. John's author and investigator. He declared: "Now, sir, this nursing business is definitely settled. The bitches suckle their young, the same as any mammal."

But when I asked Mr. Chafe he said, "The mother seal exudes the milk from her udder and the young one laps it from the ice."

So there you are!

All I know from personal observation is this, that while in the icefields I many times beheld the old mother seal lying on her side, with the whitecoat nuzzled up to her, head on.

Later I used to enjoy trudging out over the ice of the harp nurseries. The woolly little beggars look up at you with a couple of ravishing dark-brown eyes continually suffused with heart-melting tears, needing only a ribbon round their necks (if they have necks, which doesn't seem apparent) to fit them for prize winners in any beauty show. The eyes are flat, or very slightly curved, the nostrils open and close with each breath. Splendidly watertight those nostrils are. The ears are not apparent in the young. Even the old seals' ears are trivial, and seem a trifle dull. An aquatic life must injure the sense of hearing.

A whitecoat would make a splendid pet, at first. A more confiding creature doesn't live. You can hold it in your lap, turn it upside down, carry it by one flipper; it never budges, yelps, or shows any interest whatever in the proceedings.

These youngsters possess astonishing vitality; enough to compensate for an almost total lack of brains. If their mothers have fed them for a few days, they can sometimes survive being orphaned, live till "dipping time," get into the water, begin fishing, and make a go of life.

Normally, at the age of about twenty-five days, the whitecoats' pelts weigh from forty-five to sixty pounds. Gradually the colour changes to pearl gray with brown spots, and with the change the young seals usually lose weight. As "the seals' birthday" is about February 28th, and the young "dip" in about a month, the old seals are usually free to disport themselves by the first of April—perhaps a little sooner.

This sporting time of the seal is one of nature's most entertaining spectacles. The old seals appear to revel in their freedom—freedom not only from nursing and from fishing for the young (by which I mean catching enough fish to maintain a milk supply for those ravenous youngsters), but also from strenuous labours of ice boring. It is no trivial task to keep the bobbing holes open in gales and "nips" and zero weather. But that has to be done, or the young will be left unprovided for. The door of the seal's house must never be allowed to close.

Just how that door is constructed, the best authorities differ.

"Dey swiles can bite rate up troo de ice wid deir teeth, an' bore troo wid deir fippers," one old hunter assured me.

Mr. Chafe asserts:

The method of making the bobbing hole is well known. The first duty of the seal is ice-boring. A small hole is clawed in the ice. Then one flipper is planted firmly and the body is revolved around the hind flippers.

Mr. M. T. Flynn, another expert, declares:

Seals choose thin ice, just what they can break through with their heads after one night's freezing. They keep the holes open day and night till the ice gets strong enough to mount upon, to bring forth their young. Of course there are always two seals for every hole, male and female, and they will follow this ice wherever the winds drive it.

I have seen it stated that they mount the ice and bore down. Nothing can be farther from the truth, as they make the hole from below, and no matter how hard the frost, they keep it open. By the middle of March, or the 20th, the ice is perhaps fifteen or twenty inches thick, with a few extra inches around the hole.[1]

Once this bobbing-hole task is ended, along with the cares of maternity, away all the old seals go to "ride de ice an' go away an' clane dereselfs, an' have an enj'yin' time." They post sentinels and take life easy.

"Dey putts a big white dog on watch, up on a 'ummock, in evvery patch," a gunner told me, "an' dat'm de feller you'm got to kill, first. Got to shoot un. Den de odders see un lay quate [quiet] an' dem bide on ice. But if him go, dem ahl goes."

At this time, so great is their lassitude that sometimes the hunters can hardly drive them down. On a fine, sunny day, the herd will often prefer to stand and deliver its life, rather than exert itself to flee. Sometimes a seal in this stage is unwilling to take the water because its pelt gets sunburned and so tender that it tears. I have seen

---

[1] *Newfoundland Commercial Annual*, for 1921.

"burned" skins that could be ripped with the finger. A sunburned seal, if forced down, will sometimes cry with pain of contact with the cold brine; such a one is called a "screecher." The herd rides the ice early in May, when the northward trek begins. Until then, old and young alike drift with the ice, seemingly indifferent whither it may carry them.

One very curious instinct is this: that as soon as the old seals mount the ice for their annual picnic the bedlamers flock away by themselves to patches of ice ten or fifteen miles southeast and southwest of the main breeding ice; the dogs to the former, the bitches to the latter. There they stay till their elders and betters forsake the main patch. Why is this? Who enforces this discipline and what possible significance can it have?

The "rusties" and "bedlamers," or second and third year seals, appear to be the "cut-ups" of the family. They love to congregate in parties and play. Active, fearless, inquisitive, they get into all kinds of trouble. Hunters say that on the northward migration, the bedlamers run wild, do not obey the traffic laws, and as a result often get themselves shot, or netted, or caught by bears and sharks along the way. The older seals, standing off farther at sea avoid trouble. But who gives orders for the seal army? how are they transmitted? how understood?

Newfoundland has a name for every age and kind of both harps and hoods. This nomenclature is important for us to know. In the first place, "harps" are so called because they have a patch of brown hair on the shoulders roughly resembling a harp. These seals are from five to seven feet long, and when full grown are a kind of indigo blue-black, fading into gray, and with a white belly. The face is dark gray, the muzzle black; whiskers or "smellers" long and curved; eyes a liquid brown and so beautiful that many a girl might envy them. The flippers bear nails of bluish hue. Sometimes harps are called "half-moon seals." The marking looks like a broad curved line of connected dark spots, starting from each shoulder and meeting on the back, above the tail. Only the dogs have this marking, and then not till their second year.

"Whitecoats" we already know about. When "dey rolls de white off, an' gets spottedy," they are said to be "buttoned up the back." As they start migrating, they are called "baters," *i.e.*, beaters. "Quinters" is another name for the beating seals. A whitecoat that has not lost all its white, is known as a "ragged jacket." Beaters for a while suffer a good deal in struggling back on the ice. Sometimes the fur is torn from under their flippers by their efforts to mount the pans; lumps and sores occasionally form there.

Second-year harps are "rusties," or "rusty jackets." A "rusty ranger" is a second-year seal with rounded spots that have not yet opened into the harp shape.

"Bedlamers" are third-year seals and now of breeding age. These grow fast. Seals grow greatly their first, third, and fourth years, but very little their second. As Joe Stirge assured me: "Dem rusties ain't a farden [farthing] bigger 'an dem was de end o' last year. But dem *grows* when dem gets to be 'oppin' beddamers!"

The fourth-year harps are "black backs," "saddle backs," or "saddlers"—"de saddle dogs an' de rale ole bitches, de rale ole 'ers." From that time onward, they are all "old harps." After about five years of age, the gray tint becomes bluish, with brown patches on the shoulders. A "smutty bitch" is a female harp that has never pupped. Nobody knows exactly how long a seal lives. Most of them don't live long, if Newfoundlanders

St. John's, as it looks when the fleet sails (*from England's files*)

Photo. by Vey

Sealing-fleet preparing to sail.

Not lovely to look at, and infernal to live on, but built for the job is the oak-hearted old *Terra Nova*.

The departure of a sealing-vessel is always a great event.

The dingy blue sea-chests go to the steamer on odd native "slides."

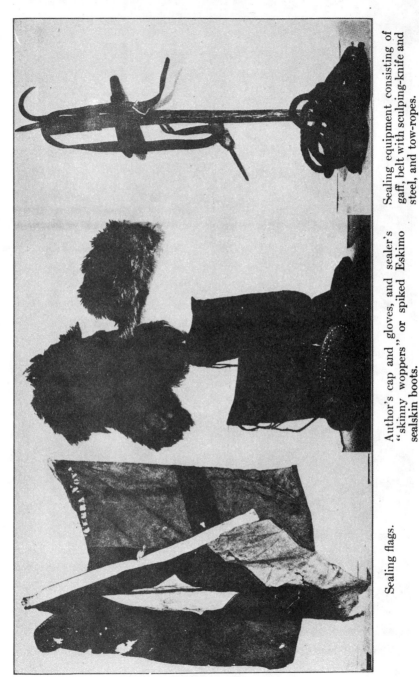

Sealing flags.

Author's cap and gloves, and sealer's "skinny woppers" or spiked Eskimo sealskin boots.

Sealing equipment consisting of gaff, belt with sculping-knife and steel, and tow-ropes.

By permission of Curtis Publishing Company

The Admiral of the Fleet
Cap'n Abraham Kean, on bridge of *Terra Nova*.

Cap'n Abraham Kean, with *Terra Nova*. Note very rough ice through
which ship ploughs.

In this cabin of the *Terra Nova*, Scott and Shackleton once lived.
Several master-watches at table.

Group of hunters on deck of *Terra Nova*

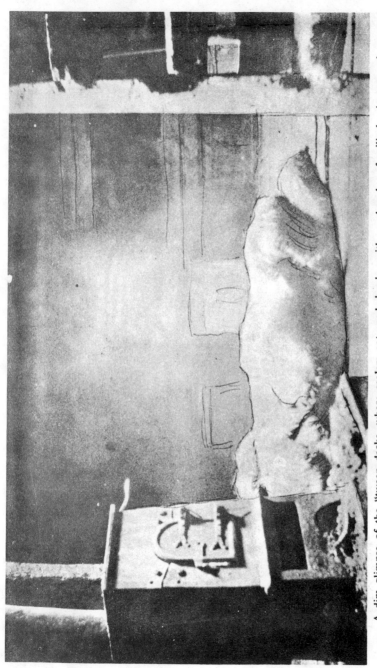

A dim glimpse of the "tween decks, where sealers eat and bunk, with seal-sculps familiarly juxtaposed and often dead-ripe. Bogey, at left where in British fashion they boil tea and make toast on the points of their sculping-knives. Somebody's always having tea and toast. (Photo and caption from England's files)

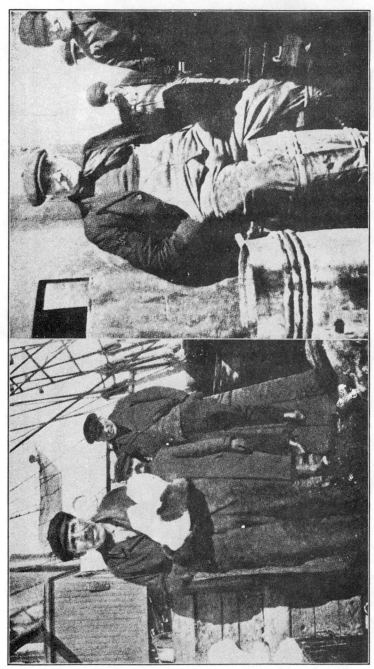

"The Standing Man" with ice for tea. (Background, Doctor and Chief Engineer).

Carpenter, Edwin Tucker, who slept on a bare board to give me his bunk. My best friend and chum on board.

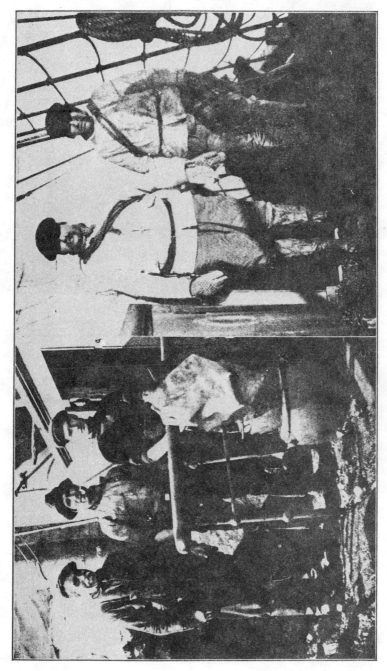

Preacher, Cook, Baker.   Bare arms, below zero!   Two master-watches.   With men like these, one does not argue.

Men preparing for a "rally" at the seals.

A "rally."

Gunners and "dogs" going away.

White-coat, or young harp seal, probably about two weeks old.

Mother seal trying in vain to induce white-coat to escape down bobbing-hole

Harp bitch and pup or white-coat.

By permission of Curtis Publishing Company   *Photo. by Vey*

Here's a dog-hood, anything but a passive resister. The baby has just been killed (at left). You have to look alive, in tackling a dog-hood.

Photo. by Hollands

The surface of the moon must look like some of the sunset views
of the arctic ice.

Photo. by Hollands

The death of a harp.

Photo. by *Hollands*

Marconi-man, 3rd engineer, and George Allan England, with white-coats.

Not too loose for hunting on, if seals are sighted.

Photo. by Hollands

Men "copying" over loose ice. "Dog," in centre, holds cartridge-bag in hand. These men are awaiting a chance to jump and scramble aboard.

Man "copying" aboard. Lively work to board moving ship over small cakes, without a ducking.

One rally is over, and the men are crowding to the forrard galley for a "mug-up" of bread and tea.

Master-watch John Kelloway. A giant in strength
and daring.

Typical seal-hunter.

Seal-hearts in the belt of a young Viking.

From pinnacles like these the men chop fresh ice, to make their famed "pinnacle-tea."

Out in the hazy fog goes an early morning army of seal-killers.

Joe Stirge, "swatching."

The winch bringing a tow on board.

Making a pan is heavy work; even in zero weather and with a gale blowing, you'll sweat.

A good day's catch, like this, fills the decks with quivering redness and the air with rarest perfumes.

Mucking into a huge "pan" on the ice.

Dragging sculps over coal-grimed deck of *Terra Nova*, to "tally down" in hold. These are old harp skins.

The chopping-up of seal-carcasses, for packing in barrels, transforms the forecastle head into a butcher's-shop.

Joe Stirge, who has to sleep on his face to keep the tobacco juice from running down his throat, is an expert gunner and a hardy man. Here he is standing on a pile of sculps of seals he has shot. The men grease their boots by wading in warm pelts. *(This photo and caption were not in the original book. They came from England's private files.)*

Attaching bombs to poles to blow up a jam.

Photo by Vey

Sealers at work with stabber-poles, clearing out jam blown up by bombs.

A long tow.

Four of the fleet nipped in solid jam.

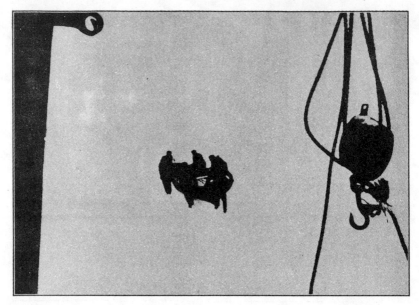

After many days the mysterious sixth sense of navigation which the Vikings have will enable them to come back straight to this boat, put out as a marker, and pick it up.

One of the flags that mark pans of seals.

This man has just hooked his kill to the rope in right foreground, which the ship is pulling in as it surges along.

Sealers in action, towing-in.

The "nit" coming aboard, with ice, on misty day.

A "tow" of sculps being hauled aboard by the winch, which is steaming freely.

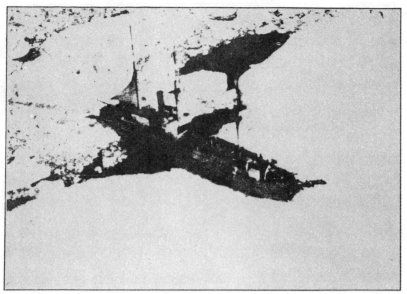

Terra Nova from aloft.   A toy ship on a birthday cake.

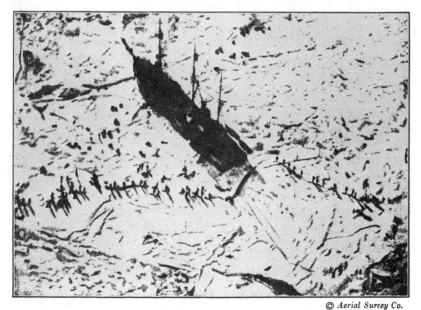

Unique photograph of mutineers on ice, near *Diana*.

The last of the *Diana*.

© *Hollands*

The transfer from *Terra Nova* to *Eagle*.

get "nigh an' 'andy to 'em." But sometimes seals are caught in nets, mere skeletons of age, very gray and without teeth. Buffon claimed a seal might live a hundred years.

The hoods, for their first four years, are "young hoods," "bedlamers," "curriers" and "old hoods." And "old dog hoods" or "old bitch hoods" they remain. Like the harps, they are hair seals, not fur seals. The bag of tough, hard skin on the dog hood's nose is an extraordinary object. When blown up, it protects the dog at his most vulnerable point. No use hammering that bag with a gaff; it doesn't hurt the seal in the least, and meantime he is more than likely to bite your leg off. The sealers tell many fearsome tales of men losing leg or arm by dog-hood bites. Even the carcass, they say, will bite you after the pelt is off. They also claim the skinned carcass will slide off the pan and swim away.

The only thing to do is shoot the dog hood at the side of his formidable head and a little behind it. Some of the old ones may grow as long as ten or twelve feet, and weigh up to eight or nine hundred pounds. It takes two good men, without rifles, to kill a dog hood. One distracts his attention from the rear by whacking him on the scutters, while the other shoves a gaff down his throat.

Old hood fat is not so valuable as old harp, but the young fat is practically as good. I have never eaten hood meat, but those who have say it is good. I noticed on board the *Terra Nova*, however, that all our seal meat was harp. The hood seems a tough customer all round.

Once in a while a "jar" seal is sighted, and even a "daughter," as the dotard is called. Perhaps twice in a blue moon a "square fipper" also heaves in view; but as these are not commercial species, let them pass with the simple mention that the dotard, otherwise the "bay seal," never comes far south. It stays on the Labrador and pups as late as July. "Dem better eatin', dough," a gunner assured me, "'an narr nudder kind." One oddity is that the Gulf seals, found to westward of Newfoundland, have a somewhat different shape from those on "the front"; shorter and stouter. Who knows why?

And who understands why, alone of all mammals, the seal has a cleft tongue? The V-shaped slit in it must serve some purpose, but nobody knows what. Does it in some way help the seal catch the fish that seem to make up its principal food? Another question!

Newfoundlanders dispute at great length the exact diet of seals. "Swile bait," Uncle Edgar assured me, "is ahl kinds fish—whitefish, capelin, cod, an' flat fish; an' dem can go to de bottom, too, an' get mushels." I have, myself, seen a bucket or two of whitefish in a ripped-up seal's stomach. Some hunters deny that a seal can crack mussel shells and eat the contents; or at any rate that they ever do. Most authorities believe that cod is the staple. Herring and squid are also said to be on the bill of fare, with salmon caught in fjords. Right Hon. I. C. Morris, ex-premier of Newfoundland, makes some interesting points. He says:

All kinds of fish are welcome to a place on the seal's bill of fare, but cod is the favourite item. It is rare to kill a seal without finding inside him the remains of a codfish. The seal may therefore be regarded as a real enemy of the cod; and allowing, say, one codfish per day for 2,000,000 seals, we have 2,000,000 codfish consumed every day, or 730,000,000 a year. Calculating 120 fish to the hundredweight, over 6,000,000 hundredweight are annually consumed, or four times the annual catch of the Newfoundland cod fishery.[1]

Seals are also said to move offshore in a gale that urges the fish "outside." They probably have a pretty ac-

[1] "The Romance of the Newfoundland Seal Fishery."

curate idea where the fishing is good. They almost always devour their food under water—or at least in it. Only very rarely are remains of fish found on ice. Chafe says the seals always eat *under* water.

Strange mammals, these!

CHAPTER IX

THE HUNT CONTINUES

THE ship "burned down" for the night, and all hands rested on their laurels, eager for more in the morning. Down in the cabin the Old Man was sitting at the table fiddling with his sextant, which somehow in the "fruz" had got out of kilter. He bade Gearge fetch him a "turnscrew," which is English for a screwdriver, and tinkered away with considerable anxiety; for once the sextant gone wrong, how could he work his positions?

Presently Marky came in with a sealed envelope, saying:

"I've got a sad message for one of your master watches, sir."

"Sad message, eh? What is it? Sad, you say?"

"Yes, sir. It's for So-and-so. His niece is dead." And Marky handed over the envelope.

Cap'n Kean summoned the master watch and handed over the envelope.

The man read his message, slowly. Cap'n Kean spoke a few words of sympathy. A moment the huge fellow went slack; but instantly he rallied. He said nothing but, stolid as an ox, withdrew silently into his cubicle.

The conversation, a moment broken, knit up again.

"Well, well, well, that's a bad job!" exclaimed Cap'n Kean; but he was referring to the broken sextant. Unable to repair the damage, he bade Gearge carry it back to his cabin. And presently out came the master watch

162

who had received the message, and comforted himself with bread and butter and with cups of scalding tea.

The Old Man had fipper for his evening meal, and with great gusto devoured two plates thereof. By way of very special favour, he gave me a plateful, too.

Not bad, not bad at all, if every particle of the fat is carefully skinned off. One fleck of fat, however, makes it inedible. In colour it is a dark mahogany, with long stringy fibres. The taste resembles that of very strong wildfowl that has been fed on fish, exclusively, if you can imagine it. A penchant for fipper must be an acquired taste; though perhaps Newfoundlanders have it born in them.

There can be no doubt that seal meat is highly nutritious, and that if the world could get accustomed to it, such might become an extremely valuable article of commerce. In addition to great numbers of seals wounded or even killed, and never taken aboard the ships, millions of pounds of carcasses are every year thrown away on the ice. This constitutes a wanton waste of life and of commercial values. In this hungry world, the sheer flinging away of these immense masses of edible meat is downright criminal. Almost all of it is left for gulls, sharks, bears, foxes, and eventually—when the ice melts— for fish. Though St. John's and the outports eagerly enjoy "fipper suppers," these consume only a very small fraction of the available meat. If cold-storage ships could follow the fleet, they could each year bring in unlimited supplies of rich meat. Canned seal meat and fipper might become as familiar an article of commerce as canned corned beef. No doubt it would merely enrich the capitalists, as the workers would (in the good old way) get only the husks; but at all events it might help feed a necessitous world.

Between mouthfuls, the Old Man told his little circle of admirers one of his favourite stories—how he had once befooled a rival captain.

"There was three other ships chasin' me. I could just make out their smokes astarn. I had me squares'ls on her, an' evverythin' topped aloft, an' jammed through a hard knot. The seals was in livin' squads on the ice. I didn't go to killin', though. If I had, them other ships would of come up, too, y'see. I burned down in the seals, as if there was nothin' round me, an' in the mornin' them other ships was ahl gone. So I got evvery man's mother's son out, an' we clapped a lickin' to that spot o' seals, I'm tellin' you!

"Some way, the other ships must h'a' got wind of it, for pretty soon I see seven smokes comin' like a terrified horse. But my batsmen an' gunners cleaned up thousands that day, before them others could get to me. Short and sweet, me sons, that's my motto!"

In high good humour over such happy memories, the Old Man chuckled joyously. The others all boistered approval. No matter how often the Cap'n repeated his stories—and I counted one at least six times—they always created enthusiasm. His tale of another captain claiming his seals, ending: "I only had 2,000 sculps in me hold, an' damn *me* if that man didn't swear 4,000 of 'em belonged to him!" was an infallible hit.

Among the men, a similar principle held, of clinging fast to the well-tried old witticisms. "I see one swile on two pans," and "I 'spects I'll go down town dis evenin' an' go to a nickel [movie] an' see if I got arr letter," always drew a laugh. "Evening," by the way, is any time after 12 M. Unlike Lotus-land "where it is always afternoon," there is no afternoon in Newfoundland. Till noon, it's "morning." After that, it's "evening" up to 6 P. M. From then on, it's "night."

My sketching gave considerable play to brilliant repartee. I found it hard to draw the men unaware, because the crowding and laughing of an invariable audience always warned my intended victim. And he usually wanted to see the picture before it was half done. The hunters never failed to wonder at the miraculous performance of "markin' out de likeness o' he."

The verdict always was: "You lines dat off wonnerful good, me son. You comes pretty handy to it. Couldn't be no nigher 'n dat." But the victim himself never admitted it. "Shah! Dat ain't *me!*" Or: "Hell's flames, I don't look like *dat!*" Whereat, personalities leaped out afresh. The word "sketch," by the way, they didn't know, save as applied to photography. Drawing was always "markin' out," and taking photographs was "sketchin' off." Every man I photographed demanded a copy of the picture.

Some of the men were so unsophisticated they thought my little hand camera was a motion-picture machine. They would pose with fully as much vanity as any Beau Brummell, and exclaim:

"I 'lows him'll 'ave ahl we sketched off now wid dat t'ing 'fore de spring's out. I 'spects some o' doze odd days us'll see ourselfs in de nickel!"

In high good humour the Old Man played checkers that night. The fact that we had already perhaps a thousand sculps aboard, added to his happiness. Not even the streams of smoke pouring down the bogey funnel, so that we had to keep the cabin door open and nearly froze to death, could damp his elation.

It was a sight to watch him, his cravat sagging far down, pince-nez precariously slipping, as he studied the next move and hummed one of his favourite ballads, such as "Roamin' in the Gloamin'," "After the Ball," or

> "On the five-fifteen,
> On the five-fifteen,
> We *ahl* are computed on
> The five-fifteen!"

whatever in the world that might mean!

A wonder at "manning down" his opponent, the Cap'n was. With swift swoops he would ravage his enemy's pieces. Sometimes in the heat of battle he would make unlawful jumps and sweep away checkers he had no right to, but in that tense excitement no one noted such trivial details.

"your Move,
Sir!"
S/S TERRA NOVA

A wonder at checkers,
the Cap'n was.

Gearge used to get rather excited over checkers. Sometimes he would leave his pantry, where he always seemed to be eating or drinking something in a hurried, nervous way, pop out like a jack-in-the-box, give advice, and pop back again.

But little advice the Cap'n needed. He would sweep all before him; and winning, would shadow-box and loudly exult: "That will be glory for me!"

Losing, as once in a way happened, he would lament: "My, my, my, I've lost the pass!"

A picture, he and all the group in the cabin. One of the most taking figures there was Cyril, the grandson. A ruddy, handsome boy, possessor of a pipe well-smoked. In secret he smoked cigarettes too, but luckily for him his grandfather never found it out. He was old and strong enough to perform incredible feats of agility and slaughter, but too young as yet for cigarettes! Worth looking at twice, he was; with intensely red lips, a classically straight nose, heavy brown hair brushed straight back and, though hardly more than "a choil," his forehead deeply wrinkled like most of these people. A man already, in some ways. In others, a very boy. He used to lie in his bunk with a dime novel, a lighted candle and a bottle of "pop," and revel in Wild West stuff—he who every day beheld and lived thrills surpassing any possible Indian-killing!

Came now Marky again with the blue envelope. The Old Man abandoned his checkers, fixed the pince-nez more firmly, and read:

Thetis jammed in 55–30 W., 48–45 N., 40 miles east of Cape Bonavista.

W. Winsor.

"Gearge, get me my blue chart!"

Then, when the chart had been fetched and spread, with all hands eagerly and joyfully looking on (for the jamming of a rival ship was famous news indeed), the Cap'n brought his dividers and parallel rulers into action. All at once he burst into an explosive laugh.

"That's not the truth nor anythin' like the truth! It's ridiculous! Billy Winsor wants to get another navigator. Whoever his navigator is, he wants to go to school again an' learn to take the meridium!"

"What'm astry, sir?" asked Uncle Edgar. "Made a miscrack, 'ave 'e?"

"That's what he have! Why, he've got the *Thetis* in a wonnerful muckery. 'Cardin' to his statement, he's 155 miles out on his reckonin'—a good bit to putt on a man's nose. A good many miles in the difference, me sons. He 've got the *Thetis* 90 miles ashore, 'way over in back o' Main River! ''

Tremendous merriment. The Old Man shared it.

"Dat navigator ain't got a corn," they decided (*i. e.*, was without sense). " '*E* ain't no smart rooster. Dey putts some quare hands navigatin', doze days [now]! ''

In high spirits the Old Man ordered his sextant. That must certainly be repaired. Much of his prestige depended on his magicry in being able to "shoot de sun and come down wid un unner his arm."

"I'll take this danged sexton apart now, me sons," he declared, "an' find out what's wrang with it."

For an hour he fiddled with it, but he couldn't make it come right. At last, nothing availing to put the sextant right, he gave up in despair and was about to put the diabolical thing away when he discovered that it had been adjusted for what he called "a morning sight," and that he had that afternoon been trying to take "an evening sight " with it.

Here now *was* a situation! In the most profound consternation he cried, seven times:

"Well, well, well, well, well, well, well! " and added: "I must be whitecoat crazy. What an old fumbler am I! ''

Awed silence fell. I judged it wouldn't be healthy to laugh and went up 'on deck to escape the tension. Nothing more was ever said about Billy Winsor's navigator.

Up early, the morrow morn, I found the ship in high spirits, for the day was certain to see rivers of blood flowing.

Already preparations were under way for a more extended hunt than that of the day before. Bosun Mike Donovan brought a number of pocket compasses in brass cases for the master watches. That meant they and their gangs were going far afield. Arthur Roberts, as competent a master watch as ever trod in a skinny wopper, tucked his compass into a tin case in his hip pocket, saw that he had coloured glasses, and tucked some hard-tack and spun yarn into his "nunch bag," This bag is a canvas or burlap sack used on ice, sometimes to carry cartridges in. The yarn, he told me, was for "staying-up" flags on "pans" of skins. He also showed me his "ticket of servitude," whereof he was justly proud.

"We'm ahl ticket men," said he. "Us master watches ahl has to have stifkits [certificates] from the Gov'ment. It takes ahl of a man to be master watch. If anyt'ing happen your men, t'ink of ahl de widders y're 'sponsible fer, an' de little ones. When you'm master watch on one o' doze [these] ships, you got somet'ing on you, my dear man!

"De master watch is de one dat say: 'You begin 'ere, stick y'r flags 'ere; an' *you* begin dere.' He got to go to de hindermost end o' de flags, an' got to see de men placed out rate, an' each man wid a flag. Den double de pans, an' wait till de swell come an' break up de ice. If dey pans on big ice, mabbe de men has to drag de sculps fer miles. It 'm de master watch's judgment as save 'em work, an' mabbe save deir life, too!"

A few more seals had already been dragged in and sculped. Some of the men were greasing their boots and mittens by shoving them down into the reeking, smoking pelts. The cold was devilish, and there was a high, piti-less wind which seemed to peel the very skin from the face. I had off and on to retreat to the "jacketwarmer" (warm place) of the cabin.

Men out on the ice, some with "hatchets" (axes) and chisel bars, were chopping ice cakes. They tossed the heavy cakes from hand to hand, and on to men standing on the side-sticks. These passed them to men on deck, who in ant-like procession were "fullin'" the port life-boat, aft.

Diana, Eagle, and *Neptune* lay in sight, one far, the other two within biscuit toss, their side lights and mast-head lights glimmering. Odd, how they dogged us! Cap'n Kean appeared a "jowler," indeed, to judge by the anxiety of the others to keep an eye on him.

When enough ice had been loaded, the men clambered aboard, talking and laughing, as they leaped down from the rail on to "soft seals" or frozen sculps. Pinnacles grew plainer; shadows slowly faded; gray and white pans floated in the leads; and overhead masses of clouds began to gather. The air shimmered over the ice that gleamed above the slow swells and opening breadths of sea. The ocean, as Newfoundlanders say, was "panting."

Open water showed an oily swell, by reason of billions of ice spicules, the night's freeze. These kept waves from building. Detached ice masses drifted; fantastic shapes green-dripping, arched, eroded, gnawed into dream extravaganzas. As the sun's naked shoulder thrust itself up, the distant icefields grew darker than the sea, flushed by ineffable tints of rose. Lovely, pellucid blues, diaphanous pinks, and stipplings of delicate green appeared; tender shades of sheer wizardry. Ghostly horizons loomed, and as the sun dazzled on leads, the *Terra Nova's* shadow flung itself seemingly miles to westward, trailing away across the plain of wonders. Long blue lines of ice barricades flanked us, with a huge berg lying in farthest distances; a berg that looked flat, all in two dimensions, ghostly and white and like a jagged hole ripped in the violet haze of the skyline.

An old hunter in a jacket of ship's canvas and with a yellow sou'wester told me some lore of the bergs.

"Dem islands of ice looms more 'an what dem is," he

asserted, fingering a porcupine bristle of whiskers. "Dem
has mud an' dirt on de bottom, mostly, an' lang starts
[points] under water, too, so it ain't safe to get nigh ner
handy to 'em. Dem nine times bigger below 'an above.
I minds de time in my remember when de *Portia* got
kitched by one o' dey, an' de berg rolled an' huv dat ship
cl'ar o' de water an' kep' 'er up five seconds, sir, an' den
rolled back an' let 'er down agin. De ship took no harm
but springin' t'ree plates. But gi' 'em a wide bert', says
I. You'm 'll most allus find good fresh water on a berg.
Lots o' times, ships has landed men on dey an' took
water. An' I 'ave yeard tell o' ships makin' fast to islands of ice, an' gettin' towed troo de standin' ice. I've
yeard of men on bergs, an' de bergs rollin' wid dey, an' de
men gettin' a wonnerful duckin'. Ye'll not get *me* on
one o' dem islands!

"See dem gulls, now?" he continued with a wide sweep
of the hand. "Dem shows us gettin' nigh de patch,
searchin', searchin', to get de whelpin' bags. De gulls
don't know where to look, no more 'an de man dat med
'em; dey ondly has deir opinion, same as you an' me.
What us wants now, sir, is a good whitecoat patch.
Dat'm de big end o' de spring. I t'ink us got a head lead
on dem odder ships, now, an' got 'em on toast, sir. Dem
got our wake, sarnly. We'm havin' a fine, smooth time
alang. Most gen'ly it'd poison ye wid frost, out yere,
but now we'm havin' it pretty moild. An eas'ly wind,
sir; east-nar-east, wid a light breeze o' narth. We'm
goin' on fine. Look like us might have a good, fine
spurt now, an' a clean-up. Us'll be into de young fat
now 'fore lang!"

Still northward bound, we skirted a gigantic icefield
dotted with whitecoats and bitches, and with old dogs

bobbing in the water with a startled and anxious air, yet not unduly frightened. They seemed more curious than anything else. To me, seals appear essentially friendly. Of an investigating mind they certainly are. Hunters tell how in the old days, when sealing vessels used to come out from Scandinavia, the Norwegians used to play concertinas to them, lull their suspicions, then butcher them. *Si no è vero, è ben trovato.*

A good many of the whitecoats were woggling about on every hand; but not enough to stop us for a rally. Forward we ploughed, looking for more populous nurseries. On the soppy black deck, all a muck of coal, ashes, fat, and blood, a sooty-faced fellow was sprinkling salt. Another grinned from the "goat's house" or "lobby," near the aft winch. He gestured at a rival ship, afar.

"Us got ahl dem sons o' brutes tied up in a shoestring, sir!" he declared. Shoestring or otherwise, it was nothing in *his* ragged pocket—nothing save pride. But aboard a sealer, how very large that bulks!

I heard the men with keen interest discussing what George Barbour's men "in de *Nipshun*" had been doing. The keeness of intership rivalry is incredible, the *esprit de corps* amazing. Pretty much the same crowd goes on the same ship, year by year; or so the men say. The "Cap'n's men," in the cabin and the top house, frequently sign with the same master for a long time. Some of Cap'n Kean's men have been to the ice with him for twenty years and over. Crass treachery, they'd think it, to desert him for another.

The stowaways were at work, bringing breakfast for the firemen and messing round the top house. The common hands' breakfast, ladled out by Adam Hawley the forward cook and by Matt Mulley his assistant— "de man as does ahl de droudgery"—looked far from appetizing. At the forward galley door a surge of grimy, grease-smeared men pressed close with foul kettles and kit pans. From within sounded a singsong:

"Fish an' brewis, how many youse?" It rhymed, for brewis is pronounced "bruise." "Anny man don't get up to braffus got to go widout un!" As the men told how many portions they wanted for themselves and for those they were serving, the cooks slopped out the famous dish renowned in Newfoundland lore: hard-bread boiled with cod. "Putt a little grase on un, b'ys. An' gi's us a drap o' tay, too, ye sons o' guffies!" Liberally the cooks drenched the fish and brewis with liquid pork grease and bits of crackling. With this, the sealers jostled away to their foul, underdeck quarters, to crouch and eat.

An old, familiar provender to me was fish and brewis, from previous rambles in "The Oldest British Colony." You can boil the hard-bread and fish in water or milk; condensed milk if you can't get fresh, which generally you can't. To thousands of Newfoundlanders it furnishes a staple, the hard-bread substituting for vegetables. As for "fish," that always means cod. The story is time-worn of the old livyere exclaiming: "If ye can't gi' us fish, gi' us haddock!"

Breakfast over, the Cap'n walked up and down the cabin singing, vastly contented with our good progress. His selection that morning was:

> "There's a good old Scottish custom,
> That's stood the test o' time.
> It's a custom that's been handed down
> In evvery land an' clime.
> Where brother Scots foregather,
> 'Tis aye the usual thing
> Just before ye say good-night, ye know,
> Fill up y'r glass an' sing:

Just a wee dock an' doris,
A wee one, that's a'!
Just a wee dock an' doris
Before ye gang awa'.
There's a wee wifie waitin'
In a wee butt an' ben.
If ye can say, It's a braw, brecht
Moonlicht necht,
Y're a' recht, ye ken!"

It was all right for the Old Man to smoke cigarettes, but when I lighted one, Gearge poked his head out the pantry door—he had been eating bread and butter there in his usual anxious, furtive manner—and informed me that cigarettes were "infectious," and that they would " 'nocklate" me. To save myself from being 'nocklated, which must be something painful, I gave Gearge some of my cigarettes; and these he smoked freely, taking all chances with indifference.

Joe Stirge warned me not to be over free with my donations.

"You better save y'r baccy, me son, an' not jink y'rself. Ye'll need un wonnerful bad, later on."

But he accepted a pipeful of my cut plug, "fulled" his pipe, "litted" it, and sighed with deep content as he leaned back in his hellhole "synagogue," as he called his bunk.

"Ah, dat'm de rale ole baccy," he approved. "Me pipe draws so good now, I got a job to kipp de smoke from comin' in me mout'. But don't be too free, b'y. You'm goin' to be in an awful tangle, bime-by. I mind one spring in de *Roarer* [Aurora], us run shart an' was ahl prayin': 'O Lard, gi' us just one smoke!' Us 'd took de boots off St. Peter an' sold 'em fer baccy, or went down on our naze to any man wid a smoke. 'E could of sold baccy fer a shillin' a puff. My dear man! Dey was ahl gamblin' fer baccy, fer gumbeans. Gumbeans? Dem's small little pellets o' baccy. Well, me son, I cut off swiles' tails, an' burned 'em to look like baccy, an' rolled 'em up in little pills. An' I gambled wid dem, an' won twenty-two gumbeans, just by playin' dem swiles' tails! 'Twas dark in de 'tweendecks, an' nobody never knew a t'ing 'bout dat. But after me gumbeans was ahl gone, I had narr pick o' baccy an' couldn't get none. *Nobody* had un or dey'd of been riots. I turned to an' smoked evvery pocket out o' me pants an' coat an' vest, an' smoked ahl de plaster rags out o' me patch bag, an' smoked 'lassy an' tea, an' spruce bark an' coffee, an' didn't I have wonnerful lips?

"When us got in to St. John's, us was to de rail like flies, me son, swarmin' over an' away fer baccy. I'd sooner putt a match to de divil 'an get kitched de like o' dat agin!"

Many a painful hour would I have dodged, had I but heeded those words of wisdom. Plenty of tobacco, yes, and rum, ought to go on every sealing vessel. Though a prohibitionist at home, I believe in all the comforts possible when at the icefields. If there's any place in this world where red liquor is excusable, it's on a seal hunt, and I'm willing to be quoted to that effect.

Apropos of this, my notebook says:

It is amusing to see the odd childishness of these big-muscled, huge-boned men in trying to conceal from the Cap'n their slight alcoholic peccadilloes. When I was dispensing hard liquor, the other night, the men sneaked timidly into the hellhole where I had my precious bottle. They reminded me of schoolboys stealing jam. They drank furtively, hiding their heads in far corners, after an anxious glance out into the cabin where sat the august Cap'n. Their voices were husky whispers, half smothered, as they muttered:

" 'Tis a martal hard t'ing to be cut off right-a shart from de stuff. Well, me son, 'ere's to ye!" I was amazed when they bade me hide the bottle under a mattress.

If ever I go on a sealing trip again (which heaven forfend!), I reckon the proper equipment will be about 950 quarts of violent liquor, 900 bottles of limejuice, 850 pounds of the rankest plug tobacco made, 800 boxes of cigarettes, 750 boxes of cigars, and a banjo. The other things, usually considered essential, really don't matter.

Sam Ballam, our wireless man, invited me to the Marconi room to have a look at his apparatus, which turned out to be a one-half kilowatt English standard cargo set.

Of more vital interest than his equipment was the story he told—a story that shows something of the Newfoundlanders' amazing ability to overcome unexpected difficulties. Aboard one ship he served on, the main injection pipe in the engine room broke, flooding the engine room and threatening to sink the ship. There was no way to make repairs, so the carpenter built a stout box around the broken pipe—a hurry-up job if ever there was one—and braced this box with a beam to timbers overhead. Then the box was packed with hard-bread and nailed tight. He finished: "That there hard-bread swelled up, by crimus, into a mass as hard as concrete, and stopped the leak. We'd already sent an S O S, and expected to leave the ship in four hours, but we didn't have to go, after all. That bread did the business, and we got to St. John's that way. How's that for a story?"

While I was still wondering at it, the *Terra Nova* stopped for another rally at the seals, and I arrived on the bridge just in time to see the hunters going over again.

Standing at the stern, I found myself peering away up the long slope of water, without waves; up a glassy swell dotted with islets of ice; water so smooth that every detail of the ice crags stood mirrored with loveliest shades of blue and green. And even as I watched, the scene changed. I was not conscious that the ship was rising or falling. As in a balloon, from which the earth seems merely to sink away, so the ship appeared to hang stationary, while the whole world either fell from it or rose about it.

In open ocean, you can feel the heave of the ship. Not so in the ice. You suddenly find yourself on top of the world, looking down tremendous declivities. Then the cosmos bends up about you with a dizzying rush and swoop, and on every hand you are overtopped with ice. Four times to the minute, as I counted it, the ice swell heaved; a massive, ponderous, irresistible movement of the white Sahara.

Not every day does the swell run. Betimes the icefields lie as the novice usually pictures them, rigid, motionless. But always after a blow out in "the blue drop," the swell gradually sets in; and though no waves can ever build in the ice, the mighty shoulders of the Atlantic thrust and heave and strain, so that the field ice curves like a white carpet shaken by Odin's self, and the blue growlers plunge their sphinx-like heads, then rise while slow surfs foam and leap along their streaming flanks.

Singularly, the ice swell so impresses itself on the beholder's brain—or so, at all events it did on mine—that when one closes one's eyes, one still sees the gigantic onward march of the icefields.

Out on to this majestic, moving floor of ice, once more the men were ordered; though not much ordering they needed.

"Jump, now!" the Cap'n shouted from the bridge. "Jump out, me sons, an' away. Make a quick dispatch and a good clean-up. Get alang an' God bless you!"

Away they swarmed once more, leaping, running, slipping, but ever scurrying on and on.

One man slid, plunged downward, whirled in a little maelstrom of foam and vanished. No one minded. He fought his way up again, hooked his gaff to a pan, scrambled out—and, dripping brine, ran in that bitter wind after the others.

Mother seals here, there, were rocking up and down, climbing low ridges, crawling, sliding, twisting about. Some were coasting curiously on their bellies, with head and tail raised high, searching for the infants they could no longer recognize. They hunted a while, sniffed at the carcasses of their babies, and at last slid away into the water with a flip of the scutters.

"Dem bitches don't bide on ice lang after de white-coats is killed," said the steersman. "I 'spects dem feels disgusted [sorry] a spill, but after dem snoffs de carcass, dem draws de hatch over 'em an' goes away, an' don't heed no more to un. But if a swile's wounded an' go in de water, her'll come up agin on ice to perish. An' see dem swiles jumpin' in dem loose lades, sir? Dat'm a sure sign of a whitecoat cut—a killin', as you'd say, sir."

My notebook, now:

Hunters are sculping on deck. One seal proves very full of milk; the richest, creamiest of milk. Billy, our plump good-natured store-keeper, carries a dangling, blood-dripping carcass aft, to stow it in a barrel. His free hand holds a pulsing seal's heart. "Look, dere's life in de heart, yet!" he smiles to me and passes on, to return in a couple of minutes with a pipe in fingers incarnadined. A fortnight ago, I could not possibly have dreamed anything like this; and now, at times, I ask myself: "Is it real? Or is it only, after all, an amazing dream?"

Young Cyril, when I go below, is loudly boasting that he has killed seven seals so far, to-day. The master watches are having a "scoff," or feed; and an amazing picture that makes—the huge men in dirty, blood-stained, and grease-soaked, once-white canvas jackets, with belts and knives on, with nunch bags and bloody skin boots, slouching, hulking and sprawling on benches at the table. The boy, cramming and laughing with them, is in his element.

Presently we strike another patch, and all hands gather in the waist, with gaffs, bristling flags, gear like crusaders. Soldiers they seem, indeed. The canvas jackets, slung ropes, high boots give them a mediæval military air. "Take y'r watches an' go," commands the Old Man. "Starburd over. Go on, me sons!"

Away and away the hunters run; they become mere dots that crawl over the dazzling fields, among the monstrous masses that swing, advance, retreat. To me they look like skirmishers on solid land; in New England meadows, perhaps—meadows of winter. Hills of ice, lakes, brooks, valleys; one looks for a red barn, a cow, a white farmhouse with green blinds. And yet, the slow rhythm of this landscape numbs the illusion.

CHAPTER X

AN EVENING WITH THE MUSES

ALL, however, was not blood and ugliness and death. Betimes the Muses twanged their lyres and Euterpe, albeit a trifle blue and shivering, favoured us with a fugitive visit.

Perhaps the most memorable of those occasions was on the night of "Sheila's Brush," which is to say the 18th of March. Newfoundland has two "brushes," Patrick's and Sheila's; that is to say, storms supposed to be connected with the birthday of St. Patrick and that of his wife. Equinoctial storms, I suppose we should call them. Any storms at about that time, are named in honour of those two saints. The word "brush" is not always used, however; you will hear Newfoundlanders say: "We have our Sheila dis time o' year," or: "'Bout time for our Patrick."

My seal-hunting experience was signalized by "a good stoutish block of a night," to mark Sheila's brush—"shockin' cold wedder, that'd moider a man, an' de snow wonnerful t'ick." But though the elements battered our ship and all outside was "dark as a buryin'-ground," we were cozy enough in the hellhole.

Our champion singer was Jardine, third engineer: a humorous, amicable chap. He really had a voice. He sang in the Cathedral at St. John's, and was amazingly versatile; could carry bass, baritone, treble, anything, with equal facility, and improvise harmonies. Sam Ballam chipped in with a recognizable alto. The doctor's bass rolled out grandly, most of the time very near the right key. Others sang, too, including even me, "de quare 'Merikin," who furnished an occasional barber-shop chord.

We ran the gamut of hardy adventure and soft sentiment—"come-all-ye's," mingled with "Carry Me Back to Ole Virginny," "Swanee River," "Where Is My Wandering Boy To-night?" "Silver Threads," and "Old Black Joe," which Joe Stirge acknowledged as a special compliment to him. "Rag" and hymns all resounded with equal fervour. Jovial Billy Richards accompanied some of the livelier passages by drumming on a kettle with two knives. Billy could drum with anything. His skill with a tin can and a pair of whetstones could not have been excelled. Such prowess, such virtuosity of the drummer's art was never elsewhere heard. Such roulades, ruffles, rataplans, and *coups de tambour*, such tuneful time and dexterity have never graced any symphony. The company applauded him to the echo, and even the Old Man came and stood at the door, smoking his cigarette, gravely smoothing down his beard.

A folklore collector would have revelled in some of the native masterpieces, now, alas, being driven out, exterminated by the tireless music of the "garmaphone," as they call it. Nearly all the Newfoundland pieces were mournful, in the habit of the race. As a rule this northern singing is moist and funereal. Shipwrecks and drowning finger most of the stops of the Newfoundland pipe; for what family but has lost menfolk in what Pierre Loti calls "marriage with the sea"?

Uncle Edgar Tucker, being called upon, protested that he was so hoarse he could " 'ardly glutch." Still further urged, he declared:

"I don't know how to sing, me sonny b'ys, no more'n

a fooley. I'd be in wonnerful punishment [embarrass-
ment] if I had to. But I can word out a piece for ye.
I can just mind 'Willy March,' an' I'll rhyme it off——"

"No, ye got to sing!" insisted Gearge. "Go on, now,
Uncle. Hayve ahead!"

"Oh, I couldn't putt a song togedder, whatever. But
I can get handy 'bout to de words."

And this being his ultimatum, it was accepted. He
cleared his throat and recited:

WILLY MARCH

"De home of his childhood, in Nothren Bay,
  He quit it fer pleasure, much more 'an fer pay.
On de icefields he ventured, most yout'ful an' brave,
  Whereon he sought death, but his life could not save.

Dat cold night in March he lay miles from de shore,
  From friends dat was watchin' to see him once more.
But alas, human aid may be looked fer in vain,
  Fer life was too sweet on de ice to remain.

At dawn, Easter Saturday, ahl happy they would be
  If in de Bay of Conception a sail dey could see,
But no sound from de ocean could bid dem rej'ice,
  Or lead dem to think he was safe on de ice.

Wid courage undaunted he set out anew,
  To reach Cape St. Francis, de object in view;
When three of his comrades whose number was four,
  Lay on deir cold beds, not to walk wid no more.

He an' de odder set out fer de Cape.
  How hard it must dwell on dat poor feller's fate!
He found himself weak, as he got near de shore,
  An' he said to de odder, I cannot walk more.

He said to de odder, Go on fer de Light.
  Tell dem at de house to come fer me to-night!

Dis man reach de lighthouse, which bein' quite nigh,
But little he t'ought he layve Willy to die!

Oh, rugged Cape St. Francis! re-echoed de v'ice
From him who fer aid called loud on de ice.
He expected assistance, but none did resayve,
An' he died near de shore, where de lost might be saved!'

This was received with due appreciation, Uncle Edgar explaining:

"Dey sove de life of one feller, but not de odder, an' 'twas an affliction case."

"*You* sing, Joe!" demanded Jardine.

"Me? I can't sing no more 'an a crippled beach bird!" Joe disclaimed.

"Can, so!" disputed another. "I yurred ye singin' 'Uncle Lukey's Boat,' more 'n once. You knows dat song ahl to pieces, an' why wouldn't ye, in 'gard of ye makin' it up in de first place?"

"No, me darlin' gozaroo, me mind's not into singin', dat night. I can't make much of a hand at singin'. You took me too much on a nonplush."

"Go on, sing! Or us'll sculp ye!"

"Sculp away. If I can't live, I'll die, an' dat's ahl about it!" But none the less, after a little violent persuasion, he loosened up on his own composition, "Uncle Lukey's Boat." It began:

"Lukey's boat was painted green,
De finest boat dat was ever seen—"

and ran on like Tennyson's brook. Fifty-seven verses, I think.

It being my turn, I recited "The Cruise of the *Nancy Bell*," but somehow didn't make much of an impression. Marky gave us:

> "Madame, have you any good wine,
>> Paaaar-lez-vous?
> Madame, have you any good wine,
>> Paaaar-lez-vous?
> Madame, have you any good wine,
> Fit for a soldier of the line,
>> With a hinky-dinky parlez-vous?"

This ran to some length. He followed it with: "Après la Guerre Finie," and:

> "Come, listen to me and I'll tell you
> Of the Spaniard who blighted my life!
> Come listen to me, and I'll tell you
> Of the man that ran away with my wife!—"

and so on, quite *ad lib*.

"Hold on, now, till I get me t'roat clear," volunteered a master watch, "an *I'll* gi' ye a little spurt o' singin'. How about 'Come on Down, Morine'?"

He launched into an interminable political song, all directed against someone of whom I knew nothing. Every stanza, however, drew applause from the sealers:

"Roll 'er out, b'y!"

"Hold to 'er. Good fer ye, brud!"

"Good fer ye! Lane 'ard on it, me son!"

He sang it to the end, then popped his quid back into his mouth—he had been holding it in his hand all during the song. The last line of every song is always *spoken* among these people. When you hear the spoken line, you know it's "Finis."

Our Chief contributed:

> "Oh, the day we left St. John's, me b'ys,
> It was a very fine day!
> Our wives an' sweethearts on the quay
> Says they, ye'll understand,
> Farewell, says they, remember me
> To the swiles o' Newfoundland!

Our duff was hard, our pork was bad,
We had to drink pinnacle tea![1]
Hurrah, me b'ys, we'll make a noise,
An' by our gaffs we'll.stand!
Me rope upon me shoulder,
Me gaff all in me hand,
Both day an' night 'tis my delight
To kill swiles in Newfoundland!"

After the applause for this had "quietened down," a bridge master gave us:

"Uncle Bill Teller died las' fall,
Young maiden, where ye bound to?
We jigged t'ree days an' niver got one,
Acrost de Western Ocean.

Oh, Billy K. is de divil fer fat,
Hang to 'er, b'ys, hang to 'er.
He can allus smell where de swiles is at,
Hang to 'er, b'ys, hang to 'er!

Billy K. got a fine old bark,
Hang to 'er, b'ys, hang to 'er.
He'll strike de patch afore it's dark,
Hang to 'er, b'ys, hang to 'er!"

Another followed this with a ballad most extraordinarily pronounced:

"Oh, come list a why-dle, an' you soo-dn shall hear,
By the rod-ling sea lived a maiden fair.
Her faaa-ather fod-lowed the sum-muggling trade,
Like a war-dlike hero,
Like a war-dlike hero, that niver was afraid!

This maiden, she sai-dled with her faaa-ather so brave,
An' dey met some pirates, afloat on de wave.
Dem pirates, a crool attack on 'em made,
On de geerl an' de sum-muggler,
De gerl an' de sum-muggler dat niver was afraid!

---

[1]Melted ice.

Now, dey kid-lled dem pirates an' took deir store,
An' soon returned to Newfoundland's shore.
Wid a kag o' brandy marched alang, dis maid,
Did dis female sum-muggler,
Did dis female sum-muggler dat niver was afraid!"

Then Jardine joined in with his rollicking:

Betsey Brennan's Blue Hen

"Good people, attention to what I will mention
Of a little blue hen that I bought in the fall.
Some villain he stole her to sharpen his molar,
A low dirty scoundrel with plenty of gall.
This hen, I did pride her, though often she'd moider,[1]
The universe round I would roam for her then,
But some wicked habbage[2] to grease his white cabbage
Walked off with my dear little beautiful hen.

May his pipe never smoke, may his teapot be broke,
And to add to the joke may his kettle not boil!
May two dogs and a crackie[3] chew up his tobacky,
And his long Yankee goatee may run into oil![4]
May his eyebrows turn red; may the quills in his bed
Prod him till he's half dead!
And imprisoned for life if he's put in the Pen!
May two girls from the Nor'id
Stick pins in his forehead,
The villain that lifted my little blue hen!

This hen, she had dozens of nephews and cousins,
The universe round I would roam for her sake.
But some wicked creature in form and in feature
He lifted my pullet to sharpen his beak.
He left me sad-hearted since me and hen parted,
And worn to a shadow and thin as a wren,
When some sneaking shooler[5] his coppers to cooler[6]
Walked off with my darling be-eautiful hen!

---

[1]Vex, annoy.   [3]A small dog   [5]Evil fellow.

[2]Savage.   [4]Spoil; be ruined.   [6]To fill his kettle.

May his whiskers turn blue! May his chimney and flue
Smoke him out of his kitchen, and choke him, and then
May corns and soft bunions as big as small onions
Make him walk on his softs[1] before women and men!
May his hens have the pip and himself take a nip,
And his goat have the mumps, and tormented, and then
May himself and his daughter half choke, drinking water,
The villain that lifted my little blue hen."

This remained a favourite all the spring. Many in
time learned it, and the *Terra Nova's* rafters used to ring
—if a ship has rafters—with shouted curses on the pur-
loiner of the Brennan poultry.

"And can't you sing, Tom?" I asked the cook, Fillyards, who sat there in blue dungarees,
listening.

"Well, sir," Fillyards answered, "I
hates to answer dat, but when a man
ask me a civil question, I'll try. But
I may tell ye a lie. I can't, sir. Not
whatever."

Jardine, our prize
"songster."

"Y're anodder!" someone retorted.
"Ye can whip it fine! Gi' us Johnny
Burke, an' don't be nonsinse!"

"Well, I don't 'eed much to singin'," answered Tom,
"but howsomever, if ye're determined on it, here go!"

And having made one or two abortive starts, he struck
the right key. His voice rose up, droned, lengthened out
the words in a surprising way. With the crash of ice for
accompaniment, the shudder of the tormented hull beating irregular tempo, he chanted to a strange-minored,
droning tune:

JOHNNY BURKE

"Come ahl ye good people, I pray ye draw near!
'Tis a sad lamentation, de troot' ye shall hear.

---

[1]Walk barefooted.

188

Been of a young yout', in de 'ites of 'is bloom,
'E 'as lost 'is swate life in a watery tomb.

'E was not yit married, ner orvis[1] ner time,
Ner riches ner orvis could alter 'is mind,
Till crool sad misfartune, which caused 'im to sleep
On a cold bed o' sand where de water run deep!

May curse on you, Uskan, an' ahl o' your breeze![2]
You would not 'elp young Johnny in de time of 'is need;
You l'aved 'im to roll an' to tumble in de deep,
On a cold bed o' sand where de water run deep.

As we were a-walkin' in fear[3] Courage Bay,
To view doze fine flowers, how dey ahl faith[4] away,
Dere birds dey l'ave deir singin', an' de flowers dey do 'cay,
W'iles young Johnny lies drownded in fear Courage Bay.

Dere's de day of 'is funeral, 'is true love come 'ere,
Ahl drissed in rich robes an' her scarlet so fear,
Fer to view 'is dead body goin' down to de grave,
As a due to you, young Johnny, an' dey ahl took relief.

Dere's 'is friends an' relations lamentin' in de Bay,
Likewise 'is tinder mudder, lamentin' fer 'e;
De lost of 'er dear son, widout spoth or stain.
'E's de flower of 'er fam-bi-ly;

(Spoken)
"Johnny Burke was 'is name!"

Native genius for narrative poems the Newfoundlanders indubitably possess. And nowhere can it be better studied than among the sealers. Lacking a written literature, they have innumerable chanteys, "come-all-ye's" and longer poems—regular sagas. Many must have perished, these latter years; but others still survive,

[1]Harvest.   [3]Fair.
[2]Breed.   [4]Fade.

chansons de geste that should be garnered into literary treasure houses before it be too late.[1]

Many of these songs are a bit unintelligible to the novice, on account of the archaic dialect, but the songs themselves are gems. In passing, let me say the dialects vary a good deal from one bay to another. But in them all, ancient Elizabethan and even Chaucerian words are still in use. "Bide," and "tarry," and "even so"; "prent," and "gobbet," and endless others persist. The Newfoundlanders themselves are singularly sensitive about their speech. The recorder has to "catch it on the fly." Ask them to repeat a word or sentence, and they will try to cast it into their idea of conventional English.

Beckles Willson, in "The Tenth Island," called the Newfoundland dialect "one of the most marvellous composites on earth." It is all of that; or rather, "they" are, for several dialects exist. The Colony, having been populated by English, Irish, French, and Scotch, can trace all these influences in the dialects of the different bays. Only a highly expert investigator could classify and tabulate them all correctly, with their various intermixtures.

One doesn't have to talk long with a Newfoundlander, no matter where one meets him, to discover his nationality. Even though educated Newfoundlanders will indignantly deny that any dialect exists, the very words they use in their denial will sometimes betray them. Among the illiterate, the newcomer is puzzled, at first, even to understand. The educated classes of course speak conventional English, with many Americanisms, all their relations of life and commerce being closer with the States than with the mother country. But even among

---

[1]Students of folklore are referred to Burke's "Sealing Poems," "Holiday Poems," and "Comic Songster." These little books, published in St. John's, are rare and hard to come by; but if the student can manage to get them, they will most amply repay him.

them, certain words are rarely used correctly, as, for example, "fipper" usually in place of "flipper."

Some odd turn of thought makes many of the Newfoundlanders use diminutives. A gale becomes a "breeze," oars are "paddles," an axe is a "hatchet," and a schooner is sometimes a "skiff." A two-masted vessel may be called a "punt," a cable is a "string," and a heavy steel hawser is a "wire." The wickedest kind of weather is often only "dirt," while the finest is but "civil." A man sick abed is merely "puckerin'" or "turned over." And yet, when some of these hardy men turn loose, they can draw the longbow with the best.

"Yes, sir," one told me, of a fine day, "dere'm clifts in Europe makes ourn look like nothin'. I seen 'em on de Mediterranean, nineteen hundurd t'ousand foot high."

"That comes to about three hundred miles," I objected.

"Don't matter, sir. I seen 'em wid me own heyes, an' 'tis sow!"

CHAPTER XI

LABOURING ON

A FINE night's sleep after our evening with the Muses brought me back to the world at half-past five. As I lay there in my bunk, which excelled King Tutankhamen's tomb for hardness, I pondered on the mystery that one can enjoy restful slumbers in such, with a lamp burning all night long, lacking any ventilation whatever, and with two other men sharing the place. The whole secret lies in getting used to it. By measurement, our little cubicle contained only 216 cubic feet of air; yet three of us slept there. And under the lower bunk, much of the time, reposed a couple of "cat" seal skins, peacefully "perishing," which is Newfoundlandese for rotting. "So they'll soften up," Cyril explained, "an' skin easier."

Odd, but when I got "inside" again—*i. e.*, back to St. John's—I couldn't sleep at first. That is, unless I kept my underclothes on and shut the window. I had to take several baths, in the first place, to get off the grease, dirt, and coal dust that were baked right through my clothes, making me all shiny like stove polish. Bathing gave me a fearful cold, and so did pajamas; and the soft hotel bed kept me awake; and having ventilation and darkness disconcerted me. I wanted to dress, turn on the light, and sleep on the floor. No joking, I did. Only after three or four nights could I make comfort seem even tolerable.

All night long, before the day I started to describe at the beginning of this chapter, the engine throbbed, to keep

191

a little water open at the stern, as we lay in our "cradle" of grinding ice. And at 5:30 it awoke me. What the hour was in "bells," I don't know. The *Terra Nova* didn't use bells, but told time by the clock, as if ashore. The only bell ever rung aboard her was the dinner bell, except for a metal bar hung in the engine room and now or again struck with a bolt; perhaps to try to keep up the nautical tradition. For that tradition needed bolstering.

This wasn't seafaring so much as hunting: a land hunt merely transferred to the ice. The men, "human paradigms of perpetual motion," were hunters, butchers, stone heavers, coal miners, anything but sailors. Except for tricks at the wheel, many of them had no contacts with ship work at all.

Lying in my bunk, I listened to the awakening of the ship, the questions of the Cap'n, still abed:

"Whose watch comes on at eight o'clock? Who takes on, then?"

"John Domeney, sir."

"Good. We'll start that coal again. Open the hatches an' get the men to it."

"Yes, sir. But some o' dey gummed foolies kickin' 'bout shiftin' coal."

"They is, eh? Well, sealin's a done game when the men begin findin' fault. The law's ahl wrang. It protects the old seals instead o' the young, an' gives the men such notions! My, my, my, it putts me on end. It's ahl a humbug—ahl this gov'ment inspector business, to keep the men's bunks clean, an' ahl that!"

"Oh, dem likes to kick, sir," someone answered, "but wedder come wahrm, make 'em sing like a canary."

"Edgar," ordered the Old Man, "you go alang an' find 'em out, an' ask who's kickin' an' slindgin' [loafing]. I'll do the rest!" And so on, quite *ad inf.*

Marky chirked me up a little by saying that on a previous sealing trip he'd made, the first fortnight was the hardest and longest. I hoped he was right. Marky predicted a quick loading and return. "So mought it be!"

The ship smelled dismally of oil and garbage, especially in the 'tween-decks. Down there, at the aft end, weltered a "pound" of sculps. A fearful place, that! On black, greasy chests men equally black and greasy were lying, lolling, snoring; they looked like so many niggers, with eyes and mouth alone distinctly visible. Their whiskers had grown jetty with grease and coal. I could hardly distinguish where their clothing ended and their necks and wrists began.

Conditions on deck and aft were deplorable. Swill and grease, blood, fat, and gory slush make unpleasant walking. Ice was being dragged over all this filth and pitched into the top tanks; melted there and used for drink. Coal pounds on deck kept everything a black muck. Ashes blew everywhere, as the ash-cat gang tipped their long steel buckets over the red rail and pitched ashes hissing out on ice. Boxes and barrels of fipper and carcass added to the crimson drip. Seal flesh in the lifeboats made long lines of red "conkerbills" (icicles) festoon the boats' keels with fringes of frozen blood. Incidentally, thought I, those boats must leak prettily to let blood run through like that.

We took few seals that day; but the weather bettered and the ship made fair progress.

Tea was enlivened by the Old Man's scolding because some of his men, during a little afternoon rally, had not killed where he had sent them; and also by heart-stopping news that one of the other ships had taken more seals aboard than we had. This caused almost a panic.

I lost caste by refusing a plate of fipper. My status on the whole was steadily declining. Though I stood long hours at the wheel, dumped ashes with the ash-cat gang, and peeled innumerable potatoes for the cook, such labours could not rehabilitate me. I had not yet taken a gaff and knife.

No wonder the Cap'n sniffed:

"A man as'd prefer to chip potatoes rather 'an go out killin'!—I got *my* opinion of him!"

That opinion, however, did not prevent his letting me help him take time for the ship. Every day I would note the exact minute, second, and fraction of a second; and by some magicry of mathematics the Old Man would later know our exact position. The value of such, out in that wilderness where one place was as good as any other to find seals, seemed just about nothing at all to me; but the Cap'n set great store on knowing that the ship's position was Tweedledum instead of Tweedledee.

"Bosun," the Cap'n that night ordered, "get the ice claw an' hold her 'ere to-night. An' when you get the claw out, tell the engineers to start ahead, easy." We often, by the way, anchored to ice with a claw, or sometimes even to a pinnacle with a "score" cut deep, casting a wire cable around it. Occasionally the cable would decapitate the pinnacle and we would go adrift, but in the ice a ship doesn't drift far.

Night was filled with many labours, after the ice claw had been made fast. Big gangs fell to work, dragging in the pans of sculps and loading them. On deck at almost any time, even in the wee small hours, harsh toil always seemed going on, by raw flares of torchlights that half revealed frost-blackened faces, gleaming eyes, teeth glinting like gnomes'.

An immense and spectral vacancy ringed us round. Under the everlasting cressets of the sky, night's limitless mystery folded us in. Black blurs of open water slowly breathed. On the horizon winked glimmers of other ships; nearer, wavering gleams flared blue as the wind tormented them. Torchlights on pans, these were, marking piles of skins that the toilers had not found time to drag in, by day. Such torches, with loose-woven wicks, will burn all night till the sunlight quenches their ineffectual flame.

Alongside the ship lay vast piles of skin and fat. Some of the men were toiling among these heaps, with "pries" or pointed sticks. Others came wearily plodding, each dragging his toilsome burden, each snicking the ice with his gaff to help himself along. As they drew near, I could see the limp bundles of laced-up skins trailing along paths that now looked black; a strange world indeed, where roads were black and all the rest gleamed white!

Beside those roads, dotted irregularly, lay seal carcasses with staring eyes and vague white ribs. From very far, a dim something advanced; took form as a kind of centipede, crawling among pallid and improbable hummocks such as fancy descries on the moon. Nearer still, I could hear the scrunch of gaffs and sparables; could make out that the centipede was composed of men, plodding shipward. The breath of toil sawed in their throats. Now, again, one unit of the centipede stopped to smear sweat with bloody hands. A gay life, my masters!

The toiling sealers piled their sculps on the edge of a little open water where we lay. Blazing torches showed them labouring, demons, a-reek with blackness. From their group, shouts beat up against the ship. Ropes

whirled out. Yells echoed. The "gurdy" chattered.
A dim blot of darker shadows came scuttering over ice,
then plunged into water and trailed a hurried wake.

That sinister bundle slithered up the side, lagging as
men hauled back on the whip-line. A shower of water
starred the rail where stood a sculptural figure gesturing,
with hoarse shouts.

Plog!

In the lurid gloom, the "strap o' swiles" hit the rail
mushily, flattened, swung clear. The swinging dangle of
sculps slid down the quivery mass that filled the deck
from rail to hatch coaming.

Shouts echoed, winches banged, steam blew. Black
figures cast wavering, grotesque shadows as they dragged
sculps, stooped to unstrap the pelts, wallowed in fat,
and threw out the strap-lines again. On ice, others strove
mightily over the black heap of skins.

"Go 'eed de winch!"

With a *rrrrr-rak-rak-rak!* a roar, a gush of steam, in
sagged immense weights of quivering fat; in again, over
broken ice, sloshing through inky water, dripping up the
side, swooping above the reek and slaver of decks not nice
to picture by any light, now sheer hellish in that dancing
inferno-glare of torches.

A fling of the reverse lever by a half-seen, steam-
wrapped figure.

Plop!

Another mass of wealth slumped and slid upon the
mounds already sloping to the rail. Fearful welters of
water, ice, gurry, skins, and grease filled the scuppers,
where men toiled feverishly to clear the way for more.

Everywhere sealers swarmed. When their hands got
too reeking, they wiped them on stiff jumpers. They
shouted, laughed, fair frolicked in their inhuman labour

of stench and filth. Slog and slip and wallow, the fat landed. Torch smoke's acrid fumes blent with stench of blood and seal fat. Waters guttered and surged.

"'Eed, de winch!"

How they toiled and sweat amid that muck of slush and red rawness!

Across the rail, ice was cascading in huge chunks, pitched from hand to hand. Two or three men were chopping it fine, with axes, nigh to the forward hatch. Others were shovelling it into flat osier baskets, tossing the baskets down the yawning hatch.

Still others were "tallying down" sculps cold enough for stowage. The fresh ones, though dead enough (God wot!) are called "live seals." But the older ones, stiff and stark, clammy and half-frozen, were ready for undiscovered depths where candle flickers wavered. Men dragged the cold sculps away, some using "gobsticks" to

"Ice, dere, me lucky b'ys!"

carry them. Into the riot of turmoil arose their warning cries to comrades under decks, who were stowing—cries of:

"*Hunder, below!*"

Shouts blared from lower deeps:

"Ice, dere, b'ys! Come 'eed de salt!"

"Salt," they called the ice; "fresh salt." Down it rained, to be sprinkled between the layers of sculps, laid fat-to-fat. The empty baskets flew up, spinning.

"Dat's enough on de salt, me sons! Dat's ice enough, b'ys!"

"Hayve 'em down dere fresh, me sons, an' snow 'em over!" shouted a vague figure at the hatchway, tallying the sculps. He held in his hands a "tally stick" and a

clasp knife, and cut a notch for every five pelts, a groove
for every twenty-one, that in the final reckoning would
count only as twenty. In a country of few schools, the
old-fashioned tally sticks serve best. And then too, such
are the filth, gloom, confusion, and cold many a time when
tallying must be done, that no one could efficiently handle
writing materials.

When the pan was all aboard the last hunters on ice at
the ship's side swarmed up, black-faced and red-handed
in the torch glares. Others would be coming, soon; and
all the turmoil would once more awaken. Meantime, the
stowing down would continue.

Half the night it might be, or all of it, before the dragging in and stowing down might cease. No matter; that
was "ahl in de swim o' de day's work," a day that often
lasts four-and-twenty hours. And on the morrow the
Terra Nova's iron-shod prow would once more crush the
floes to pick up the more distant pans, then again turn
Northward Ho! along her endless trail of red.

CHAPTER XII

PAST AND PRESENT

IF EVER an extraordinary captain trod deck or bucked ice, killed seals and generally made himself notorious, that man was Cap'n Hickson. On the *Rosalind*, going to St. John's, I had already heard many of his exploits. While in St. John's, I collected more. And aboard the *Terra Nova*, a still greater wealth of anecdote came to me.

Among the sealers, though Hickson has long since gone to his reward—which for good or bad must be a whacking one—he still looms gigantic. While I was at the ice, hardly a day passed wherein his name was not mentioned; and always with respect, admiration, almost with awe.

It was Hickson who once, when he had an infected finger, called for a "tom'awk" and implacably chopped that finger off, "standin' dere on de ship's brudge, sir, bare-handed an' in a green split-tail coat. Ah, what a clever lookin' man he was, too! Had a heart like a bloody gert puncheon an' a carcass on to him like a wheel [whale]!"

"Not a smarter man ever jumped on a pan of ice," put in another of the hellhole gang. "I mind one time he says to a feller on a ship he was master of, says he:

"'You'll get off dis brudge, 'live or deed!'

"An' den he kicked un off back'ards an' tore his coat off. He peeled his own coat, an' went fer un, an' hot [hit] un between de eyes an' knocked un flat. Den drag un in de fo'c's'le an' huv un in dere. But dis feller didn't have enough yet, but cursed on Hickson, an' Hickson

199

entered his 'eed [head] in de fo'c's'le an' dis feller grab un. Hickson burst his 'old an' huv un in de bunk, blood runnin' out of un evverywhere, an' ahl naked, wid narr shirt on un. Well, sir, dis feller rayched out o' de bunk an' bit a piece out o' Sandy Weller's shoulder, an' he jumped out o' de bunk an' kicked un in de face an' cut scollops o' flesh out of his face. It tuck t'ree or four men to hold un'; evvery 'ar [hair] drapped off his 'eed. Dey lashed un two or t'ree times, but he bursted it an' went screechin' crazy.

"'I don't care who was de best man 'ere afore I come,' says Hickson. 'I'm de best un now!' An' he was, too— one hell's-flames fine man!"

"I'm sayin' de same," agreed another. "He used to take [get angry] at de laysses' little t'ing. As fine a man as ever wet a line! He'd swear at ye one minute, an' give ye a piece of his heart, de nex'. One time one of his men had de toothache an' ask un:

"'Cap'n, can you 'aul a tooth wid a pair o' nippers?' He was fair raisin' to get dat tooth out, 'gard of it bein' so bad. De more pain in a tooth, ye know, de more venimis you is to take un out.

"'I can,' says Hickson, 'yes, an' wid a pair o' tongs, too! Carpenter, bring me a hand hammer an' a tenpenny nail!'

"De carpenter brung 'em, an' damn' if Hickson didn't knock de tooth out o' dat feller, quicker'n you'd cock a gun! Oh, dere was no better barn from woman, an' him."

"He was de roughest man in de world," a third contributed. "But on de inside o' he, a rale man! I mind one time anodder cap'n, to de ice, got shart o' coal, an' Hickson took twenty ton an' putt it out on a pan fer un, dough he didn't 'ave none too much his own self. An' couldn't he curse an' swear, dough; an' what wonnerful bad language!

But smart! One time when his funnel got ripped off by a blizzard, he built a wooden funnel an' made a fine spring of it. Oh, he was a wonnerful perseverin' man, an' had a gert hold-out. If he didn't get de young fat, he'd go after de ole an' make a fine bill. An able man as could 'aul me an' me tow!'"

"As fine a man as ever huv gallus over 's shoulder," another joined in. "Ye mind how he used to go round wid his coat tied together wid w'ite t'read? I minds de time in my remember when he fulled his ship wid fat in sight o' Cabot Tower [at St. John's]. He used to fool ahl de odder swilin' cap'ns an' clane up de patch afore dem could rayche it. Seven foot high an' wid a hand on him like a foot—like a bucket!"

"I putt gert faith into un," said Joe Stirge. "He could do any martal t'ing. De rightest man ever was. A nice man, out o' liquor. An' he could carry a barrel o' *dat* 'fore he'd get in de tantrums wid drinken'. A wonnerful able man! I minds one time he struck de swiles of a Sunday an' two men wouldn't kill. Dat was afore de Sunday law. He says to 'em:

"'What you do, Sundays, when you'm home?'

"'Oh,' dey says, 'go to church.'

"'An' what den?'

"'Get our dinner an' take a walk.'

"'Well,' says he, 'you get out on ice an' bide dere, or *I'll* give ye Sunday!' An' he huv 'em on ice ahl day, an' den sent 'em to de wheel till midnight, an' den med 'em shovel coal till darn [dawn]. A fine man, ahltogedder!"

"He didn't have no Sunday on his calendar at ahl," reminisced the carpenter. "Had it prented widout narr Sunday on to it. But evvery night, had prayers. Never wanted no rum on his ship. A bloody hard ticket, but a whole gintleman. He was de 'eed of 'em ahl. A gert bear-lookin' stick of a man, honest as de sun an' true as steel."

"Be jakers, dough," added another, "a very peculiar man, he was, so. Never let his men shave at sea. An' he had to be inside de Narrers hisself afore he'd shave. One time I was shipped to un, some fellers shaved, an' he says:

"'So y're shavin', eh? Goin' home, is you?'

"'Yes, sir,' they says. 'Why, dis one is borin' up fer home now, ain't it, sir?'

"'*I'll* show ye!' he says, an' turns round an' bides out anodder fartnight. He was de Ole B'y's rale limb when he made fire [fought]. He'd be like a ole dog hood wid his narsls [nostrils] split abroad, an' in twenty minutes be laughin'. A smart man. He could heave a line wid any man dat iver went round de heads. *He* knowed liniment from red rags, Hickson did! Nothin' barn to-day any better; an' he niver got licked, needer."

"He did, so," disputed a master watch. "A Scotch engineer 'armered [hammered] un proper. One time he had dat engineer in de cabin an' said de engineer was drunk, which he wasn't, whatever.

"'Man, y're wrang,' says de engineer. 'Don't be jadin' y'rself wid such nonsinse.'

"'Come down, sir, come down,' says Hickson. 'Y're full as a tick.'

"De engineer got vexed on it, den, an' says:

"'Y're foolish as a she-capelin, sir. What you tryin' to do? Haul de cod off me?'

"'Y're sopped!' says Hickson, 'an' if you deny it, you'm de divil's own liar!'

"'Now see here, Cap'n, ye stunned fool, sir,' says de engineer, 'you ain't got de sense of a suckin' pig. You may cut a hell of a sway wid de common hands, but it don't go wid *me*. Your thoughts is too far aft, sir. You ain't well in de 'eed!' An' he start to layve de cabin, where him an' Hickson is ahl alone.

"An' be dat Hickson lock de door an' putt de kay in his pocket. An' he says:

"'Y're a double-dutch liar, an' drunk, too, ye puckaloon [fool]!'

"De engineer was ahl tore up in mind, wid dat, an' he turned pure liverish wid how mad he was an' not wantin' to have no muss wid de Cap'n. He goes to de door, an' he says:

"'Cap'n Hickson, sir, you open dat door, or I'll open *you!*'

"Hickson's hair begun to stand up straight, an' de sweat begun to fly out of his 'eed, an' he turn black, like he allus did when he was vexed. He says:

"'You'll get my fist in your eye, you'll niver come up agin! You'll get de bloody Scotch block knocked off ye! You'll find y'rself in de missin' colyume!' Oh, Hickson was fair ready to jump down his t'roat.

"'No damn fear I won't!' says de engineer. 'You lay a hand on me, an' I'll hayve you over de table, an' you'll go across where de sweet oranges grows!'

"Den Hickson call un ahl de foxy sons o' guns, an' start to make fast to un. Still de engineer try to sheeve [back-water]. Can't strike de cap'n of a ship, ye know. Why, dat's manus [mutiny]! De engineer say:

"'Now see here, Cap'n, I declare to ye, such a beatin' I'll give ye! I'll hammer de 'eed off ye. I'll moider ye!'

"An' be dat, Hickson go stark roarin' an' grab de engineer, an' dey sarnly has a bit of a fuss. De engineer get un by de collar, an' clane un rate down; an' when dem troo, Hickson's as sick's deed. Hammered un stiff, de engineer did. An' my sweet man! Hickson loved un fer it! After dat, dem two was so wonnerful chums 'twas fair beyend ahl. No squarer man ever was afloat 'an Hickson!"

"No, ner no better one fer politeness," another chipped in. "Wonnerful polite he could be. One time he says to a man he was fightin':

"'Please don't come a-nigh me or I'll have to split ye wid dis hatchet!' He was de best of 'em ahl. He made up to seven t'ousand dollars a year"—fabulous wealth for Newfoundland—"an' died bare [broke]. Give away evvery cent, he did. His funeral procession was de langest iver seen in St. John's. No better man ever went on de sea. Oh, dere niver was narr un like Cap'n Hickson!"

"These modern days, now, ain't like the old uns," declared Cap'n Kean, who had drifted in and stood listening to the end of the Hickson narrative. "Sealers to-day ain't hardy, like the ole-fashioned breed o' greasy jackets! If I had an ole-time crew, I'd get out of a jam, swell or no swell; I'd get a load, whether there was seals or not! Ah, them was the days when men *was* men! The rale seal haulers, they was!

"Some o' the men I used to have would go away on ice afore daylight an' never putt foot aburd till lang after sunset! Why, those fellers could jump over swatches [open water]. They could jump over a ship without touchin' narr rail. They'd come in with a tow o' fat over one rail an' go rate out over the other!

"Not much socialism an' ah-ner-chism, in them days. The handiest ever I come to it was one time when me men grumbled about haulin', an' someone said: 'We'd haul, ahl rate, if the ship was going on the rate jife [direction].' I come rate down from the barr'l to the bridge an' called for silence an' give 'em a piece o' me mind. An' just then a whitecoat went '*Baaaa!*' an' you never see such a change. An' ahl hands went into the fat, an' I was cock o' the wall!

"An' once," he continued, "I see twenty-one ships ahl near, an' I took in fifteen t'ousand in a single day. I once went on ice meself an' helped pan twenty-one t'ousand an' get ten more into the ship. I killed eleven on one pan, an' struck me toe, an' me an' a whitecoat fell in together, down a rot-hole, an' I went clean under, but I got me seal!"

Much laughter and appreciation.

"Dem was de enj'yin' old days, sir," declared Uncle Edgar.

"Ah! Men as went in any other ship but mine was in bad luck." Something epic, thought I, in such boasts.

The Cap'n beamed with sublime self-satisfaction. "Way back, we'd go sealin', in seine boats off shore, 'an sometimes we didn't even have boats to get seal with. I mind one spring, I and my brother went out from Catalina with some others at 1 A. M. on the ice, when we heard the ole ones howlin' out there. T'ick fog it was too, me sons. We walked rate out to sea, an' there, sure enough, was the ole seals. Ahl we could do was take a tow, an' that would settle it, we thought.

"But a iceberg come alang, an' we hauled lots o' tows to that. The wind come up, an' the berg floated to land, an' we got 'em ahl. The men had plenty o' rum, in them days. 'Twas their god. They'd drink an' fight an' scratch an' kill one 'nother. Had to cut it out, it got so bad. But, ah, them was the good ole days!"

"Must ha' been, sir, wid pliny rum!" sighed a master watch, regretfully.

"Too much luxury, nowadays, that's what," the Cap'n continued. "I mind the first barr'l a ship had aloft. It made a wonnerful lot o' talk. Scunners an' spymasters used to cling in the rig."—Fancy that, will you, with such bone-piercing gales!—"Too much luxury, that's what's the matter with sealin', now. Why, I remember when we didn't even have stoves aburd, as the owners said the men'd stay an' warm themselves instead o' goin' after seals. We used to cook on the ballast in the ballast locker. We'd cover ourselves with sails at night, an' the lucky ones might get a chance to sleep in the after cuddy. An' no ilcskins, neither. Now, sealin's a pure luxury, with engines to do ahl the work, an' with bunks, an' hot food. Pooh! It ain't a man's game at ahl, now! Why, even the shore men thinks they got to have motor boats. They'd ought to be ashamed o' such weakness!

"I minds hearin' how in 1850 Sam Winsor had his ship dismasted. They didn't have no steam engines, them days. They rigged jury canvas an' putt a cable out, an' fifty four-oared boats towed her to Greenspond. In four days they had new masts in her an' topped her again. 'Twas ahl a loyal fitout an' they left again fer the ice on the fourth day, an' was first men in with a full load. Now if a ship met that misfartune, their spring 'd be done!"

" 'Twould, so," agreed Gearge, nodding his gingery head. "Oh, tapers, yes!"

"Then there was my uncle, William Kean, 'lang back in 1845," pursued the Cap'n. "He chopped a whole vessel's frame, yards an' spars an' ahl, an' built that vessel with the stem to the water, an' putt in spars an' blocks an' ballast, an' was ready to go. 'Twas a full-rigged brigantine o' farty-nine tons, with four stays'ls between her masts. When it come the day to la'nch her, he had a line an' measured the distance so this line 'd bring her up before she struck the other side o' the tickle.[1]

---

[1] "Tickle," one of the commonest of Newfoundland words, means a narrow passage between islands and the shore, between islands, or, in general, any small waterway.

"'Bill,' said my father to him, 'if you don't putt somethin' before her stem, she'll burst it out.' But my uncle had a new line and an' anchor set well in the solid earth, so he didn't pay much 'eed. He la'nched, an' when the strain come the line snapped like a string o' tow an' bursted the stem out. He putt men on the pumps an' had to go to Greenspond to refit, an' pumped her ahl the way. He rigged a purchase an' hove her down, an' putt a new stem in her, an' went to the ice an' got two trips o' seals. No men like that, the day, I'm tellin' ye now!"

"Narr un, Cap'n," affirmed Abram Best. "De body bulk of 'em ain't worth shootin', doze days."

"I mind the time," continued the Cap'n, while our timbers creaked and groaned under increasing pressure. "when the men didn't use to get no soft bread at ahl, an' had to be friendly with the cooks, for to get flour enough for a little thick'nin'. An' now they gets soft bread, an' even sugar on Sundays. Then they got pork an' duff three times a week, an' hard biscuit an' tea. The ships only carried salt pork an' beef an' tea. How'd ye like that, eh? An' molasses an' a little sugar, but no vegetables. Not even peas! Now ye have beans, potatoes, an' turnips, peas an' cod, soft bread three times a week, an' even butter!"

"'Azy times, now, sir," nodded Uncle Edgar. "I minds dem ole days, in my remember, I do!

"We had lamps with train oil—'rotten oil,' we called it —an' a pipe to 'em like a kettle, an' a wick yarn. Now we have kerosene, an' sconch lamps; an' in the ole days the men had a bread box back o' the wheel, an' ahl the hard-bread as got broken an' half used was dumped back in there, an' it kept gettin' worse an' worse, all blood an' fat, an' that was the cook's plunder, an' he sold it at the end o' the v'yage."

"Ye mind, sir," asked Roberts, "we used to have a kind o' cakes made o' fat pork, flour, an' molasses, called 'bitch an' dogbody'? An' de broken hard-bread was called 'slut'?"

"I do, so! An' glad enough the men was to get it, too. My glorianna, yes! An' in them days we used to use hatchets an' saws on ice, an' tow through. Cut a score on an island of ice, to hold a line, an' tow in the wake of it. An' scale them cliffs on the bergs to see a spot o' seals. Ah, wasn't the seal thick them old days? What killin's! An' we had tillers an' wheel ropes, an' sometimes the men used to get knocked out. There'd be three or four men on each side, tailed on to the ropes. We had ice saws an' hatchets to split the ice, an' always a barrel o' rum."

"Ah!" from a scunner.

"An' the men 'd make pans of hundreds o' seals. An' some o' the steersmen didn't know starburd from port, so we had to tie a red rag on one rail an' a blue one on t'other, or putt a new boat to one side an' an old one to t'other. An' 'Caboose' or 'Galley' was for 'steady.' So I'd call me orders: 'Red rag! Blue rag! Caboose!' or: 'New punt! Ole punt! Galley!' Ah, them was the days!"

"Ye mind, sir," asked John Domeney, a master watch, "how they had wangles for the men to jump an' ride on under the bowsprit, an' push away the ice jams wid their feet an' wid poles?"

"I do, that! Seal haulers was real men, them days. I mind when they had no cabins like o' this. They had open skiffs or gang boats—so me father told me—with pork an' hard-bread an' ice water; an' ahl the cooking, such as 'twas, had to be done on flat stones under a cuddy in the bow; an' the men slept out in the rain an' snow.

Real men! I remember, meself, havin' rams'-horns on ships, an' me men passin' ice to looard. An' when we'd come to a lead, we'd putt our rail to the ice, an' the ice 'd come rate over!"

"Stuns'ls an' r'yal t'gal'n s'ls!" ejaculated Joe Stirge, his bloodshot eyes gleaming with brave memories. "Shearsticks an' rams at de bows! Swilin' in barks, brigs, an' brigantines, an' in ships wid four yards on 'em. Crews in small boats 'aulin' de ships troo de ice, an' gangs on de barricades wid tayckles to h'ist 'em up! Men hangin' to ropes on de foresprit guys!"

"Yes," chipped in Uncle Edgar, "an' men wid chisel bars to cut de ice an' nudge troo. 'Aul up spanker, 'aul down stays'ls, an' spin her round. Port an' starburd mainbraces, ahl day lang! One watch to work de canvas an' one to kill swiles. Crack evvery stich o' canvas on 'er, an' wear round. Ah, me sons, dem *was* days!"

"I've fired a ship to port, when coal run out, with sharks' livers," affirmed the Cap'n. "Sharks' livers, old harps' shoulder-blades, punts, wooden davits, an' even planks off the decks. We got thousands of livers; gaffed the sharks on pans, where they come attracted by fippers for bait, an' by tarchlights too. I've seen as many as eighty sharks round one pan. An' what a fire sharks' livers make! My dear man!"

"Ye mind de time, sir," asked Arthur Roberts, "ye sove de *Roarer*, afire?"

"Ah, yes, yes, indeed I do, that. Ah, b'ys, what a time that was, to be sure. We see smoke comin' out o' the galley, an' lifted up the booby hatch, an' oh, my, my, my! What a burst o' flame!"

"Farty mile from de ice, dat was," chipped in Joe. "An' de smoke fled rate to de sky. Swile fat, wonnerful stuff to burn. I melted a bogey one time an' bursted de pipe, just wid t'ree small pieces o' fat, an' won't de smoke blind ye, dough?"

"Way out in the blue drop, me sons, farty mile from de ice," the Cap'n narrated. "An' with the wind dead agin us. The fire caught from the engine-room bulkhead. 'Twas the fat run to oil an' leaked through to the furnaces. It set the bunker afire. Well, me sons, the wind chocked to the sou'west an' come on a hurricane, an' we made a run for the ice. I putt men down with coats round their heads an' our Chief cut a hole an' went in with a tarch. We got a hose on the fire. Had four thousand sculps on deck, mind ye, an' a full load in the 'tweendecks. Lost a lot o' fat, but we reached the ice an' hove our deck load over, an' sove evvery sculp an' the ship, too. Ah, me sons, we was rale men, them good ole days!"

CHAPTER XIII

A TOUCH OF NEAR–TRAGEDY

ONE night we came near to having what the Old Man called "a very miserable affair." Long after tea, presages of serious trouble threw the ship "rate in a fruz."

Down in the cabin, under the smoky lamplight, high-pitched, scolding voices, or gruff and hoarse ones, were reviewing the day's events. And it was all what "*I* done," and what "*he* done"; what I or he didn't do, and why; or what we should have done, or why not; and so on.

"Ye done good, the day, me sons." This from the Cap'n, treating himself to a slice of cake and a glass of stout. The cake came out of a pasteboard box kept in his cabin, was hard-frosted as the icefields' own selves, and lasted for weeks. The stout had, of all things, "a little drap o' sugar in it"! Sugarless ale didn't tickle the Old Man's palate. "Ye done good. It's not as good as we *'ave* done, but better times comin'. By the way," he added, "where's Arthur Roberts an' his go [gang]? Seems like we got a lot o' men missin'. Where they to?"

The babel quelled. Joe Stirge answered:

"Someone say dem alang [on board]."

"*I* ain't seen fedder ner bone of 'em, not since dem went away," volunteered master watch Abram Best.

"When did we putt Arthur down?" the Cap'n asked. "'Lang about two o'clock, wasn't it? My, my, my! Somethin' 'stray here, sure."

"Him an' his fellers was gone on ice afore two, sir,' the bosun volunteered. "Last I see of 'em, they was into some loose, pummely stuff, off to narwest."

"If dem ain't aburd by now," said someone, "de divil don't know where dem to. It might be a hard fuss to get in, if de ice go abroad, an' *I* t'ink us goin' to have scuddy wedder, too."

"Gentle Moses!" the carpenter ejaculated. " 'E've de look of it, de wedder 'ave. Dem can't bide on ice a night like dat, wid wind comin'!"

"My, my, my!" the Old Man repeated, sure sign of perturbation. "I charged ahl hands not to bide out after dark. "It's the devil, ahltogether. The devil's own to-do! Get a couple o' tarchlights, bosun, an' putt 'em on this pan where we are now. Marconi, call the *Sagona*— that's the 'andiest to us—an' see if Roberts is aburd of her with his men. 'Pon me soul, I don't see how we missed 'em. They must be on the *Sagona*. They'm 'board of her, sure."

"Dere'm a gert way, wherever dem to," pessimized a bridge master. "*I* t'ink dem made a jink of it, dat time!"

"If they *is* on the *Sagona*," put in Shipper Nat, the second hand, "we must get under way again, an' take 'em off. They must be aburd the *Sagona*. I knows what Roberts an' his crew has done—they've went to that ship, sure. She wasn't no more'n a quarter mile from our flags, or handy 'bout that, when we was up there to west'ard! That's where they'm to!"

Whispered consultation followed. Not even Skipper Nat could reassure the ship. The Old Man bundled on his furs to go on deck.

"They'd have a hard rowt," judged the Cap'n, "if they was to bide on ice to-night. A murderin' time! They might take wonnerful root [damage]. I think we better go back to that place they was. That's big water, y' know. We got to find them strays, sure. They got anythin' to make a fire with, out there? Got arr matches?"

"Must have," judged Stirge. "Some of 'em's baccy smokers. An' dem'll have no trouble to make a shelter by dis reason, dat dere'm pliny pinnacles."

The Old Man looked extremely worried as he ordered the bosun to go up and light the sidelights. "Roberts is an experienced man," he added. "Not like a youngster. But the weather looks t'ick. We got to give this one a shake-up an' get alang toweard where we last seen 'em. This may be a wonnerful do! An awful tear it may be, s'help me, b'ys!"

The engine was prodded back to life; and away the *Terra Nova* snailed, thumping and bucketing through heavy ice. Behind her, as a landmark, she left two torches on a barrel and a whipping flag. Her sidelights gleamed—an unusual occurrence, as they were rarely kindled—and on her barricade an oil flare wildly blazed, shooting wild shadows along ice and snow, and roaring in the gale. Weird fantasies of blue, of red and black played hide-and-seek among the pinnacles. "Fire spanels" (sparks) skidded along the floes. Funnel and masts, black silhouetted, stood up against the flickerings of pale, frozen stars. Men clotted along the rails and on the barricade, murmuring together, peering out into the ghostly and infinite wilderness that enfolded the labouring ship.

The answer from the *Sagona* plunged the Cap'n into consternation: "Your men are not with us."

With such a gale building, the ice might at any time "go ahl abroad" and Roberts with his crew be lost. Wind shouted. Blistering cold lashed in and in. Here, now, we knew we had the makings of a first-rate tragedy.

"Run up a masthead light!" the Cap'n commanded. "What's the matter wi' us, anyhow? Whitecoat crazy? Double full speed ahead!"

I know not what that means, for already the ice-racked old ship is flogging on through the floes and against the wind's weight, with every ounce of steam her condemned "can" will carry.

Up jerks the masthead light.

"Putt out dat galley light!" bellows the Old Man, reverting to speech that betrays his emotion. The light is extinguished, so that he can better pierce the gloom. On, on we thrust and toil. On toward what disaster we know not, we dare not guess. From every quarter we hear the whitecoats bawling, but now they wake no interest.

A few faint stars die as the weather thickens and the hour draws on to midnight. More slashing grows the cold; keener the gale. But I cannot go below. I crouch behind the scant shelter of the top house and keep vigil with the others. Grim memories of sealing tragedies come trooping.

All at once a murmur rises, a cry:

"*Light a'eed, sir!*"

Very far a glimmer has begun to tremble on the night. Toward it the ship thunders.

The glimmer brightens. It flickers, as if something were moving all about it. Cries of hope and fear and exultation burst out. Gradually the glimmer brightens to a fire, and by that fire, black figures become visible.

"Dat's dem!" the Old Man exults. "We found 'em!"

Cheers arise.

We nose through broken ice and jetty waters to the edge of a phantom floe; and now the dim adumbration becomes a fire, with men all about it and with a broad black pan of sculps.

We hail; are answered. Gradually we win to under-standing distance. Wild words ring and figures troop toward the on-crashing ship.

And what does the Old Man shout? Words of pity, of apology for having forgotten to pick up that crew? Com-miseration, inquiry if any damage had been taken? None. He yells:

"How many seals ye got, me sons?"

Amazing Cap'n; and astounding men!

"Sixty-one sculps, sir!" shouted Arthur Roberts, proudly. He seemed to think nothing of what had happened; less than nothing. Apparently, for all he cared, he might have been having a picnic on the midnight ice.

Soon the skins were loaded, ghastly under torch flares; and the black-faced men came swarming up the side sticks. Gaffs waved—such as were left, for many had been burned.

The ship backed away, and the men crowded to the forward galley for their mug-up.

Cap'n Kean returned to the cabin. Down came master watch Roberts, with some others; and it was:

Master watch Roberts, almost apologetic.

"Doctor, gi' us a drap o' rum to save our lives!"

Happy am I to say that all who asked, received, that night. They didn't drink; they simply opened them-selves and poured it in. Probably that was what they called "glutching." Rum was rationed out by the doctor from a milk pitcher, every man taking his whack at the same stone-china mug. Their faces were parboiled with frost; their jackets frozen. The doctor ordered them to "turn right h'in, as bloody quick as you can, after you get a wet [a drink] an' that there."

The Cap'n was jovial again.

"Well, well, well," he exclaimed, "you must ha' been 'way to the other end o' the flags. 'Way off to nardeast, eh? I *was* a little chafed, but now we can ahl be safe enough. One time, though, seemed as if it like to ha' been a most miserable affair."

"We'm ahl rate, sir," Roberts assured him. He seemed almost apologetic for having nearly lost his life through the Old Man's forgetting to go after him by daylight. "We was to de nardenmost flags, on de far end o' where we knocked off yesterday. I got out on de black stuff [thin ice], sir, meself, an' den cut back agin. After it come dark, we couldn't see to go an' didn't 'tempt on raychin' de *Sagona*. An' I kep' me men runnin' back an' forth over de fire an' round it," explained Roberts, "to make un flicker, an' 'tract y'r 'tention, so ye might see un. When it come duckish [dusk], de wind chopped to de narnarwest, wonnerful sharp. But I don't want to intrude on [bother] ye. We'm ahl rate 'cept fer bein' a little cowed out [tired]. Knowed you'd come alang fer we."

"We was burned down for the night," explained the Cap'n.

"Yes, sir. But us knowed ye'd come."

"Y're a man of humgumption," the Cap'n approved, and ordered him another tot of rum.

CHAPTER XIV

A VISIT FROM THE AIR

IT WAS a morning destined to be memorable in sealing annals—the first day that ever the fleet was visited by airplanes with directions where to find seals. The Old Man, it seemed, was in bad humour. He felt that laws protecting the men had bilked him of some of his prerogatives and was freely airing that opinion:

"It's ahl nonsense, ahl these laws about the inspectin' of ships! What good do it do? I just been alang through the castles, an' you can talk o' dirt! Why, what do that inspectin' amount to? Nothin' but trouble fer the ship!"

"Dat's so, dat's right," someone agreed. "Dem new laws is ahl draf' [rubbish]. De law's a cod, sarnly."

"It's ahl codology." The Cap'n waxed still more wroth. "I never seen them castles dirtier in my life. If we *got* to have an inspector, it's his duty to keep the food an' bunks clean, but do he do it? No, sir! It's ahl taken out o' my hands, now. Them new laws an' me can't saddle at ahl. Evverybody thinks they owns the ship, now. I ain't got arr'n 'tall authority like in the old days. Gi' me a good ship an' crew, an' plenty o' seals, an' I won't ask for no more heaven, below! But how can I have heaven with ahl them laws an' inspectors an' such? I ask ye, now!"

It was a relief to get out on deck. A frosty morning, but not too piercing. The life of the ship had long been active. Steam was bubbling and sputtering in the siren. Shovels and slice bars clinked far below. A gang was

217

heaving out ballast rocks, making place for a "wing
pound" of sculps. Pitching ballast on to the ice, now,
would not bring back luck; but if any had been thrown
over before we had taken seals, it would certainly have
jinked us.

In the forward galley, some horrid-looking brown stuff
was bubbling on the range; it smelled worse than it looked,
if possible. Men with "spikes," or pry sticks, were dig-
ging frozen sculps apart. The doctor came along with
an ice-blinded man following him, hands on the doctor's
shoulders, eyes bandaged. "Studdy [steady] me alang,
sir," said the victim. "I find [feel] it like sand in me
eyes."

Long lines of hunters departed, and now a new note
came into the hunt: gun play!

For out went Joe Stirge, "swatching." Swatching
means shooting seals in open water. Some say the word
comes from "seal watching," but this seems fanciful.
The thing itself is sufficiently dramatic. Joe had been
carefully preparing for it, oiling and cleaning his precious
rifle; pulling rags through the barrel with his teeth and
quoting Scripture when they stuck. Now he stood,
motionless as any statue, beside a lake that shone like
burnished bronze.

The lake swung in vast curves as the swell ran. On its
far side, craggy pinnacles upstood, so that it seemed a
lake on land, ringed in with little white hills. But those
hills, reflected in the undulant surface, grew distorted as
never did reflections in the world of reality now so infi-
nitely far away.

Unmoved save for the heave of the swell, Joe stood like
a dog at point, his ears on the stretch, under all that
majesty of colour and light. His rifle was ready, every
muscle tense for the kill. Even did he make that kill,

results would be problematical; for thus late in the month, seals when dead do not always float. As the fat leaves them, they lose their buoyancy and often sink.

A striking figure Joe made, with his dark, saturnine face, his tangle of grizzled hair, stubble of pepper-and-salt beard, keen eyes that never missed their aim, as he stood black, squat, muscular, with high-laced boots revealing his knotty legs; a fascinating figure, a hunter born, if any ever lived!

Splash!

A huge saddler emerges! Startled, it tries to plunge. But——

Crack!

Swifter speaks the rifle. Its crash is echoed by a slapping, spasmodic fling of the seal which hurls itself almost clear of the water and churns the surface to a bloody froth.

The victim leaps, turns on its back, thrashes. Its wild convulsions fade to rippling tremors of flippers. A rosy foam spreads all about. Joe picks up a gaff, waits till the seal—just awash—drifts in near the lake's edge; then hooks it out, lax and dangling, on ice.

Again he waits. From aboard, shouts of encouragement ring through keen morning air. Up from the calm purity of the lake surge two more seals.

Crack! Crack!

Joe's rifle bags them both. Both sink and are lost.

"Dem'll perish, dough," the cook assures me. "Dem'll crawl up on a pan an' perish, later. Us might get 'em, an' den again, might not. Dat Joe, now, he'm a bit of a rooster wid a gun, ain't he?"

Since the ship was making only slow way through a wilderness of alabaster and pearl, of purple and pale, shimmering argent, I decided to go overside and do a little hunting of my own. Under the thrust of the stout prow, fissures and crevasses kept constantly opening, through which the sea boiled up, with tangles of slob. I needed spiked boots; but having none, was constrained to go in my plain ones. It was not too hard, sliding down the ropes and over the sticks; though the leap to an up-tilted pan of ice, spikeless, is none too enjoyable.

I rounded up a whitecoat and shot it—with my camera. I visited a number of the engaging infants, found some of them getting lively about hunching over the ice, and was glad to discover at least one that growled at me. Anything was better than that bland stare of indifference.

After I had enjoyed my fill of whitecoats, I took a turn at hauling in a tow of fat. A lathering job, dragging the huge, quivering bundle along the crimson trail! Half an hour of it was enough for me; but sealers will haul for a whole day long and come aboard ready to take the wheel, shift coal, or heave out ballast.

I found it none too easy to swarm up the greasy rope and over the rail; besides which, it sadly deteriorated my raiment, already notably impaired. Then I stood two and a half hours' trick at the wheel, where for some time I had been officiating as a common hand. My jobs on the *Terra Nova* were, for weeks, steering, emptying ashes, peeling potatoes, taking time, counting seals' tails (whereof more, anon), helping load ice, and doing a bit of doctoring, as well as selling tobacco. I hope I earned my keep! Inasmuch as more than once the Old Man, spying me at the wheel, cried out to me: "Y're ring-bolt to the job, sir!" perhaps I did.

The matter of bucking arctic ice is none too safe for the men at the wheels. Backing up for a charge at the floes, the rudder often strikes a pan and slaps back against the hull; the wheels tear loose, and woe be unto you if caught by a spoke! All hands jump clear while the wheels spin. No four men living could hold them. If they get you, with luck you may escape with nothing more than broken bones. At the wheels you have to keep your coat buttoned lest some loose flap get entangled; and every minute you have to "watch yourself."

Different times, while helping steer, the men told me a variety of horrific tales about injuries inflicted by the wheels of these old tubs. The irreducible minimum, allowing for all exaggeration, was quite bad enough. Peary, you will remember, got himself smashed up in that way. He was at the wheel of the *Kite* (one of the sealing steamers) in the late summer of 1891, off the Greenland coast, when he was caught and had two bones in his left leg broken. The sequel is heroic. He had the leg strapped to a board; and on a stretcher was carried ashore in that bleak, desolate land. He ordered the ship and the surgeon to return to the States, lest they might be imprisoned there by ice for the winter, while he himself stayed in the North. Eventually he crossed Greenland, with his leg freshly knit.[1]

The screw caught a whitecoat on a pan, flung it into slush and water, spun it helplessly.

"He'll live, sir, ahl rate," one of my wheel companions grinned. "An' de mudder o' he—her'll come an' find un, ahl rate, even if him out in de cl'ar drop [open sea]. You can't jam an ole swile, sir, when it come to findin' de young un, not no ways in dis martal world! But," he added, seeing me sweat, "don't take to 't so 'ard, sir. 'Ave a spill [rest]. Ye know, one of our gang 'ere is de minister." It chanced that preacher Levi Butts was with us. "He'll drill [work] ye to death. Ye know what min-

[1]See *National Geographic Magazine*, April, 1922.

isters is like, me son!" The first, last and only bit of anti-clericalism I ever heard in Newfoundland.

I gave the grizzled patriarch a little tobacco, which he received with touching gratitude and stowed in a box that in brass letters bore the motto: *Gott mit uns*.

"My feller [son] bring dat from de wahr," he explained; and when I told him what the motto meant, he viewed me with admiration of such profound learning. "It's good o' ye to 'elp we simple folk."

While the old man at the wheel was warning me not to overtax myself, a great outcry from forward, supplemented by hoots from the siren, announced the sighting of an airplane. You never beheld men more excited. Most of them had never seen a 'plane before. Yells and cheers greeted the visitor as it came skimming far above the ice, like a midge in the blinding glare.

Swiftly it drew near, and swooped twice about our barrels, with its ice skids—in place of wheels—almost grazing our spars. Those skids, of course, were for emergency landing, if the pilots could find a smooth enough place. Another 'plane flickered along farther distances, but did not approach, and gradually faded into the blink.

"Our" 'plane had a message to deliver. Down fluttered a long red, blue, and yellow streamer of bunting weighted with an iron bar; it fell on the ice, perhaps a hundred yards away. Old Uncle Absalom was first over-side. He picked it up and proudly brought it in—the very first message ever dropped by a 'plane for a sealing ship—and gave it to the Cap'n, who read:

> Large quantities of seals about three to five miles ahead of you about one point to port.

Roughly pencilled that message was; but an imperial rescript, embossed on vellum, could not have produced a more profound impression. I thought the men would stare their eyes out, after the retreating 'plane, till it vanished beyond the ice world's ragged edge; I thought they would never have done talking about that miracle of the air.

"Not t'irty yard above de h'ice she come, 'ard as she could pelt. An' she was takin' off vifty knot if she was takin' off one!"

"Close aburd to dat, brud; an' goin' like a bloody blue-tail fly. An' her ingine sound like de rote [roar] o' de sea. Ye can travel fer de spring's len'th an' ye'll niver see de like."

"Dat'm de rig-out she drapped de message in. Now I 'spects dis-un 'll get squads o' swiles!"

"Yes, b'y, she huv dat message overboard rate on our quahrter, an' I 'ad a wonnerful geeze [look] at she! It were fair beyend ahl."

"So it were, how dat-un went round us like a carkscrew an' turned off to loo'ard! Dem hairyplane can skirr [hurry], sarnly. I'm fair charmed wid 'em. But what kipp 'em up? Dat'm what I can't fadom out!"

"I'm dyin' about 'em. When I first yeard about 'em, I t'ought folks was coddin' me good an' tough. But dat'm where I was making de cod of it, meself."

"Alang she come, about of a hundurd foot 'igh, desperate fast, me sons."

Everybody had to see the message and either read it or hear it read time and again.

We tried to reach the seals indicated. Alas, impenetrable "knots" of ice reared themselves in our way. We got no good of the message.

Levi G. Chafe, in his 1921 "Report of the Sealing Fleet," gives this quasi-official account of the first attempt to locate seals from the air:

The aëroplane that was introduced this spring for the first time, by the merchants and the government, to take part in the hunt . . . did not prove satisfactory. The managers had endless trouble in getting the machine in working order in time to locate the young seals. It was only on March 23d that it made its first flight from Botwood, when parts of the machinery gave out. . . . The 'plane was valueless . . . as far as locating the seal herd was concerned.

The 1922 "Report" gives the following:

. . . The 'planes made an extended patrol, and large patches of seals were seen, sufficient to load all the ships. . . . Parties directly interested in the venture took quite a time to decide what they would pay Major Cotton for his information. In the meantime, the ice and seals were driven a considerable distance. When arrangements had been finalized, and the ships wirelessed the position of the seals, needless to say they could not be located where first seen. Major Cotton was prepared again to locate the seals, but the ice was from 50 to 60 miles offshore, and the remuneration for his services was not sufficient to warrant his flying again.

Though as yet without much practical value, the fact is noteworthy that modern methods have at last definitely invaded the seal hunt. The air service for sealing was organized in 1921 by an Australian aviator, Major F. Sydney Cotton, of the Royal Flying Corps, under the name of the Aërial Observation Company. Headquarters are in St. John s; the flying base is at Botwood. Associated with Cotton are Captain V. S. Bennet, and Captain A. S. Butler. The enterprise is daring, to say the very least.

The ships carry charts marked off in squares; the 'planes carry similar charts. On spying seals, they note the square, and undertake to notify the ships of the location. To me it seems almost an impossibility to identify one's position in the air, over the icefields. It is also hard to "spot" seals, especially whitecoats, from aloft. Some of the sealing captains have faith in the plan, others scoff at it.

So far as I could see, we got no good of the service. Major Cotton claimed to have reported the "Main Patch," Mecca of all sealers—the patch that none of the captains in 1922 reached. This came to be known as "The Cotton Patch," and caused oceans of talk, considerable jesting, and not a little acrimony. The Cotton Patch may have been where Major Cotton claimed it was, right enough, but it happened to lie where ships could not reach it. Thus the principal herd escaped for at least one year.

CHAPTER XV

ODDS AND ENDS

LATER in the spring, when conditions grew much worse and the voyage too long, a little murmuring developed, but not much.

If to labour is to pray, then the sealers are praying all the time. Their one standard of value is a man's capacity for hard manual labour.

Oh, they may grumble a little because there is too much salt junk, too little tobacco, and practically no adequate rum. They may grouse a bit concerning the low price of fat and the extortion of "tare," or "back weight," for adherent flesh that sticks to the fat; that is always reckoned as sticking to it, no matter how clean they peel the sculps. That tare is counted off at the rate of from a pound and a half on white coats up to seven pounds on old dog hoods.

They vaguely recognize that the merchants are cheating them, and have formulated a telling proverb: "If you lose your grapnel in the spring, you're sure to find it in the fall"; *i. e.*, on the merchant's ledger, where it will be charged up to you. But how to remedy conditions through concerted action they do not even dream.

A good many of the sealers mentioned annexation to the States as a consummation devoutly to be wished. I had already heard the same from various kinds of people at St. John's, including some merchants; and later, on my return, I heard the matter broached on the very steps of Government House, which I visited to witness a session of

226

the House of Assembly. At least one Member of that House told me he stood committed to working for such annexation. The question arouses bitterest debate in Newfoundland, the pro's and contra's right royally denouncing each other.

The Newfoundlanders seem to gauge others by themselves—as we all do. One day a good-humoured fellow showed me his steel and explained: "Dat's fer steelin' a knife, sir," as if I were a small child needing enlightenment. They used to expound the most obvious matters to me, the "quare fish," who was probably supposed to be not quite right in the top hamper. Their idea of humour is the discussion of derogatory personalities and localisms. As in all small countries where inland travel is hard and where life clusters in bays (*cf.* ancient Greece), they cling to local attachments and think of themselves as, for example, "White Bay men," "Bonavista Bay men," "Conception Bay men," and so on.

Some of the more clever ones will poke fun at their more backward brethren, telling perhaps how So-and-So always kept his money in a tin can. This So-and-So happened to be a "planter," or trader, who had really amassed a pile, but with it, little knowledge of the world of affairs. Well, one day a St. John's merchant told him his canned money could be earning interest; explained it all out to him, and for the first time in the planter's life made him understand what interest was. The planter, only half convinced, sent part of his money—still in a tin can—to the bank; and only after he had really got a little interest let the rest go.

Then they tell about the livyere who wanted to send money by mail and put it in a sealed envelope on which he inked a mourning border—the idea being that nobody would dare open a mourning letter. They tell about the Government once sending a pedigreed bull to an outport to build up the local breed of cattle, and the outport men holding a meeting to decide what to do with the animal.

"Kill de son of a one rate where he is, an' give evvery man his sheer o' de meat!" was the resolution that finally carried.

They tell how, at the time of a bank crash, the outport men demanded: "De gold wid de gallopin' harses on it!" —their description of British sovereigns. One old fellow related how a certain lightkeeper at Gaultois had a light on a little trackway, so that he could pull it up every day to fill it. Navigators who missed the light on several stormy nights made a complaint, and the government inspector got this excuse from the old keeper:

"Fine light like dat, sir, I couldn't see de force o' layvin' un out in de starms to get dirty!"

Such stories are innumerable among the Vikings.

Queer beliefs some of the men have, and curious fancies. That icebergs sink in Southern waters is a firm article of their faith. Nothing will convince them that ice always floats. A doctor aboard one of the other ships told me that whenever quarrels used to arise, he had only to play on a little zither he had, and sing a bit of a song, to have the combatants all happy and peaceful in a very few minutes.

*　　　*　　　*　　　*　　　*

On deck [says my notebook], I find a magnificent berg visible, perhaps a mile off, blocking off a long section of the skyline. A splendid object, with blue-gray water surging all about it; a mountain of ice, gray, blue, and gleaming white. I get a snapshot of it with the *Neptune* directly in front of it.

"I wish that berg would keep still so I could get a picture of it," I say to a hunter. He never smiles, or understands, at all; merely says: "Oh, dat'll kape still ye, sir, whiles ye sketch un off." "And is it true, do you think," I ask, "that all this sheet ice is wheeling round the North Pole with the Pole sticking up through it like an axle?" He gravely opines it may be true; probably is. Unable to get a good shot at the berg, I undertake to sketch it as we draw nearer. This sketch I caption: "The most splendid object I have ever beheld."

A deal of exaggeration has been written about bergs. Fanciful authors tell how an iceberg flashes, sparkles, throws out iridescent lights, and all that. I saw very many icebergs on my journey into the North, and not one ever sparkled at all or shot out lights of any kind.

They look more like immense chalky masses; like mountains of frozen snow, rather than ice. Some are lovely grays, others, hazy blues like smoke. Usually enormous surfs are bursting against them. Spray sometimes explodes fifty or a hundred feet up their flanks; and all about their bases a maelstrom usually boils, beyond description.

The implacability of a berg appals. Winds fret it not; waves and tides dash impotently against it; icefields in vain oppose it. In the grip of cosmic currents it moves, sublimely indifferent to the frettings of the world. Only one master it acknowledges, before whom it bows and perishes—the Sun.

A growler, sometimes called a "roly-poly," is a baby berg. It may have been born small, or it may have melted from a huge one; but at all events it is little, perhaps no larger than a brick block or the Woolworth Building. It is called a growler because it makes a grumbling noise as it rips through the pack ice, leaving a long "slick" behind, full of floating fragments.

News came one day by wireless that the *Diana* was "in an awful fudge," jammed and unable to move, with her propeller shaft broken and her bows "bet in."

Enheartened by this our men flung into the hunt with redoubled energy. The prospect was full of seals, all sizes and conditions, bobbing, flopping, swimming and splashing, sliding down holes and rifters, or tobogganing off the edges of floes.

I saw one kindly act that afternoon; so rare an act that it must be recorded. In a pause, loading sculps, Joe Stirge went overside to swatch. He was just about to shoot an old bitch on a floe, when he happened to spy its young one.

"*Too* young!" quoth he. "Poor little feller perish if I kill de mudder." And to my amaze he lowered his rifle.

"Very good creature, dat Joe!" said a steersman. My amaze increased.

Remarkable luck we were having. Not even the fact that Billy Richardson, the storekeeper, had that morning killed a rat in the flour barrel seemed to have any effect; and everybody knows that killing a rat brings bad luck. The whole frozen plain, as far as eye could reach, was speckled with men and flags. A wonder day!

Out of the confusion in the cabin that night the fact emerged that we now had more than 2,000 seals: 1,300 stowed and above 700 panned. This, I calculated, was perhaps one tenth to one fifteenth the number necessary to "full dis one" and make her "bore up." At this rate, we wouldn't get back to St. John's till sometime in June. Fortunately, however, we should soon run into thicker patches; and anyhow, the law went "on" again, May 1st. There was always that, as a last resort, to depend on.

Some of the master watches reported that the white-coats were beginning to show signs of being "scruffy"; *i. e.*, of losing their white fur and showing the dark. That meant, of course, that before long the young fat would be "dipping" and would disappear. Undoubtedly the young seals were starting to turn. I could see that their heads were growing dark, also their scutters, and that their bodies were becoming patched and mottled. This meant that the *Terra Nova* would soon commence her chase, primarily, of the old fat. That rifles would begin to crack in good earnest; that the great gun hunt, on the trail of the northward-beating migration, would very presently be under way.

A new phase of life—and death—was to be opened to my sight. New marvels were to be shown. Behind the fleeing herd the cry was soon to be:

"Northward! Northward, Ho!"

CHAPTER XVI

THE SEALER AND HIS WAYS

JOE'S life, as bit by bit, in the long weeks, I gained some knowledge of it, seemed so typical of Newfoundland that I must give it here, pieced together from what he himself told me:

"I went fishin' when I was six an' niver see de inside of a school. But I had a gun when I was so small I couldn't 'ardly carry un. I minded me ole man, you bet! If I didn't, he'd get it out on me, no matter if 'twas t'ree days. I ain't got narr pick [of learning]; can't read ner write, whatever.

"I worked 'ard ahl me life, I 'spects. I've lugged ice enough in me time fer de whole bloody main patch to pup on. When I'm well, ain't narr marn [morning] kitch me in bed at darn. Summers, I go down de Labrador. Oh, yes, I knows de Huskimaws, good. I knows deir dogs, too. Ahl nice an' friendly dem seems, but by de Law Harry, if you falls down amongst 'em, dey won't layve enough o' ye fer God to judge. I can talk Huskimaw, some. *Naulyer* is what dem calls a gull, an' *tucktoo* is de vog [fog], an' *lipshoot* is a fork. Ain't dat a sensible word fer a fork? Lipshoot! Wonnerful fine, I calls it!

"I niver had much luck wid de women, but some day I'm goin' get me a 'luninum ring an' slip un on de finger o' some woman when her'm not lookin'. 'Cause I don't give a damn 'oose finger I puts a 'luninum ring on dey got to 'ave me! I niver had much luck, me son. When I do get arr pair o' mitts, it's belly an' back [odd ones].

I made me own livin' iver since I could work cross-handed [alone], an' 'spects to till I straighten rate up fer Cap'n Jones [Davy Jones]. I been shipmates wid a good many few loads o' swiles, an' I don't like nothin' better 'an to get me toggin' on an' go on ice, gunnin'.

"One time I got to know a New York sport, an' he said he'd take me to de States an' rise [promote] me, but I'd rudder bide yere where I knows what's what. He'd of putt me on de fat pig's back, mabbe, but I loves me swiles an' me fishin' and birdin'. Dat'm me life, brud—swilin', fishin', an' birdin'. I knows where to find dem birds! I knows where you'll 'ave y'r eyes bate out wid puffins, turrs, an' gulls, in July month—ducks an' white-wing divers, too. I got a house, down Narth, an' a motor boat, an' I goes ahl alone, birdin'; an' don't I 'ave de enj'yin' time, dough?

"Man, dear! I load up me ole birdin' gun wid a span o' two fingers powder an' more 'an a t'ousand shot, an' wad 'em wid tarry oakum, an' go down to me gaze [shelter], an' de birds pitch [come down] by t'ousands just after de sun risin'.

"I've worked 'ard ahl me life," says Skipper Joe.

More de vapour fly, dat'm de best time at a good smooth-water place. A gaze is a battery, me son, same as where ye got a fort to. I go pick up me birds by de boatload. Jeeze, what a big burst o' birds down on de landwash! I strick 'em down an' snick 'em down by de t'ousands! Baulks, haigdowns, scurwinks, ahl kinds. Yes, sir, in summer de heft o' me time is birdin' an' duckin' an' salmon kitchin'. A gert life, b'y!

"I loves swilin', me son; an' after I'm on ice, I loves to lay back in me synagogue an' dror de vog [draw the fog,

i. e., smoke]. Ain't narr nudder t'ings but a gun an' me
baccy I sees a bit o' use in. Evveryt'ing else is lobscolla-
meed an' wag-me-chin-water talk [nonsense]. I don't
let narr man vex me; 'cause if a man get vexed, he 'ave
to bide vexed—someone always 'andy to 'im. Ahl I
minds is me rheumatics. I got a wonnerful appetite fer
meat, an' if I don't get plenty fresh meat, I'm no good
—can't 'ardly carry round me clo'es. I can eat a dog
hood in t'ree meals, an' not much out. I get two 'elpin's
o' swile, evvery meal; an' what I'm off a dog hood meself
is a small lot. Love mammy, love daddy, love y'rself
best dis time an' ahl de time—dat's me!"

One night the Old Man waxed wroth about a young
fellow named Jonas, accused of "slindging."

Cap'n Kean called the bosun away from a job of cutting
spun yarn, to see about it.

"Bosun, I charge you, get a list o' their names that
don't get out in their watches," he fumed. "Them men
has got to be cut. Get their names an' I'll do the rest of
it. If I let this slindgin' go on, it'll knock things higher
'n a kite!"

"Yes, sir," answered bosun Mike Donovan, quietly.

"Now then, Bosun," asked the Cap'n, "have you called
the crowd forrard? Have you got the bunkers full?"

"Yes, sir."

"How many you got stowed in the forrard pound?"

"Seven hundred, sir."

"Ahl rate. That's fine! An' we want to get some ice
for the cook. Tell the eleven o'clock watch to do that.
Tell 'em to get it as fresh as they can. There's a big
lake o' water rate ahead. If we can make out the western
carner of our pan, that's our best policy. How's the
ice?"

"Soft, sir."

"So? Well, if there's any seals to be panned up yet, they can pan 'em up in the mornin', an' we'll do our gleanin', later. An' now about this slindgin'. Go alang an' take down the names o' the sick men an' the slindgers. We got to get the rights o' this!"

"Dat Jonas," volunteered the bosun, "ain't doin' a thing. He ain't worth his salt, sir. An' if ye speak to un, he mind ye of a squid squirtin'."

"Oh, he do, do he?" The Old Man bridled with virtuous indignation. "'Oose watch is he in?"

"Mine," spoke up one of the master watches. "An' he'm no good, needer. Dat gozaroo don't mind no one. I told un I'd putt ye on un, Cap'n. If iver a man deserve to be cut, it'm dat un. Ye ought to give un Ole Link, sir, de martal son of a scaldy!"

"I agree with evvery word of it," proclaimed the Old Man. "He was putt aburd here against my wishes. You ought to enter your protest about this thing, about the way men are putt on this ship!" The Cap'n's indignation was blazing. "The only way is to give the Cap'n the right to choose his own men. *Then* I'd get men that wouldn't be laid up if they wasn't really sick! If I'd of known such fellers as that Jonas was goin' to be putt aburd, you wouldn't of had *me* in this one as Cap'n!"

"If he'd get on ice, he'd feel better," volunteered one of the men, "or shovel coal wid any o' we. But no. Ahl he do is go sick, an' lay in bunk wid his hocks [boots] on, workin' de coaleys [playing cards]. He'm useless on y' earth. He'm foreright [careless], an' don't 'eed to nothin' He do not one livin' tap, dat feller!"

"Coaleys, eh?" snorted the Cap'n. Here was a horrendous crime. Who doesn't know that cards are the devil's picture books? "I'll soon see about this. He'll get cut sure, then. If ever a man was cut, he'll be. He thinks he's got the cod o' me, do he? *I'll* show him!"

He consulted the ship's register, a biggish book wherein was entered every man's name, number, address, where signed on, and remarks.

"There's his name, now," he announced, "I got him! Rate here. This man's name is Jonas Ecks, an' I've already got him down here, 'No good!' Master watches, you ought to cull y'r men an' cut 'em, evvery time!"

"I got some wonnerful fine fellers in *my* go," boasted master watch John Kelloway. "I had one feller on de ice, yestiddy, wasn't 'ardly able to stan' up. 'E was ahl w'rout [worn out] runnin' troo slob. Slim an' slight, but 'e got a 'eart like a dog. 'E'd take on anyt'ing! 'E went down troo rifters an' was ahl pantin' an' blowin'. I t'ink he'm in de fringes o' de yumonia, but him work, jus' same!"

"Hadn't ought to," the Cap'n reproved. "I'm very scrupulous about not tellin' a man he ain't sick when he is. But you got to watch these fellers that monches [play truant], an' that goes out an' comes in with one seal when other people's gettin' two! I seen a couple o' fellers out yesterday, an' I told 'em to clear up some seals widin a hundred yards o' the ship. They got none, an' I couldn't see where they went to, neither. Know where them angyshores [worthless fellows] was to? Hidin' behind a pinnacle. They fired [lighted] their pipes, an' was chewin' the fat [talking] rather 'an haulin' it in! It's the bad laws we got now as stews [corrupts] the men. Slindgin', I tell you!"

Presently Jonas entered, twisting his cap in both "sprayed" [chapped] hands.

All eyes, eager, hostile, and hard, fastened on him as he stood, mazed and quite alone—a tall, pale young

man, very much afraid, who didn't look quite bright.
He dared not so much as raise his eyes to the august majesty of the Old Man, or to the stern ranks of his accusers
grouped on benches round the table, standing along the
blood-smeared panels.

The Old Man for a long minute held silence, then,
levelling an accusatory forefinger, commanded:

"Come rate 'ere, you! Stand 'ere! You won't get
cried down till you had a chance to talk. What ye got to
say for y'rself?"

With a kind of twisted, apologetic smile, Jonas made
shift to stammer:

"I be's wake, sir. I knows me own feelin's." He fell
silent.

"Feelin's! I never the devil ever!" shouted the Cap'n.
"You big useless! Why don't you work?"

"I be's wake, sir."

"Did you respond when your master watch called
you?"

Silence from Jonas.

"Have you been layin' in bunk, playin' cards?"

More silence.

"Do you think you can go [defy] Skipper Abram Best?
An' *me?* What ye got to say fer y'rself, now?"

"I be's sick, sir."

"Sick, eh? Let me tell you, you'll be cut!"

"Me back's bruck, sir. Ye won't kindim me fer dat,
will ye? I be's ahl bet out."

"Bet out! Uh!"

"I knows me own feelin's, sir."

"Feelin's! The doctor says you're ahl rate!" Delec-
tation gripped the audience. Every eye was fixed on the
trembling wretch. "It's time somebody was puttin' me
on you! Y're no good, that's what's the matter with

you! Now see 'ere, Jonas, you can either work or slindge, whichever ye like. If you work, you'll get the benefit of it. But if you slindge, you'll get mighty few dollars out o' the bite. I got as much compassion as any man, but I won't 'ave slindgin'. It's got to be putt a stop to. I won't 'armer [hammer you], though ye deserve it. But if I had any guts, I would. You, playin' cards an' layin' in y'r bunk, an' not jumpin' when y'r master watch says jump! Well! In them old days, the old-time cap'ns swore, kicked an' cuffed an' booted their men! That's what you'd ha' got! You, slindgin', an' this tearin' crowd o' men workin' their heads off to feed you!"

"I niver had to lay back in ahl me life, sir, not since I had me remembrance, till now," pleaded Jonas, his eyes on the floor, cap twisted to a rope. "I ain't tarred up wid no lazy stick, sir, but I be's wake."

"You ain't got the sense of a she capelin!" the Old Man vociferated. "If you slindge any more, I'll make a sample of you! A sample as you'll never forget. Ye may 'pend on it, I'll cut ye! You'll only get paid 'cardin' as you work. Sick! Uh! You'll come into collar, from now on, an' when you're tailed off to do a job, you'll do it?"

"I be's helt too hard, sir," Jonas mumbled.

"Helt too hard! I'd fix *you*, if I was what I used to be! But I'm too easy. I won't kick or cuff you; no, ner give you the tongue-bangin' you deserve. But you got to live up to your agreement or smart. I got ahl the pity in the world for a man in bunk, but you're ahl rate. You're nothin' but a lewerdly slindger as won't hold up the harm [acknowledge it]. Why, there's some men as 'd slip through a knothole, an' ask to be paid, too, on the heel of it!

"But now," he concluded, "I'm not goin' to keep this

thing draggin'. It's goin' to be putt a stop to. You slindge from now out, an' you'll dance to the pipes o' my cuttin' you, an' don't you forget it! Now, go forrard, an' if you don't do your duty, you'll hear from *me!*"

Jonas, more scared than ever and not even daring murmur that he was "wake," departed into outer darkness.

"The merry-me-got!" exclaimed the Cap'n, wrathfully. To call a man a merry-me-got seriously reflects on the legitimacy of his entrance into this sorry world. "It's enough to make a saint swear, so 'tis! Don't let me forget this Jonas feller, now, when we goes in. Master watches, you'd of had more 'an one like him, if I hadn't had ahl the names o' the slindgers took down."

And now mark you, as a result of having thus been shamed in the eyes of both cabin and fo'c's'le, Jonas became the most reckless daredevil aboard.

Astonishing but true. The Old Man's tongue-lashing and the reprobation of the others must have turned the iron deeply in Jonas' cringing soul; for from that day out he became a paragon of industry and zeal. He ceased to loaf or indulge in other heinous misdemeanours. Instead, he assumed the rôle of leader in many a daring deed.

He took wild chances over the ice, and spared himself no peril or hardship. He became an Attila for slaughter, a horse for towing in enormous loads, a maniac for sculping. More than any other he longed for "a gert rally," with infinite work, and "wished to de Lard we'd get a flash at de rusties in a jam." No "hard rowt" was now too tough for Jonas.

On one occasion he jumped overboard after a seal without any gaff; jumped from the moving ship to slush ice, raced across swaying pans, and chased the big old dog harp barehanded. The seal fled. Jonas ran faster. Amid the uproarious cheers of a large company clustered on the ship, he caught the dog harp just as it was about to dive down a rifter.

He caught it by the scutters. The seal flared round at him. He held fast, kicked it on the head, stunned it; then still by the scutters hauled it back to the ship. Shrieks of delight acclaimed him.

From then on, he was no longer classed as a slindger and a merry-me-got, but as a prime, A-One man. With new dignity he stood erect and took his place among the other men, a man.

All he got from it was praise, and very little of that! Perhaps his greatest reward was a master watch's:

"Dat feller Jonas, he'm as good as vifty, now. De like o' dis I never seen."

"De stone dat was rejected by de builder," quoted Uncle Edgar, "has become chief o' de carner."

CHAPTER XVII

BOMBS

DAY by day and night by night, except when we were "burned down" in the ice, our rugged old ship fought her way on, in all directions and seemingly in none. And ever sculps accumulated, were tallied down. Sense of location vanished. Time was lost. Gales swept us, fogs enfolded us, snows wrapped us. Rains came, and the hunters disguised themselves in black or yellow oilskins that gleamed as they *tramp-tramp-tramped* the decks, or tailed on a rope hauling up ballast. Even under the coldest drizzle of misery, they laughed and sang.

We left markers: returned to them by miracle. We "done a barbarous act—killed 3,000 swiles an' didn't get 'em aburd, 'fore dem went abroad."

At times, when no killing offered, some of the men would drive a couple of "sheet knives" a few paces apart in the filthy, splintered deck, and with little circlets of rope would play ring toss. This sport, however, was not looked upon with favour by many. To play games before the ship had a logger load would drive away the seals and probably jink the ship.

For all that, the *Terra Nova* kept lagging ever deeper, as the fat filled her pounds. Ever the stench of blood and oil strengthened, dirt and disorder thickened; but while the ship grew fouler, Nature kept revealing ever fresh beauties of sun-glories through dazzling banks of cloud, of glowing vapours that tinted the ice to melting rose. Often the aurora's blazing spectrum, like heat lightning slowed to hour-long glories, wavered and rippled. "Sun dogs" gleamed, mock suns glowed, mirages lifted, floated. Bergs jostled us; we elbowed them, indifferently.

One night the sturdy old vessel jammed fast. Not all the Cap'n's "Easy 'starn!" and "Full speed ahead!" could budge her. And presently, such were her labours that her rudder chain snapped and we were "in a fruz" for fair.

"Looks like we'm handy to a fix," judged Uncle Edgar. "If dis un get froze in yere, solid, de divil himself couldn't get us out. We might bide a fartnight in dis jam."

"Ain't got much of a slant [chance], an' dat's a fact," said master watch Roberts. "De ice is shockin' tight. We'm snug, b'ys! Pinched up bad, I 'lows."

"Might take root [damage]," agreed Skipper Nat, "if dis jam was to increase anythin'. Come on, ye guns o' sons! Got to blast!"

The whole ship began to buzz like a poked beehive.

"Putt a rackin' in the wheel chain! Bosun, fit [fill and trim] plenty lanterns an' tarchlights. The wind's a good sign to bring 'er off if she don't get jammed *too* tight. A good bit of ice 'ere, though. Skipper Edgar, bombs! We're just out cl'ar of some growlers; that's a blessin'. Come on, me sons, let's give this one her liberty!"

All hands looked alive. Masses of men grabbed "star-ber" (stabber) poles and tumbled over the rails from the barricade. The engineers meantime attacked the broken link in the rudder chain, making repairs by torch wavers. Down in the ship's waist, indifferent to naked flames of torches near, Uncle Edgar and Bosun Mike were filling bombs. Tin cans, these, with tin wings and with a hole at one end for the passage of a waterproof fuse. Each must have held about a quart of high-powered blasting powder.

Heavily the engine laboured, to win perhaps an inch of freedom. Whatever happened, the boiler must not be allowed to blow off, as, if it once started, the defective old safety valve wouldn't close till the pressure had run far down; and with our "barbarous" coal it might take hours to get steam again. Then, too, water must not be wasted —the precious fresh water whereof now only a fraction filled the boilers.

Now axes were hurled overside and men began making the ice ring. Uncle Edgar and Bosun Mike nailed long poles together; and to the end of these they spiked the bombs.

"Now, bosun, me son," the Old Man shouted from his bridge, "get y'r best line ready! An' get six more tarch-lights 'ere!"

Excitement waxed keener.

"Tarches! Tarches, yurr!" From barrel, bridge, and wheel, cries echoed. Vague ropes sprangled through the night. Men, swarming like bees, dragged out a long cable. Some, on deck, sank almost to their knees in the fat slither of sculps, as they paid out the rope.

"Hayve un over, me lucky b'ys!" bellowed the second hand. "Hot de poker fer de blasses [blasts]!"

"Tarches, dere, me sons! Bosun, got arr big pries aburd? Well, get 'em out! We goin' to blast an' pull troo wid de winches. Dis is young ice—a night's work to get cl'ar of it. Cut a score on dat pinnacle, some o' you men! Now, de hawsser! Seize on y'r eyes an' pass un out troo de runs!"

Vague forms rig lines out through rouse-chocks and make them fast to thumb-cleats; lead them to the winches;

shout unintelligibly. Meanwhile Uncle Edgar is inserting fuses in the bombs and coating them well with butter where they enter the tins. Buttered bombs—a new one, for me!

In the forward galley the poker is being "hotted." Outside, they are chopping with vast energy to rend a hole for the bombs.

When the bombs are ready they are passed overside, with raw and wavering lights glinting from their metal.

"Putt 'em rate in dere!" shouts the Old Man. "Poker?"

"'E's ready, sir," calls a voice from somewhere forward.

"Poker! Poker!" echo loud yells from the ice.

Now "Ole Glass Eye," our forward cook's assistant, runs to the rail with the cooler end of a long poker in hand. Its other end glows almost white hot. Glass Eye thrusts it over the rail to clutching grips. Swiftly it descends. A gnome runs with it, scrambling, sliding, leaping.

Fzzzzz!

The fuse leaps to spitting fire. A dim toiler thrusts the bomb, on the end of its pole, deep down through a chopped hole in the ice, far down, below water. Men leap, pile ice blocks hurriedly over the hole. Everybody turns and scatters to safe distances. Aboard, we cringe down back of the rail, under the bridge, behind galleys.

B O O N G!

The ship quivers. She groans and creaks. The splintered bomb pole flies far. Up heaves the ice. The detonation hurls a rain of fragments, some higher than our mastheads. All hands duck. Last year a huge block crashed down on Cap'n Kean on the bridge and crippled him for more than a fortnight.

As the ice bombardment clashes over decks and houses,

sulphurous odours float and mingle with the stench of blood and oil.

Pans heave and grumble apart. Up between them boils dirty, cork-like ice. Specks of phosphorescence glow in troubled rifters. Yelling, the stabber-pole crew come running back and fall to work. Cooks, stewards, all the shore crew line the rails, shout advice. Violent though the blast was—so violent as well-nigh to throw us all off our footing—it appears to have produced not much more effect than a firecracker.

"De h'ice settled in on de land!" someone shouts. "It'm nipped on de land!"

"Me sons," the Old Man exhorts, "we got open water not half a gunshot away. We blowed out de divil's bulk o' dem worst clumpers, dat time. Got to take to 't, agin. Stop chin-waggin', now, an' get to work. Ye won't make arr hand, just talkin'!" So loudly eloquent does he become that a man near me grunts:

"'E've gone fair screechin', dat's what 'e 'ave!"

His "screeching" produces results. Again the sealers shout, prize with their long poles. Still the jam refuses to break.

"She won't go 'less 'n us gives 'er nudder shot, me b'ys," opines Uncle Edgar.

He makes ready another blast, and once more glowing poker rushes overside, ship reels, ice and water fly, men leap again to the attack.

"Dat's well enough, now," the mate finally vociferates. "Now fer de line! Mind ye don't get un round de propeller. Now, den, over dat score! Sheen [shin] up dere, you, an' putt un over. Now, den, de winch—let un go!"

The cable is made fast to a pinnacle ahead, led aft and through a rouse-chock, then wound on the drum of the after winch to pull the ship ahead.

246

"We ain't spun out, yet!" the second hand exults. "No jinker aburd o' dis one. Rise up dat string, you—hayve un off dat clumper—so! No, no, *dat's* not in it [not the way to do it]. Come yere, you two—I want 'ee! Bear a hand, dere. Fire dat string to 'ell's flames out o' dere! Ah, *dat's* it! I'll call *ye* complete hands! Now den, yere she go—'dout [unless] somethin' burst!"

The *Terra Nova* shudders as an acre or two of ice begins to creak and shift. Perilously the hawser tautens; vibrates like a fiddlestring and seems about to snap, but holds.

"Give 'er 'nudder shot," advises Uncle Edgar.

"Half de len'th of 'erself she went!" triumphs the Cap'n, while I watch amazed. "Now she's hayvin' rate into de ice—squattin' un rate in! No need to cast off dat line, me sons—we'll trail it an' let de winch take it in. Now den—ahl ashore—*ahl clear!*"

A couple of days after we had blasted our way clear, we ran into an immense patch and everybody had to get out. Bosun, carpenter, scunners, bridge masters, preacher, firemen, even the baker himself, went overside with a rush.

All day, anywhere and everywhere, our hunters kept jumping out or scrambling aboard. Sometimes they landed on hardly more than slush; but little they minded that "loose, pummely stuff." They scrambled up and out of it, gay-hearted as boys playing "tiddledy-benders" on a shallow puddle, indifferent to the whole Atlantic heaving beneath them. And ever from the Cap'n rang shouts:

"Jump out! Over agin! Come on, b'ys!"

Every few minutes we slid up to a pan, made a kill, loaded. My arms ached with the constant drag of *starboard, steady; port, steady!* We killed many while on the move; and if the men failed to get aboard, the ship left them far behind, dwindling on the frozen plain. Hours afterward, no doubt the ship would garner them.

And in the midst of it all, as I stood at the wheel, lo! I caught another glimpse of the hunters' mentality.

"A power o' blood, sir," a grizzled old fellow beside me murmured. "A 'ape of innocent blood. You t'ink us got much chance o' heaven, spillin' so much? But, den," he added, looking very serious, "don't de Bible say as how ahl de animals was sent down fer de use o' man, in a nit [net]? I 'lows dere must of been a swile in dat nit, sir. An so we'm sove from sin, from de sin o' killin' dey poor swiles, an' ahl dat crool business. My glorianna, I 'spects de good Lard must *want* us to kill dey!"

Blessed be theology!

Mid-morning brought news that the crippled *Diana* was beginning to have trouble with her crew and that mutiny threatened. A few of her hunters were still "working scattered seals on the sheet" in which, with broken tailshaft, she lay imprisoned; but most were beginning to demand relief from other ships.

The Old Man tried to assume a simulacrum of regret; but the satisfaction of his: "You don't mean it!" when he read the message, sufficiently betrayed his delight. One competitor entirely down and out meant our better chance to come in high-liner. All hands joined in wishing the *Diana* the worst possible bad luck and all felt new enthusiasm.

Most of the whitecoats were now plainly beginning to "shade" (shed) their birthday suits and assume more rusty coats. At times the seals lay thick; again our men went over for one or two. Lots of energy and labour were sometimes expended for just a single whitecoat; now and again the skilfully handled ship would ram a lot of slob ice together and hold it firm for hunters to go away. When released, the slob would disintegrate to slush. Toward tea-time, Joe Stirge, who had been out gunning, came in, announcing that he had fallen into the sea; but all he changed was his socks. Just so he didn't have wet feet, the rest signified nothing.

"Wid de rheumatics in me naze I got to be careful 'bout not layvin' me feet wet," he explained. "Wonnerful bad ice, me son; gert growlers among it where I was to. I've lost me shootin.' Made de worst 'and ever I did. But I killed two wid one shot, anyhow. Dat's *somet'ing!*" He consoled himself with much toast and tea.

The wind built; ice stiffened; we slowed to a crawl.

"Gettin' very thick, me sons," admitted the Cap'n down in the cabin. He sat in his leather swing chair, the picture of dejection. With a fine patch all about, any idea of jamming cast him into doldrums of misery.

"He'm studyin'," the carpenter murmured to me. "De Ole Man look wonnerful pitiful, an' us studyin' wid un. Us ahl anxious fer dis man, doze days!"

We jammed at last; and—no danger now of the ship running away and leaving us—a little party of non-combatants went away to follow the crimson trail and have a look round. We numbered five: our Chief, "Marky," the doctor, third engineer Jardine, and myself. No knowing how long the ship might be "bottled," so we had time to spare. Men were out on every hand, questing like beagles. Our little party of slackers was not out for blood, but merely to pay a friendly call on the whitecoats.

Far from the ship, alone, deserted, we found a "nogg-head." That is to say, a motherless whitecoat, "wid narr pick o' fat on he." Poorest and most pitiful of seals a nogg-head is, spare-ribbed and starveling. In the enormous flux of the herd's life occasionally you find such a one: an unmothered baby whose dam has been killed; a youngster that, born only to suffer and die, has never known more than a few days—less, perhaps—of maternal care.

The seal mother, diving through her bobbing hole and away under the floes, miles, by chance, somewhere and somehow comes to grief. Unlike her thousands of sisters, she fails to return. They find the nursery again, far though it may have drifted. She comes no more; and her little one perishes—a hopeless, lost creature, terribly and inescapably alone with the North.

Rejected and unfed by any other, the nogg-head lies starving. It does not cry aloud. It simply lies prone on the ice, its huge eyes staring.

Sometimes a nogg-head survives. If it has had sufficient feeding before the catastrophe, it may last till "dipping time," then slip into the sea and eventually succeed in catching fish. In time it may grow to full sealhood. But this not often happens. The vast majority perish. Typically the nogg-head, while its more fortunate kin are waxing fat and hearty in preparation for the long sea trek toward Baffin Bay, shrivels to nothing. It lies inert, its black nostrils opening, closing with every laboured breath. Its flippers hang lax; its scutters trail prone along the ice. It grows dingy, and mottled, as Nature—*quand même*—tries to change its starveling coat.

I saw several nogg-heads in different scouting trips away from the ship, but not one would the men ever kill. One day a fireman brought in a nogg-head—alias a

"screecher," though why so called I do not know. So
far as I could learn, they never make any noise at all.
The fireman put it on a block of ice in the starboard punt,
or lifeboat. A hard-looking seal that was, i' faith!
Nothing but skin and bones and big black eyes and huge
tears. I made a sketch of it, and tried to feed it, but it
showed no interest in fish and brewis, and since we had
no milk to give it we put it out on ice again, to die.

CHAPTER XVIII

A BIT OF HISTORY

THE information which I obtained from the Cap'n and the crew on the *Terra Nova* I have combined with valuable data furnished by the Rev. M. Harvey, by A. A. Parsons, James Murphy, and Levi G. Chafe, and can thus give something like an historical *coup d'œil* of the whole industry. Those who look askance at history and writhe under statistics, can easily skip this chapter. It will not be long.[1]

Cod fishing has been carried on in Newfoundland waters for some four hundred years, but seal killing has been actively prosecuted only since about 1763. The uses of the seal and the most efficient ways of killing it were only gradually learned by Newfoundlanders. Previous to 1763, the common method was by netting, in "tickles" along the coast; and l'Abbé Raynal says that at about this time "English fishermen were in the habit of repairing to certain favourable places in order to capture seals in the way referred to," *i. e.*, by nets. This method is still employed on some parts of the northern coast of the island and down the Labrador. The seals, of course, were—and a few still are—netted during their migration; and the "Bay seal," which does not migrate, is often taken in nets.

---

[1] *Cf.* "The Seal Fishery of Newfoundland," by Rev. M. Harvey; "The Great Sealing Industry," by Alex. A. Parsons; and the voluminous reports of Levi G. Chafe, covered every phase of the industry for more than half a century. Mr. Chafe's reports constitute the most exhaustive body of statistics in the world dealing with the industry. James Murphy's "Old Sealing Days" contains a wealth of singular material for the investigator. All these authorities are Newfoundlanders; their works are all St. John's publications.

At the height of the netting industry, nets were placed all the way from Conception Bay to the Labrador. The nets were spread at right angles to the shore and drowned the seals caught in their meshes. Four or five men usually made up a crew to attend about twenty nets; but when seals were migrating freely, this number of nets required eight or ten men to haul them. On the Labrador the netting began in November and ended with Christmas; on the Newfoundland coast it began about Christmas and continued through the winter and spring.

Netting, as practised to-day, was thus explained to me by Uncle Edgar. The nets are hung vertically, with corks on the "head ropes" and with two long poles fastened to the upper corners of each net. These poles are secured to the nets by one end, so that they float vertically, with their tops just out of water. The "foot" of the nets is secured by grapnels, weights, and chains. The nets are often fifty to seventy fathoms long, and are placed in about fifteen fathoms of water with their tops considerably below the surface. They are made of very strong cord, called "seal twine," with a mesh of eleven to fifteen inches. The poles yield and bend over when ice comes along, later once more rising to the vertical position when the ice has passed. Sometimes as many as twenty or thirty seals are found caught and drowned in a medium-sized net.

The earliest record of seal products is in 1749, when oil to the value of £1,006 was exported. In 1767, this had risen to £8,832; in 1768, to £12,664; in 1773, to £26,388. In 1795, 4,500 seals were netted.

At the same time, men used to go out—as occasionally they still do—over the ice, from shore. They now and then dragged in a little fat, by dint of enormous hardship and peril. This shooting and clubbing by landsmen is only a minor part of the hunt, but it is worth noting. In 1894, the herd got jammed alongshore in such a way that 120,000 were thus killed. Men, women, dogs went out, with "catamarans," or sleds, and a record killing ensued. In 1917, landsmen took about 12,000, from White Bay to Cape St. Francis. At times, tugs even go out from St. John's, when the herd drives so far south. In 1922, such tugs killed 700 seals; and as for the shore killings, that year, they amounted to some 10,000. Occasionally seals are taken in Cabot Strait. Last year the *Kyle*, running from Port aux Basques, Newfoundland, to Louisburg, Nova Scotia, killed 150 seals and took them on board in less than an hour.

It should be recalled that in the early days both Scandinavians and Dundee Scotchmen came out to hunt the seal, but that eventually they abandoned the game as too strenuous. None but Newfoundlanders could keep it going. And their next development of the "fishery" was a gradual abandonment of netting in favour of going to the icefields in small boats—"ice skiffs" and open craft; incredibly small affairs with which to buck the arctic ice. These usually sailed about the middle of April, loaded with gunners. Decked boats were also used; and gradually small schooners were introduced. Some of these stayed out until June, following the herd north.

This kind of hunting proved very arduous and wasteful of seal life. As many seals were shot in open bays and leads, sinking there, the number brought in was wholly disparate with the number killed. Some 3,000 to 4,000 men were employed in this hunt; and though the risks run and hardships encountered were appalling, surprisingly few fatal accidents occurred. Some of those early schooners were of hardly thirty tons and carried but twelve to eighteen men. As they came into more general use, the date of sailing was made earlier, and the seals were taken in the whitecoat stage or—in case of the old—while riding the ice, as now. March 1st was adopted as the time of sailing, in place of St. Patrick's day which had for some years been the accepted date of departure. In these small schooners the men had no fire at all save in the galley. The skippers of some of these little vessels —gradually increasing in size up to one or two hundred tons—"became renowned as mighty hunters of seals," says the Rev. M. Harvey, "and many of them acquired considerable wealth. . . . A hundred such vessels used to leave St. John's, alone, for the ice."

The total number for all of Newfoundland ran into the hundreds. Here are some figures of sailing vessels:

Year	Number of Vessels
1805	81
1815	126
1830	558
1840	631
1852	534
1857	400

In this latter year, the crews amounted to 13,000 men; the value of the catch to between $1,000,000 and $1,250,000. The sailing vessels of that epoch usually stayed out from three to six weeks—a long stretch to go without a fire, meseems; especially if one happened to fall into the ocean a time or two.

Inevitably steam drove out sail. To-day, not a single sailing vessel goes to the ice, and with this change all the business connected with the building and outfitting of the sailing ships has dwindled to nothing. In those days, sealing was prosecuted from Twillingate, Fogo, Greenspond, Trinity, Carbonear, Harbour Grace, Cupids,

Brigus, and many other outports. Now it all centres at St. John's.

Wooden steamers were used in the beginning; were for a time replaced by steel; and now the wooden ships are back again, sadly diminished in number, time-worn and weary, but still carrying on. The fine steel ships *Florizel, Stephano, Bellaventure,* and *Bonaventure* have all been wrecked or sold. To-day only eight of the old-time wooden ships remain—the *Sagona, Ranger, Thetis, Seal, Viking, Eagle, Neptune,* and *Terra Nova.*

The best-known of the once numerous steamers, in addition to those just named, were:

Algerine.
Arctic.
Ariel, lost in 1875.
Aurora.
Bear.
Beothic.
Bloodhound, lost in 1872.
Commodore, lost in 1883.
Diana, lost in 1922.
Eclipse.
Esquimaux.
Falcon.
Grand Lake, lost in 1908.
Greenland, lost in 1907.
Hawk, lost in 1876.
Iceland, lost in 1910.
Jan Mayne.
Kite.
Labrador, lost in 1913.
Leopard, lost in 1907.
Lion, lost in 1882.

Mastiff.
Merlin, lost in 1882.
Micmac, lost in 1878.
Monticello, lost in 1872.
Narwhal, lost in 1884.
Newfoundland.
Nimrod.
Osprey, lost in 1874.
Panther, lost in 1908.
Polynia, lost in 1891.
Proteus, lost in 1883.
Resolute, lost in 1886.
Retriever, lost in 1872.
Southern Cross, lost in 1914.
Tiger, lost in 1884.
Tigress, lost in 1875.
Vanguard, lost in 1909.
Virginia Lake, lost in 1909.
Walrus, lost in 1908.
Wolf, lost in 1871.
Xanthus, lost in 1880[1]

Steamers first came into use in 1863, with the advent of the *Bloodhound* and the *Wolf,* both small but energetic

[1]The losses, out of the above list, amount to 70.7 per cent.!

and successful. By 1866, they had increased to five; the sailing vessels had diminished to 177. By 1873 the steamers had mounted to eighteen; by 1882, to twenty-five. As recently as 1894, twenty-one steamers, with a few sailing vessels, were employed. In 1905, twenty-five steamers went to the ice. This seems to have been the largest number ever sent. These steamers have all been of small tonnage—from 250 to 450[1]—and carrying from 150 to 200 men; in late years, that is, since more humane laws have been passed. The crews have for some time more or less steadily diminished in total number. In 1894, 5,000 men went out. To-day, only eight steamers brave the ice, with about 1,200 men all told.

Steam, which has generally increased the production of wealth in everything else, has oddly enough decreased the numbers of seals taken. Gradually the catch has declined. In this, some find proof of the wiping-out of the herd. To me it seems more reasonable that the lessened numbers of hunters naturally bring in fewer seals. When as many as 600 ships and 13,000 or 14,000 men went out, fancy how they must have combed the icefields! Again, the length of the open season has been decreased by law. In the old days, no closed season appears to have been enforced. The kill was ruthless. Vessels often sailed as early as the first of March. Now, they may not kill until March 15th. Badly enough protected as the herd is to-day, with slaughter of the breeders permitted, its safeguards are far better than fifty or sixty years ago. The diminution of the modern catch by no means convinces me that the herd is dwindling. With any kind of reasonable protection, it should flourish and increase, form a constant source of wealth for the Colony, and escape the fate which alarmists predict for it—a fate which has

[1]The *Terra Nova* is rated at 400 tons.

indeed overtaken some other branches of the seal family.[1]

Doctor Grenfell's opinion, however, is always worth listening to. Says he:

The employment of . . . steamships spells nothing less than the extermination of the seal herds. . . . . We are relentlessly attacking with ever-increasing ingenuity a limited species of mammals who have only a single offspring each year; attacking them with huge vessels and deadly repeating modern rifles, and at a time when every other animal alive is protected, *viz.*, when it is having its young.

We forget that from a quarter to a half million of these have been destroyed . . . and that enormous numbers of wasted carcasses are left rotting on the icefields, simply because, weight for weight, the ships make more money by loading fat and skin. We forget, also, that those interested in the actual returns are few in number compared with the population once maintained by these great seal herds. . . . It is a question of hustle and rapid returns, which cannot possibly last; for no class of mammals on earth has ever, or can ever, long withstand such an onslaught.[2]

These remarks were made at the time of the steel steamers and the great slaughter attending them. To-day, the kill is, fortunately, much reduced. Legislation is undoubtedly needed to shorten still more the open season; but even as things are, I believe the herds are now holding their own, if not increasing. In the palmy days of the sailing ships, close to 700,000 sculps have been taken in a single spring. The steamers' best year, 1902, yielded only 500,000. In 1922, the number had fallen to 126,031. It seems safe to believe that, if the herd managed to survive the unlimited slaughter of old times, the comparatively small modern kill cannot deplete it. Some say the herd is seeking other whelping grounds on harder

[1] *Cf.* "A Cruise among Desert Islands," by G. D. Hanna and A. W. Anthony, in *National Geographic Magazine*, July, 1923, which describes the absolute extermination of a once fine herd of seals through ruthless slaughter.

[2] "Seal Herds Going Fast," in New York *Evening Post*, sent to me without date.

and more distant ice. Who knows? No British census of the Atlantic herd exists, like that taken by Uncle Sam for the Pacific seals; which census has enabled our Government to keep killing within suitable limits and to obviate any danger of too far depleting the Alaska herd. In the old days, serious inroads on the Atlantic herd were undoubtedly made, but now I believe the losses are being repaired.

A "failure" of the seal hunt for a year or so must do much to re-stock the herd; as, for instance, in 1921, when only 101,452 were taken. Compare the modern figures with those of sailing-ship days:

CATCH BY SAILING SHIPS

Year	Number of Seals Killed
1830	558,942
1831	686,836
1832	508,407
1840	631,375
1844	685,530
1848	521,004
1852	534,378
1858	507,624

CATCH BY STEAMERS

Year	Number of Seals Killed
1906	341,836
1907	245,051
1908	213,863
1909	269,302
1910	333,349
1913	272,965
1917	196,228
1918	151,431
1921	101,452
1922	126,031
1923	101,770

It is evident that both the number of steamers and the catch of seals have steadily diminished. The hunters have suffered thereby even more than the owners, for whereas in the old days the men used to get half the catch as their own, now they receive only one third. We may always trust a benevolent capitalism to look out for itself.

Luck and skill remain to-day, however, as in the old days, trumps in this perilous game of sealing. Luck is the real joker. With luck, the *Wolf* once brought in 26,912 seals in only eleven days, the 255 men getting $72 apiece. Without luck, a ship may suffer weeks of misery and come home almost blanked. The high-line achievement of the fleet was made by Cap'n Abraham Kean in 1910, when he headed in through the Notch at St. John's aboard the *Florizel* with 49,069 sculps. He got in April 1st, if you please, after having been out only seventeen days. The weight of that phenomenal haul was 1048 tons of fat, valued at $90,800. Each of the 203 men received $148.

The same captain in 1916, on the same ship, brought in 46,481 sculps, which (being older fat) weighed 1,200 tons. The value of this cargo amounted to $135,848, and each of the crew of 270 men got $167 for only seventeen days' work. The Cap'n is said to have received $5,500. That *was* "swile-'aulin'"! Cap'n Kean, needless to say, is known as a "jowler," which is the reverse of a "jinker," alias a "Jonah." The next biggest hauls ever made were by Captains Blandford and Pike, each of whom is credited with having brought in 41,000 sculps. The quickest trip on record was made by the *Southern Cross*, when she brought in 30,000 sculps after a voyage of only nine days.

Cap'n Kean is justly known as "Admiral of the Fleet."[1]

---

[1]Captain Abraham Kean is officially a skipper in the R.N.R. and a commodore in the Newfoundland marine. He holds a commission from the British Admiralty for service in the fleet. He knows to a dot how many seals he has been instrumental in killing in a full half-century's work; an activity whereof he seems extraordinarily proud.

The largest "bill" ever made in the seal fishery was by the crew of the steamship *Retriever*, of Harbour Grace, in 1866. Under Captain James Murphy her 105 men cleared up $303 apiece. The largest bill ever made by a St. John's steamer was by the *Nimrod*, in 1871, when under Captain Peter Cummins the crew of 140 in two trips made $208.47 each. In 1892, Captain William Barbour, in the *Diana*, landed seals to the value of $106,148.06. The crew of 224 each got $184.30. At present a bill of $80 is considered unusually good. In 1922 the men of the two ships I was on, *Terra Nova* and *Eagle*, made respectively $74.90 and $49.22. The lowest bill made in that year, on a first trip, was the *Ranger's*, of $18.31 apiece; on a second trip to the ice, the *Seal's*, of $15.57 apiece. This gives some indication of how sealing, though still the world's greatest hunt and still second to the cod fishery as a marine source of Newfoundland's wealth, has fallen from its erstwhile high estate.

A very remarkable event happened in 1872, when the *Commodore*, under Captain Azariah Munden, not only had his ship filled below and on deck, but also towed a large quantity of seals from Bacalieu up Conception Bay as far as Western Bay, where the towed seals were winched on board. The *Commodore* was so deep in the water that her crew (200 men) could easily touch the water with their hands by leaning out over her rail. I suppose if she had sunk or turned turtle, that would have been an obvious act of God!

CHAPTER XIX

A SHORT CHAPTER ON A LONG SUNDAY

ONE Sunday I found the decks all deep-sheeted with snow—a most dreary scene. Seals, safe for the day, were bobbing in a wide bay of water just astern. Whitecoats were bleating, some alone, some in groups. A few were lying on their backs, wiggling their flippers in the most entertaining and debonair fashion. Not to-day should they die. Extraordinary, how the Sunday law holds! On the Sabbath men will work at anything but never will they kill. Some, however, draw the line at any kind of personal or avoidable work. I knew hunters on the *Terra Nova* who refused to sew on Sunday. "De Man Above," they told me, would have regarded sabbatical needle and thread with disfavour. Of course "chickers" were completely taboo. I never found any sealers, though, who carried the blue-law idea far enough to stop smoking on Sunday—or to refuse a good glutch o' rum.

Some of them seemed to entertain some faint idea that the Sabbath-keeping law, under the circumstances, was rather inconsistent. "Us 'auls in sculps an' stows 'em down," one confided. "Well, me son, might's well kill, too—might's well eat de meat as drink de gravy. But don't ye tell de Ole Man I said so!"

The Sabbath law may add vastly to the length and hardships of the voyage. Before it went into effect, most of the men killed. Even then, however, certain men refused; and these were then called "Sunday men." Now-

adays I believe the "Sunday men" are those who refuse
any kind of duty. Now, though the ship toil through
ice and storm for six days, finding but "a scatterin' few,"
and then on Sunday run into a wondrous spot of fat,
perhaps the "main patch" itself—no man will touch gun,
gaff, or blade. And if by Monday morning some mystery
of drift or ice or wind has blotted out the seals, 'tis the
Lord's will, and may that will be done! The law holds
like iron.

But to return to the Sunday I am describing.

The night before had been wild and blizzardy, but dawn
was splendid, with gold and crimson banners flying; lakes
and leads glowing; ice—no longer blood-patched, for the
merciful snow shrouded all—ivory and purple in ridges, or
shimmering argent on wind-swept plains. A fading moon
hung breathless with amaze at our impertinence of in-
trusion.

As the sun burned higher, it irradiated the world with
luminous and vivid glories. A miraculous drench of light
rained down upon the fretted ice, and a sky of tenderest
blue cupped a world of wonders.

And we struck the fat, too! Irony of evil fortune, that
was. We ploughed into so fine a spot of (to-day inviolate)
seals, that the Old Man decided to leave a marker to guide
us back to the same place on the morrow, unless in the
meantime we chanced to discover richer fields. A gang
of black-faced and muscular men dragged a lifeboat
away over the hummocky ice, tipped it over on a high
ridge, and stayed up a blue-and-white flag that cracked
in the wind.

That we could ever return again, thridding our way
through that mad confusion, locate our boat, and really
recover it, seemed one of life's most improbable contin-
gencies. And yet, days later—and in rain from a weeping

sky that smothered all vision—back through those silent miles we came precisely to that boat, and once more took it aboard.

We stopped now and again to haul in or to gather pans. Occasionally we struck open water, but progress, for the most part, was dead slow. The ice, "bound wid de land," offered hard knots to penetrate. We could "'ardly face troo de nip." *Grind-grind-grind!* then "Stop her!" and after a pause, "Back her! . . . Stop her! . . . Full speed ahead!" *Crash!* Ice and water flew; ship reared and quivered; we gained perhaps ten feet.

We had a rough time of it, trying to make headway. Our rudder was often caught; and as we backed and plugged ahead, it was "a gert job on us, me son, to get troo at ahl!"

Church, that night, down in the fetid, stifling, and overcrowded 'tween-decks, was ill-attended, for the ship jammed, and hour after hour the men were blasting with bombs, red-hot pokers, and all the rest of it; yelling, swarming, prizing, winching, with hoarse yells of: "Dere she go! Dere, now!" when as a fact she did not go at all.

One while it looked as if we were in a regular crush that, for all the *Terra Nova's* stout ribs, might bash in the ship.

At last we broke the jam and surged through into a huge lake all twinkling with stars, but presently we ran into the ice again, and found a flag set up in a barrel—some kind of signal left there early in the day. The Old Man decided to quit for the night. Right well he knew his position. I believe he could allocate any individual "ice candle" (icicle) on any clumper in all the North!

Even though sure of his ship and his own skill, the Cap'n showed worry. The nip grew serious. Blasts availed nothing. The gale built. A little more, and out on the ice perhaps we all might tumble for keeps.

That day was the Cap'n's wife's birthday, which he always celebrates in the ice with wassail and good cheer; but our parlous situation was inimical to revelry and all was omitted. The annual fiesta could not be held. All evening, after we "burned down," he sat brooding—praying, perhaps? Often, before meals, I thought he indulged in a moment of silent prayer. Now he seemed supplicating whatever powers there be that his ship might be spared—that natural laws might be suspended for our particular benefit.

"Him studyin'," Uncle Edgar murmured, as we all sat in the hellhole. "I seen a jam worse, before dat [now], but us got a hard look-up, now. Hard enough, b'ys!"

His smooth, pink, white-whisker-grizzled face grew more serious than I had ever seen it. He shook his head and tugged at his white moustache.

"Dat'm a gert man, dat Cap'n," he added. "I loves dat man!"

"It'm a quare place him'll get into an' not get out of!" opined Joe Stirge. "Ain't narr danger dis un'll get bursted."

"Sayin' is not much good, b'y," returned Uncle Edgar. "We'm up agin de divil's own knot where we'm is now."

"Yes, but our Cap'n's de rale ole silver-hair as know how to get cl'ar. He allus got a few shots in de locker. T'ings looks kind o' dark an' gloomy, but when us runs into arr lade [lead], rate away ye'll be up in y'r high heart, me son; up in y'r high glee!"

"Us might bide yere till de spring break up an' de ice go ahl abroad," put in Arthur Roberts. "Ye can see wid one slew o' y'r heye we'm in a hard take. I'm t'orough mired [exhausted] wid de blastin', dat night!"

Thus the discussion wagged along.

"Us might bide yere t'ree or four weeks," murmured John Domeney, " 'gard of a knot like dat."

"De Lard 'll see us troo," judged Uncle Edgar.

"De Lard," retorted another—one of the few Doubting Thomases I found aboard—"don't care fer we ner nobody else. Well," he yawned, "I'm goin' to have a small 'coction o' tea an' turn in. I don't care what de world say, I'm goin' to have a doss-down. Want arr cup o' tea wid me, anybody? What's de use to worry? If us sinks, us sinks—an' dis ain't narr walkin' distance from de land, needer, coarse wedder like dat!"

Some had a small 'coction o' tea, and a final smoke, and —such as were not soon to be called for duty—turned in. And, worn out by ennui and the weariness of too much ice, I turned in, too.

CHAPTER XX

POWERS OF DARKNESS

NEXT day, when one of the men addressed me as "Doctor," I began to realize that I had acquired a new title and perhaps new duties. This was a result of my having painted a man's chest with iodine and dressed a cut finger. For some time I had noticed that now and then a man would complain:

"I ain't bodily sick, sir, but I got a sore stummick."

Investigation revealed that the men's stummicks were always their lungs. So after I had painted one stummick and brought the man out of bronchitis or something, others began to come. Before long I had "a good bit o' call"—*i. e.*, business—as a stummick painter. My iodine, plus an unquestioning faith, worked miracles. Some of the men were convinced that all this talk about my being a writer was nonsense; that I must be a doctor after all. Perhaps not a "full-sledged" doctor, but some sort of one.

Many aboard seemed to have colds and coughs. That none died was a marvel.

Ministering a very little to the men's health, I learned some odd bits of native therapeutics.

"Take a mout'ful o' cold water, b'y, an' set on a hot stove till it bile, an' dat'll cure a toot'ache," one sealer told me. No doubt it might. Another Newfoundland way to cure toothache is with pebbles from a new-made grave. An aluminum ring will ward off, if not actually cure, rheumatism; and so will a potato in one's pocket. If one

266

is afflicted with warts, he need only wrap some pebbles in a cotton rag, throw them away, and trust to luck that somebody will pick them up. The minute that happens —good-bye warts! Or if one prefers, he can rub the warts with bacon rind and feed the rind to a cat; and presto! the warts will vanish.

The first snow falling in May will infallibly cure sore eyes. "Water welps," or sores on the hands and arms caused by salt water, yield to brass chains worn round the wrists.

"I've 'ad dem welps so bad," one old fellow informed me, "dat I've took me knife an' scrope 'em down, fer spite. But brass chains cured 'em. De more copper ye has in de brass, better it'll work."

If you have whooping-cough, find some woman married to a man with the same name as her own surname and induce her to give you a slice of bread and butter, and you will get well immediately. Lumbago is easily handled. Just lie down on your face and let a woman named Mary step on your back, and it's all over in a minute.

Everything has its own especial augury, good or bad, among the sealers and the outport people in general. Up there the folklore hunter finds rich ground. Some of the superstitions must be old as Adam, or older. Just as the Newfoundland dialect is made up of four elements —English, Scotch, French, Irish—so the island's superstitions have been blent of those same four; and exceptionally rich they are.

The morning brought clearing ice, as might have been expected with the good omen that ushered in the day; for on crawling out of my bunk I knocked off the lamp chimney, which fell to the floor but did not break.

"Dat mean de best kind o' luck comin'," Uncle Edgar assured me. "But if dat had bursted, it would of meant a death." Whose, he did not say.

You have to watch your step, among the sealers and outport folk, or you will certainly do or say something to blight your career. More taboos exist there than in any other country I have visited. Luck is everywhere, and it is mostly bad.

If you don't want to lose your luck for the day, you must take care not to drop your knife. You mustn't look at the setting sun or talk about it; or play cards with your hat off, for being uncovered shows homage to the Jack of Spades, which is "the very Old One himself," incarnate, whose picture book you are handling. The six of hearts is a notorious jinker, and is called "Crawley's curse." Sitting under a beam while playing cards is thought to bring bad luck. Lending money during a card game has the same effect. Some call it unlucky to kill a rat or a weasel; to pick birch for brooms in May, to rock an empty chair, or to sit in a room with two lamps burning.

It is said that in the strange rivalry existing between the two flames to give the better light, a "something" inimical to human life is going on, and I know of persons who would hesitate to sit in an apartment for a minute where two lamps are burning. It is not lucky . . . to hail in any way the setting sun, because Sol is supposed to be in communication with Erebus.[1]

Bad luck will attend you if you turn a hatch cover upside down on deck; drop a swab bucket overboard; tear a flag, even by accident; mend or sew sails on the quarter deck of a vessel; whistle on the water, or turn your boat counter-sunwise when starting from a wharf.

Fortune and misfortune lie in every triviality. Stars too near the moon bring mischance. If you cut tally sticks before you get any seals, you will probably have a

[1] P. J. Kinsella, in "Some Superstitions and Traditions of Newfoundland"—an invaluable book to which I am greatly indebted.

poor load.   Likewise, throwing ballast over before leaving port, or sailing without at least one stowaway, will injure the ship's chances of success.

If you sneeze, somebody is thinking of you or wishing for you.

A black cat may jink a ship.   To hurt a black cat is especially dangerous; but to be followed by one means that bad news will be followed by good.

To refuse to give a man a drink from a well may mean that you will die.   A bird or a bee in a house signifies death or a message of death.   If wise, you will not watch or talk about a boiling kettle; it may work you ill.   Women or parsons as passengers will bring a ship bad luck—the more women or parsons, the worse luck![1]   It is also of bad omen to sail from port on Friday or Sunday, or to reach port on Saturday night.   Sodom and Gomorrah, Newfoundlanders will tell you, were destroyed on a Friday; and Judas also perpetrated his treachery on the same day of the week; therefore Friday is bad.   Q. E. D.

It is risky to sail with a man who has neglected to pay his washerwoman before going to sea.

A window blind falling off means a death in the family; but as very few houses in Newfoundland have blinds, this risk is negligible.   It will bring you bad luck to be the first to cross the sill of a new house; you may even die of it. You must also avoid cutting the first sod for a new building—get somebody else to do it, if possible.   New buildings must be blessed by a clergyman to take the curse off, for of course Satan owns all new things.   It is bad to be first to cross a new bridge or be baptized in a new font; and still worse to be the first buried in a new cemetery!

After a burial in Newfoundland, a pick and shovel

---

[1]One hears tales of parsons having been thrown overboard to quell tempests; modern Jonah stories, with a vengeance!   Sailors have been known to simulate illness so as to avoid shipping with a parson.

should be laid crosswise on the grave. Also, a man should be kept in the bows of a vessel during a storm, to "cross" the waves. To hear a hen crow is bad fortune—bad for the hen, at all events, for she must immediately be killed.

If a livyere's wife wants to keep him from sailing a voyage, nothing simpler. All she has to do is catch a black cat and put it under a kettle; then her man simply can't go. Salt in a house will keep it prosperous, but a cut onion will draw disease from far and near. I found that the doctor, too, shared this superstition. It may be common in England as well as Newfoundland.

Our jovial doctor, equally ready with quip or pill.

"A honion," he one day said to me, "a honion, you cut it an' 'ang it hup, an' hall the disease in—disease in a 'ouse flies to it. Or keep one rolled in a paper, an' it will draw diseases to ye. They ain't safe to 'ave around, a cut honion ain't. But you'll never ketch no disease so long as you—long as you carry a bit o' camphor in your pocket, an' that there. An' there's a meanin' to every dream, too, if you can only remember the proper details of it!"

The soul of a dying man, Newfoundlanders tell you, goes out on the tide; and if a sick man can live beyond Friday, he is almost certain to get over Sunday, too. The surest way to keep one's house from burning for a year is to toss a brand from the back log of an open fire over the house on Christmas Eve.

Any girl who wants information about her future husband can do it on St. John's Day, June 24th, in this wise: She must put an egg in a tumbler before noon, and in the afternoon throw it out into the street. The initials of the first man to walk over the egg, will be those of her future spouse. Another method is for a girl to boil an egg hard, take half of it from the shell, and fill the empty space with salt. She must then take the egg and salt to bed, eat them, and leave a glass of water near her bed. In the night her future husband, or a vision of him— —authorities differ on this—will come and give her a drink.

On the *Rosalind*, going to Newfoundland, I was told about a tree in the middle of a small fenced-in plot of ground at Wesleyville.

"I was showing that place to a stranger," my informant said, "and he asked me:

"'What is that, anyhow? A burying ground?'

"'No,' I told him, 'and what's more, we'd better keep away from it, or some of the natives are liable to hurt us. See that tree? You notice it has a crook in it. Well, some years ago there was a hunchback child here, and they put it through a hole in that tree, and the child was completely straightened by it. Now some of these people would kill you if you even took a leaf of it.'"

Shrove Tuesday night, otherwise "pancake night," is sometimes celebrated in the outports by baking a cake containing a white horn button, a dime or a nickel, and a ring. When the cake is cut, the one who gets the button is doomed to remain single; the recipient of the ring will shortly marry; he who gets the coin will come into money. Sometimes a wire nail is also put in; and the one who gets that will die inside of a year, or—if a woman—will marry a carpenter.

It is not uncommon to lay a pipe on a dead man's grave,

quite in the old Egyptian manner of providing the departed with prime necessities.

A sufferer from nightmare is supposed to be ridden by something called "the old hag," and the only way to free him from torment is to call his name backward, when the hag will release him, instanter. Green is an unlucky colour; as why shouldn't it be, belonging as it does to "the little people"? The unsettled condition of the Island before the war, the great fire in St. John's in 1892, and the disastrous bank crash of 1894 are said to have been due to green issues of stamps for those years. A person or thing marked by that colour is given over to the elves. If you wear green, almost any fairy may carry you off. Above all, you must never wear green at a wedding.

Another thing you should never forget is the danger of speaking to a ghost. If you do, it can force you to do its will; and what's more, you will be very liable to die. "Corpse lights" or "corpse candles" are common—souls of relatives in the form of flames that come from the graveyard to summon the spirit of a dying man. Then there is the *ankou*, or coach of death, a most unpleasant apparition to meet on a midnight road. Night animals abound, headless or otherwise disagreeable. A Newfoundlander who had attended Harvard Medical School and was thoroughly well educated gave me a circumstantial account of his meeting one of these headless animals at Fogo, one dark night.

A drowned man may easily be found by putting a lighted candle in a loaf of bread and setting the bread afloat. The loaf will forthwith move to the body and stop there. The *modus operandi* of this procedure is that the flame represents the soul going in quest of the body.

If a wedding day be stormy, it portends a turbulent marriage. A bit of verse gives the whole situation:

If the wedding-day be fine and clear,
No cloud to the sunshine will ever appear.
If the day be stormy, dark, and drear,
The eyes of the woman will have many a tear!

The howling of a dog at night means a death.

A piece of string laid outside a house on St. Brigid's Eve will attract the saint, who will walk on it. Then a bit of that same string, tied round the foot or leg, will keep the wearer from any accident connected with stumbling or falling.

"Whistling for a wind" still claims adherents.

The gift of a knife or anything sharp will sever friendship.

Harm will surely befall any one who at night stands near crossroads or sits alone by running waters.

Haunted houses, ghosts, and "things" unidentified are common enough in Newfoundland; omens, premonitions, and warnings of evil constantly come. One of the oddest outport superstitions is that, if one of a betrothed pair dies and the other marries within a year, the faithless one will also die before another moon shall wane. Souls abandon bodies and wander about in a most disconcerting manner in those latitudes, leaving the bodies to simulate death. Buried treasures are innumerable, but unfortunately always in haunted places where he who digs usually comes to grief. The dead return to avenge injuries inflicted while living.

Phantom lights that lure ships to destruction, and phantom voices too, of like purpose, are common all over the Island. Ghost ships—some with skeleton crews—are well known. One man is known to have died of depression after having seen a ghost ship. The sealing steamer *Newfoundland* was seen sailing in Quidi Vidi Gut at the very hour she was lost in the ice. An old man whose son perished in the disaster clearly perceived her and knew trouble had befallen. Aboard the *Terra Nova* I talked with men who had themselves seen the wraith of the ill-fated *Southern Cross*. Such visions are of ill omen to a man, and may cause his death.

"I seen de ghost o' de *Cross*, plain as day," one man assured me. "De rale ship was black-painted, but dis ghost ship I'm speakin' on had white bulwarks, ahl shinin'. I seen it, an' dat finishes it! I did, so!"

Wrecks exercise a peculiar fascination over these island folk. The usual prayer: "God send ahl wrecks safe!" is supposed to be said *cum grano* in the form of a mental addendum: "Safe—to we!" One old fellow told me how he and a gang of "wrackers" went out to do a little robbery at a stranded vessel, "wid a tarch, crowbars, hatchets an' a bottle o' holy water."

Every dead man, by the way, is always spoken of as "poor Tom," "poor John," or the like. You hear "poor" applied to anybody, and you may safely assume he has passed on.

Troubled spots are common, where no house can be built without being thrown down by aggrieved spirits. Restless ghosts wander till someone will listen to their tale of woe, after which they can sleep in peace. "Eerie places" are those where goblins are to be shunned. Certain localized trouble spots exist in the sea, haunted by familiars which delight in wrecking any craft there. The sea spirits are angry if you rescue a drowning man—close parallel to the Chinese superstition of "river devils" that will drag down any who attempt to rescue a drowning man from their clutches. Ghosts often give warning of wrecks about to happen. Clouds of evil portent drift over houses destined for trouble; voices of advice or menace shake roofs; wraiths of drowned seamen stalk midnight roads. On one occasion at least the soul of a pirate was carried off by a full-rigged ship sailing through the sky.

Near Indian Harbour, on the Labrador Coast . . . many years ago, a pirate lived; and at his death a cloud came up, with a square-rigged ship in it, and the words: "The hour is come, but not the man," were heard. As the ship sailed over the house, the dying man's room was filled with the noise of waves and breakers, and the house shook as the soul of the wrecker passed away, borne in the cloud ship.[1]

"Fetches," or spirits, are annoyingly familiar at sea. They wander about vessels and try to get the crew to chat with them; also with ghostly hands they essay to remove human ones from the wheel. If the living steersman will only keep cool and quiet and hold fast, the fetch will presently disappear; if not, and the fetch gets possession of the wheel, woe to that ship!

To wear a dead sailor's clothes the same trip on which the man dies is execrable luck.

If two cocks crow together, trouble is in brew for the family of the man who owns the ground where the cocks held their duet. To work on New Year's Day is evil fortune, also to change one's clothes if one happens to put them on inside out.

Dropping a dish towel means that a visitor is coming. If the towel falls rolled up, the visitor will be a man; if open, a woman.

A new-born baby must always be raised into some higher place than that of its birth to make it fortunate— taken upstairs, or even lifted up into the arms of a person standing on a chair. A child born at midnight of a Friday will always be timorous.

---

[1]Kinsella's "Superstitions and Traditions."

A pig on board ship is a weather prophet. When logy and lazy, it foretells bad weather; when lively and in good spirits, a blow is coming. "Jinkers" are common enough: men who always carry bad winds and weather with them. Such men usually acquire nicknames like "Foggy Bill," "Heavy-weather Jack," or "Squally Jim." Plenty of disasters have been caused by incautious whistling on deck; but if you know just *how* to whistle—enough, but not too much, and with your body pressed close to the mainmast—you can usually get a good sailing breeze by a little musical skill.

Bread, called "comp'ny bread," in one's pocket, will keep the fairies away. I've tried this, myself, and know it works.

A broom nailed to the masthead, also a shark's tail on the jibboom, bring a ship good fortune. St. Elmo's fire causes both good and bad luck; good, if it rises or stays aloft, bad if it sinks. Killing a shark is good fortune. Salt in a pantry brings luck; and a coin pounded into the sill of a new house will always keep money in that house. (It will, for a fact!) The sun dances at dawn, Easter Sunday. If the moon rises in a storm, it will chase or eat the clouds. At the end of a journey, you must always throw away your old clothes and shoes; this insures the prosperity of the next voyage.

"Gi's nudder bun o' bread, yar, b'y," one day a master watch called out at tea. "I lost dis un!" The bread had fallen to the cabin floor, butter side down; and by that token, the master watch had just told a lie. Belief in that sign is firm, as in the old idea that odd numbers bring fortune. Some sealers will tell you that if you wear a ring on the fourth finger of the right hand, it will give you control over the weather. But wearing such a ring imposes certain limitations; for then you must not stay over

Wednesday ashore, or go a cruise of more than three months, or you will die.

Aboard a sealer, the first whitecoat caught should be kept alive, for a while at least, to bring good luck—a rule conspicuously broken aboard the *Terra Nova;* and think of the heavy ice we ran into! A certain amount of cursing may be permissible, but beyond definite limits it must not go, or misfortune will surely strike.

One day Joe Stirge told about a skipper he had many years ago gone cod fishing with. A storm came up on the Labrador, and the skipper's rage passed safe bounds.

"He cursed on God A'mighty an' cursed on de hangels, an' lightnin' an' thunder. He laughed at 'em, an' yelled: 'Don't you t'ink you'm goin' to front *me!*'"

"He was a gone man, entirely," judged a scunner, with conviction.

"He was, dat," agreed Joe. "Dey ahl got fish, an' he got none. Oh, a bad man! When he begun cursin' on de lightnin' an' de rain, he was a whole gentleman. A gray-whisker man, he was; a rale whisker man wid narr bit o' ha'r on his 'eed. Dat med it worse. I 'eerd he say t'ings ye wouldn't 'ardly credit. De rate carey [queer] talk he done, dat time."

"He must of went off his 'eed, to curse on de lightnin'," put in Arthur Roberts. "Ondly a gommel [fool] 'd take a chance like dat. I'd be every [very] scarrited to be in a ship wid a man as 'd curse on de lightnin'."

"So was I, b'y," assented Joe. "We had a bunch o' raws aburd, fit fer any martal t'ing from pitch-an'-toss to manslaughter, but we was proper 'feared. Dat feller was so nigh an' handy to hell's flames ye could smell un swindgin' [singeing]. An' by de Law Harry, didn't de son of a scaldy bring a wonnerful starm on we! Such wind an' rain, me sons! Dere was no let-up, an' no driet [clearing up] in de wedder, a week on end. De schooner flaus down in de trock o' de sea, like she goin' to de bottom, evvery minute. We got no fish, ahl de time bein' we was dere, had to 'aul in to Battle Harbour, an' bored up flyin' light. I don't want narr nudder time like dat!"

"If *I* heard a man cursin' like that," declared our Chief, "he'd get my fist in his gob so he wouldn't come up again."

"I can curse on a tide," added a master watch, "but de lightnin' an' rain an' de hangels—no, sir! No luck in de like o' dat!"

Many of these men are well-schooled in the Bible, if in nothing else. That book must be practically the only instruction many receive—like Joe's uncle, whereof Joe said:

"I had an uncle once as had a parrot, an' de parrot called un a dirty drunkard, an' me uncle cooked an' ate de martal son of a one, to get square-up wid un. Me uncle learned to read de Bible, an' narr man couldn't jam un on dat, but he wasn't much good on narr nudder book, an' he could ondly pick out scattered words of a newspaper."

Many of the sealers were prompt with a pat biblical answer or allusion.

"Shake off de dust off thy feet again," one day exclaimed Uncle Edgar.

"For de place where thou standest is holy!" added another.

And Uncle Absalom had frequently to hear:

"O Absalom, O Absalom, me son, would I had died fer thee!"

Bible questions and riddles were popular; knotty theological points like: "What place in de world did de sun ondly shine on once?" The answer, of course, was the bottom of the Red Sea. Another example: "What things was made on dis yearth an' is now in heaven?"

The reply: "De wounds o' Christ," satisfied everybody. "Yes, dat's sarnly so!" they agreed. The Miquelon Frenchmen speak another tongue than theirs, because of the Tower of Babel.

With great acerbity they argued obscure points. Closely some of them catechised me, to make sure I was quite orthodox—and naturally, they got me into some very hot water. When I let slip the devastating fact that about two thirds of the population in the States is not connected with any church, *i.e.*, that America is not really a predominantly Christian nation at all, I created a scandal. The men told me about Newfoundland Sabbath laws, almost as bad as our own in some states; laws with us happily more honoured in the breach than the observance, but in Newfoundland still enforced. My information that we had Sunday baseball, newspapers, motoring, golf, trains, and even motion pictures, to say nothing of "sacred concerts," filled them with pained amaze. Right cheerily they dangled America over the brimstone till I could verily sniff the fumes. Their native courtesy kept them from calling me also "a gone man, entirely," but I knew their thoughts.

Newfoundland entertains more religious prejudices than any other land I know, unless perhaps it be Italy or India. Sects swarm, and each is working for its own particular brand of salvation with the fervid devotion of a Babbitt booster for his home town. In my notebook I find:

The importance and tenacity of sectarian questions among these people are incredible to a man coming in from a twentieth-century atmosphere. I have heard of one captain who would never give a berth in his ship to a man of the Methodist persuasion. Such ideas seem naturally to be concomitants of Newfoundland's primitive educational system. The smallest outports maintain church schools; and where only one school can be supported, rival sects alternate in naming the teacher.   No non-sectarian schools exist, nor in St. John's was I able to find any public library—this, in a city of more than 30,000.   Every Board of Education has a clergyman for chairman. Sects of all sorts receive government grants.

The question of religion is a live one, in Newfoundland. Remote settlements may lack nearly everything, but they always have a church.   If they cannot afford a resident clergyman, circuit clergy and laymen officiate. "Parish boats" bring in people for services, from inaccessible places.

Beckles Willson, who knew the island as few outsiders have ever known it, has this to say:

St. John's, barring a few Scotch and Asiatic communities, is the most religious town on earth.   There is more religion here to the square inch than in any place I have ever visited.

Newfoundland has probably produced hundreds of painters and poets and musicians; but unfortunately their talents have all been stifled by the spirit of their environment.[1]

---

[1] "The Tenth Island," p. 42.

CHAPTER XXI

MUCKING ALONG

DAYS passed, each crammed with colour. The whitecoats kept getting rustier, "scrobbin' off de hair" as the time approached for the gun hunt after old fat. Weather came and went; days dull and foggy, when nothing could be seen except the ghostly pans opening before us, closing behind, in the oppressive vapour. Came "scats o' snow" when the fog fanned away and all grew sheeted with blowing drifts. "Scuddy weather" of uncertain winds sometimes set the ice "ahl in a whirl." Now and then, by way of variation, dawned "glittery" days, when the intense glare made ice glasses necessary. Again it would be "man-murderin' wid starm," and "freezin' gert guns, shockin' cold, b'y," so that the men's work seemed beyond all endurance.

The skins now began "running to oil," and the fat "goin' to pummy," which is to say, getting very ripe and degenerating to a nauseous mess. "No matter how you kipps de swiles cold," a hunter explained, "dem bound to run to hile. After a while, de new ones us gets don't kipp against de ole one us loses."

"A cent a roll, ten cents a hole," is how sealers reckon their loss. Each puncture in a skin is fined ten cents, and every roll of the ship is supposed to grind a cent's worth of value out of the cargo. Our pumps began pumping oil and blood; pretty expensive stuff to be jetting away!

It is this running to oil that sometimes puts an end to seal hunts, as in time the process begins to "come agin"

281

the cargo so that further labour is fruitless. My mentor added:

"One time we was to the Harse Islands, an' got stuck in de hice. We went ashore, an' killed ahl day. Built a fire an' bid [stayed] de night, dere. Next day killed, too, an' got a full load o' swiles in, an' away we went to Trinity Bay. De folks was ahl starvin' dere, an' we give 'em nigh ahl our supplies, an' what ye t'ink, b'y? We got jammed, an' had to live on bread dust an' fipper, an' ahl our skins runned away. We ondly got four dollars apiece, dat spring!"

Losing money on run-to-oil skins is bad enough, but the stench is worse, and now this was beginning to penetrate the whole ship.

The economic side of the skins being run to oil is worth a moment's notice. A good deal of valuable oil goes into the bilges and is pumped overboard and lost, but a lot is saved, and this belongs exclusively to the owners of the ships. The men get paid only for their sculps. I heard of one steamer with iron tanks, that at the end of a voyage had many puncheons of clear oil, bringing in the raw state twenty-five cents a gallon. Even in this way, too, the common hands are cheated.

The only really respectable pay made by any workers in the sealing industry is cleared by the skinners, at St. John's. These skinners are tremendously deft. With long knives they peel away the fat in two or three slashes, never leaving a shred of fat on the skins or cutting the hides. I understand they have to serve five years' apprenticeship, trimming flippers and such odd bits of work, before they are entrusted with sculps. They receive five cents for small sculps and ten for large, and are considered lucky men indeed, as they can earn from $200 to $500 for their spring's work. The record is held by one John Cook,

who skinned 717 sculps in a single day.   Even at five cents
apiece, this would come to $35.85—a breath-taking wage
for Newfoundland.

Time passed, as time will.   The fire roared; the light
dimmed; another day lagged to its graying close.   And
presently we stopped awhile, lying motionless in fog and
rain, with engines going dead slow.   A most dispiriting
day, that; yet numbers of the men were singing as they
slaved.

One man came aboard with a violent nosebleed.   The
doctor did his level best, but to no avail.   The sufferer
became faint.   As he returned forward, shrewd-faced
and good-humoured Tom Fillyards hailed him from the
galley.

"Bring dat jib [nose] o' yours yere, ye kenat!" he said.
"Layve me sove y'r miserable life fer ye.   My glorianna,
well, ye *are* an affliction case, ain't
ye?   Are ye lang fer bleedin' like
dat?"

"About of half an hour, Tom, me
darlin' man."

"Gentle Moses!   Have she been
bleedin' like dat so lang?   Come yere,
b'y.   Dat doctor's ondly a cod.   I'm
proud [glad] to 'elp ye, I am so!"

He took from the galley shelf a
whetstone and commanded the man
to bare his left arm.   Which done, he

"My glorianna, you *are* an
affliction case!"

proceeded to lash the whetstone very tightly into the
hollow of the man's elbow, right below the swelling biceps.
With stout spunyarn he lashed it, till the veins swelled;
and lo! the nosebleed stopped!

Explain that who can, the fact remains that in a very

few minutes the drizzle was checked and ceased altogether.
Shock of the cold stone, was it? Auto-suggestion?
Faith cure? I know not and can but record the fact.

Tom Fillyards, however, knew how it worked.

"Dere'm two t'ousand, seven hundurd an' twenty-five
veins in de foot connectin' wid de back o' de head," he
explained. I wrote down the number at once to get it
exactly right. "Ahl de blood in de body have to go troo
de veins o' de left arm. Well, den," he concluded with
entire lucidity, "if dem tied, how you goin' to bleed *any-
wheres?*"

The day wore on. Ice began to groan and shift, with
occasional grumbles of pressure changes. The *Eagle*
worked in to starboard, about a mile off, but had to
struggle out again, much to the Old Man's satisfaction.

"They're like pigs in a pound, goin' round an' round,"
he exulted. "They better go suddren [south] again, pick
up a few scattered hoods, an' burn down for the night.
It's too risky for they to come in 'ere, with the fog another
dark lantern!" But an urgent message from the crippled
Diana drove out all other discussion. The *Diana* reported dire distress and demanded that some ship stand
by and rescue her rebellious crew. This precipitated
lively argument, with much hauling-out of charts, the
invocation of sea laws, calculation of chances and costs.
No one evinced the slightest willingness to save either
ship or men. If those pestiferous rivals were in peril of
sinking, let them sink!

By five o'clock of the next morning—March 25th—I
returned to a world of harsh realities. The hellhole was
full of boots and of snoring men swathed in foul blankets;
men insensible to hardship or dirt or leaks or anything
conceivable. At 5:30 the engines began to thump again,
and after thirty-six hours of unspeakable ennui, lying ice-

bound, we tuned up for the day's run.   All seals within miles had been cleaned up; we had to move along.

Blest be the sun, after long fogs and rains in the ice!

Gloriously it arose that morning while I was very early at the wheel and while the Old Man ordered Skipper Nat aloft with a "Go now, first, an' look for flags!"

One of my wheel mates, after his pipe was properly filled with American tobacco, averred:

"De sun's risin' troo a bank fer a fine day, me son."   He shivered, an "ellery" man, in pitifully thin clothes. "We may 'ave a civil spring, from now out.   Ye know:

> "Marnin' red an' evenin' gray,
> Sets de traveller on his way.
> Evenin' gray an' marnin' red,
> Brings down rain upon y'r 'ead!"

A wonder-dawn, that!   The world seemed dissolving in palest blues, most delicate garnets, damasks, lilacs. And here was green—"the blue-green of the springing year"; there, watered silks of chameleon hues that changed even as one marvelled.   Silver plaques of ice miraculously floated.   The rain-melted and now re-frozen surface, glazed like mirrors, flung out gorgeous flashes, transplendent beyond words.

At eight o'clock, just after we had relinquished the wheel with a "Steady on as she go!" to another crowd, a shout of "*Hoods!*" rang down from the barrel.

Instantly the ship was in an uproar.

CHAPTER XXII

A BRUSH WITH HOODS

I RAN forward and reached the forepeak just in time to see a complete hood family—an enormous dog, a bitch, and pup. The ship slowed. Men began scrambling down from the barricade and from 'midships.

Guns were rushed up; for hoods are "bad fellers to get nigh an' 'andy to wid de gaff." More men jumped to ice. One plunged into water and came near being ground to bits between a pan and the ship, but others hooked him out with gaffs.

One swift gunner, Bob Noseworthy, was already leaping from pan to pan like a chamois toward the seals. He halted and fired. Another man shot from the forepeak but aimed too high. The bullet whopped into ice above the old dog.

Noseworthy, with better aim, winged the dog. Away the massive creature lumbered, while men guyed the poor shot and cheered the good.

The wounded dog meantime was undulating toward open water, "wonnerful sick," as somebody close beside me shouted. Excitement boiled. The bitch turned, slithered away with surprising speed, and before anybody could draw a bead on her, among the pinnacles, ducked into a rifter—"drawed de 'atch over 'er, an' shucked unner de pan. A rig'lar ole bitch, dat was—a rig'lar ole 'er!"

I felt astonished at her flight, for I had heard that hoods never retreated. This one partly made good such

286

reputation by immediately surging up again with a vast clutter and splash; and on the instant Noseworthy plunked a bullet into her head.

Her probable intention to stand by her pup never materialized. She rolled over on her back in the water, with a smother of blood, and vanished. She never came up again, but sank—probably five or six hundred pounds of fat, meat, and leather. What wastage of life in a world so needful! And it was typical of all gun-hunt sealing. Impossible to calculate the thousands of tons thus lost each spring.

One of the .batsmen had meantime rushed on and, outdistancing his eager competitors by some daring leaps, had with the gaff flogged life out of the pup. A final shot from Noseworthy finished the old dog.

Cheers split the frozen air.

Old dog and pup were soon dragged in by willing hands. Even the pup was so big that the hunters had to get out the "seal-dog" iron hook, jam it through the broken jaw, and hoist the pup aboard with rope and pulley. The winch had to be unlimbered, to get the dog aboard, with a great clatter and puffing. As the immense creature flattened out on deck it looked to me almost identical with a sea elephant. Its long nose, curved down like a proboscis, and its deflated skin bag on the head gave it a peculiarly formidable appearance. No wonder sealers fight shy of personal encounters with dog hoods.

Swiftly and with zest both seals were sculped. As a souvenir I plucked out one of the dog's whiskers—"smellers," the men call them. A peculiar, horn-like structure it was, somewhat corrugated, and of a peculiar gray-brown tint with darker brown spots.

The pup had a whitish belly, changing to slatey blue and to gray on the back. The dog looked spotted, mottled with black and gray. It showed a "last year's burn," or the scar of a bullet wound from the previous spring. So, then, it had already come in contact with Man. This time had been once too often. It also revealed traces of being "sunburned" as a result of riding the ice. Its skin was exceedingly soft.

Cheered by the gunplay, which presaged more soon to follow, the crew laughed, gesticulated, joked. The hunters came back aboard. The ship perked up. Now that the sun once more was blazing and the old-fat hunt, or rifle work, was approaching, spirits swiftly revived.

"Stand by on the port side!" rang the Old Man's cry, after we had crashed on a little farther. "Young hoods!" Quickly men leaped over again, killed and hoisted a brace of young hoods aboard. One had a white belly mottled with gray, a back all gray; the other was too blood-soaked for observation. At the next kill, the Old Man shouted from the bridge:

"Hayve over the seal dog! *Kill* y'r seal! Turn him belly up an' putt the seal dog through his lower jaw!" Obviously there is technique in this art! Four men were required to drag in one of the pups.

Merrily we forged ahead. Bright blazed the sun. "De moild's over, now!" some declared, meaning the foggy spell. Spirits ran high.

And there came rivalry for the desirable hood-pup carcasses to fill the barrels—each marked with its owner's initials—that now encumbered the barricade. I got glimpses of men carrying skinned carcasses, dragging them up the forecastle-head ladders, heaving them into lifeboats, jamming them into barrels. There came much chopping and dismembering of the bodies—grisly objects, raw-staring, but to these men choice and dainty morsels.

Our cheer and freedom did not last long, for presently

the ice grew heavy again, closing up with thick sludge grinding between the pans. It raftered formidably; and before long, despite all our churning, we were jammed again.

"It's goin' to be a miserable evenin' [afternoon]," judged the Cap'n. "We're on the weather edge o' the ice, an' there'll be no give-away till it moderates an' goes abroad." The sun gradually flickered out; the cold sharpened, and I was glad to seek refuge by the galley fire with my pail of potatoes. The seals that had promised so well "petered out" to only a few scattered whitecoats—whitecoats now scruffy and active.

Jammed again that night, regardless of all blastings, we had another songfest. Uncle Edgar contributed a sentimental ballad, beginning:

> "I t'ink I'll get wed
>   When de roses is red,
>   An' de wedder is lovely an' dry.
>   'And-in-'and we will stand,
>   At de altar we'll stand,
>   At de altar u-u-u-united to be!"

Tom Fillyards was prevailed upon to intone:

> "De time is drawin' near, me b'ys,
>   De narthern floe to face,
>   So we must get out 'aulin' rope,
>   De whitecoats fer to lace!
>   Our belt, skin boots an' shaythin' knife,
>   Our piper an' our pan,
>   An' rough it ah-h-h-h-ahl de month o' March,
>   An' do de best we can!
>
>   Some in de Gulf is goin' to sail,
>   De whitecoats fer to fight,
>   De *Viking* an' de *Suthren Cross*,
>   De *Nipshun* an' de *Kite*.

De warriors o' de wooden fleet,
Dey soon will sail away,
In charge of 'ardy swilin' crews,
Wid colours flyin' gay!

A few more days, an' ahl will sail,
Doze steamboats strong an' good,
To face de harp an' bellamer,
Whitecoats an' ole dog hood,
An' soon de slaughter will begin
Upon de bloodstained pan,
An' may good luck attend de fleet!
Success to evvery man!

On Patrick's Day, wid colours gay,
When in de narthern floe,
We hopes ye'll have your steamer full,
An' safely stowed below,
An' ahl return wid heavy loads,
An' buntin' wavin' gay!
Wid cheers from doze as is on shore,
When you return, some day!

Den, yere's success to ahl de fleet,
De wood an' ironclads,
Manned by de yout's of Newf'un'land,
Ahl active, hardy lads!
Fer ahl can do deir part like men,
An' face de frost an' sleet,
To haul a tow in rain or snow,
Our b'ys dey can't be beat!

May Providence guide ye, night an' day,
An' *suc*-cess crown y'r work!
Fer when de swiles is dere to kill,
From work ye niver shirk.
An' may ye ahl make tidy bills,
An' wealth to evvery man!
Fer he deserves a-a-a-ahl he can make
Who treads de frozen pan!"

Jardine followed with:

> "There's a bouncing girl in Fogo,
> That I am going to see.
> No other fellow knows her,
> No masher only me!
> She cried so when I left her,
> I thought she'd break her heart,
> And if I ever find her
> We nevermore shall part.
>
> Oh, she's the sweetest rose of colour,
> This hobo ever knew.
> Her eyes are bright as di-a-monds,
> They sparkle like the dew!
> You may talk about your St. John's girls,
> Or sing of Rosalie,
> But the girl I met in Fogo,
> She is just the girl for me!
>
> When summer winds are sighing,
> And the stars are shining bright,
> We walk around the harbour
> On a quiet summer night.
> And now I'm going to find her,
> For my heart is filled with woe,
> And we'll sing the old come-all-ye's
> That we sang to long ago,
> And we'll play the comb and jew's harp,
> And we'll sing the songs of yore,
> For Matilda Jane from Fogo
> Shall be mine forevermore!"

A lacklustre morning brought a slight heave in the ice so that the steamer rolled a bit in her cradle. A "dead cold" morning that was, too, unspeakably desolate. Through its early pallor, sparks from the galley winked up against the drift of smoke out of the funnel. From a bit of grumbling, as I helped get in ice, I suspected that some were growing weary. "We'm ondly gettin' $4 fer our fat," one man grumbled, "an' de *Ranger* makin' a second trip prove dere'm lumps of gold in it fer de owners. If us can't have $7 fer un, us better chuck un overburd!"

I heard ever-growing murmurs among the men. Deprived of killing, they turned to pessimism. Some kept going out and fetching in long-dead carcasses which they chopped up and stowed in their barrels and boxes. But most congregated together, only the lucky ones smoking, for many were now out of 'baccy. Perhaps that stimulated discontent; which after all was wonderfully slight, considering.

"Us been out too lang ahltogedder," one grumbled. "I got tons o' work to do at home. A stage [wharf] an' graypnels to make, an' a motor boat to fix. I don't like to bide yere, crackin' hard-bread!"

"Ah, gi' lang, ye ral!" another retorted. "Ral" is a mild term of reproach. "It'm ahl right to bide, if ye gets de fat. What'd ye be doin' at home, fer money, but walkin' de bank?"

"I t'inks us ought to hold up dis racket pretty soon, an' bore up!"

"Don't be havin' de bad word!" a third reproved the complainer, while forward a lively quarrel developed between two who claimed the same carcass. "Ye'll be glad ye bid [stayed], when she'm discharged. Us done better 'an arr nudder one, dat spring."

"I t'ink dat'm a lie, an' I'm goin' to hargue de p'int!" put in a fourth; and "hargue" he did. So did others. One claimed a certain other captain had been stealing our seals, which another indignantly denied. One attacked the merchants, while another defended them, claiming that: "T'ree parts o' de merchants got bursted."

Aft at the wheel, I heard the steersmen covertly "guying" the Cap'n with such whisperings as:

"He ain't got small yet!" and "De Ole Man want to be de big punch or be nothin'!" Even one of the firemen, leaning over the quarter-rail, growled. A wonderful figure, that fireman, with shabby torn cap, ragged sweater fastened with a safety pin, torn trousers, and a sweat rag like an Hawaiian *lei* round his neck. A perspiring, pale old man, sucking away at a stub of clay pipe, as he added: "De Cap'n t'ink he's gettin' dis one troo de ice, but it'm *us* as make 'er go!"

Obviously an idle day in bad ice was breeding ill-humours.

I had a little talk, apart, with a certain old fellow I had now and again helped with a pinch of tobacco. His grievance was vital:

"I'm a worn-lookin' man, sir, not in me time. I'm sixty-seven past; an' after a man passes farty, he'm comin' down de odder way. I been on ice when it was man-murderin' wid snow. A murderin' time I had, ahl me life, an' I'm gettin' pretty well up troo wid it, now. I had fourteen little ones, but dem ahl die young, cl'ar o' two. A man's soon an ole man now, an' away wid un!"

"I'm a worn-lookin' man, sir."

He sucked at his pipe, pondered mournfully, and continued in like vein:

"Me hands is ahl crippled wid work, an' not a cent. If de fish fail, ye have to go cuttin' pit props. Here I been workin' ahl me life, draggin' and 'aulin, mucklin' up grayples, sometimes bloody gert 'auls two hundurd an' fifty viddum [fathom] lang on a gurdy, an' I ain't got narr penny, sir. Not enough to babtize a fairy!" Something of the anguish of his toil-and-death-martyred race loomed in his face. "But whiles dere'm a draff in ye, ye got to go. De worst knock ever I got, dough, is now that me woman wants me to get her a set o' store teeth. Not as them costs so much, but 'cause if her has 'em, her'll eat a wonnerful lot more, an' I doubts if I can reach to feedin' she.

"Ah, well," he concluded, "some day us'll ahl shackle up an weigh anchor fer a better harbour. Us won't nade no purgatory ner washin' out. Ahl I got to do is cruise away me time till me dear Master call me. De grave's de next place I expects to find rest, an' praise de Lard it won't be lang, now. De Man Above said 'E died fer sinners, an' I 'spects 'E meant *me*. I'm a sinner, ahl rate; but I'll go to glory wid flags on, mabbe!'"

CHAPTER XXIII

GUNNERS AND DOGS

"GUNNERS an' dogs get ready!"

That cry one morning electrified the ship. For now the spy master had sighted afar an immense herd of old fat, and the second stage of the hunt—rifle-work—was about to begin.

We shall say no more of whitecoats. They pass. Another phase of the vast slaughter draws our attention. The season is over when many of the young can be taken. They have gone, either into the fleet's reeking holds or into the Atlantic. Gaff-work recedes; Winchesters come to the fore. Wary at last, beating north and ever northward, the vast herd—decimated but still incredibly numerous—is on the trek to the far places where men cannot pursue. Time is growing short.

The herd that we had sighted instantly put an end to all grumblings. It lay on a vast sheet which as yet the ship could not smash—miles and miles of solid, gleaming ice, against whose edge the sea beat in vain. The most furious ocean storms, be it said in passing, fail to break such masses—masses perhaps as big as a county. Only when the long swell forms can the sea conquer them.

The *Terra Nova*, with her shadow striding over the ice plain, laboured fruitlessly to reach the herd. On part of the floe's edge she had already lost a lot of killed seals that had somehow broken and gone adrift never to be recovered.

The *Ranger* seemed to have discovered the huge herd

afar, about the same time we did; and now she came fiercely straining through the "running ice." We beat her to a rift that fortune opened in the barrier, and plunged in at top speed. Joy swept the vessel.

"Scun 'er up to 'em, Jacob!" the Old Man shouted from the bridge. "How them bear?"

"Two p'ints on de starburd bow!"

"Good skein?"

The spy master brushed in the distances with his winking brass telescope.

"Big jag o' fat, a nice bit off, sir. A good spurt. But us goin' to have a hard dart to get among dat sheet. Tight ice, sir!" The shout trumpeted down exultantly as it ended: "I niver see but few better signs 'an dat. If it ain't a carner o' de main patch, it'm nigh an' handy!"

"Double full speed a'eed!" the Old Man cried. As if, indeed, the *Terra Nova* could do another inch an hour more than she was doing! "We're goin' to get a rally at the bedlamers, now. Goin' into the t'ick of 'em. Master watches, call up ahl y'r crowds. Get ahl y'r men ready to go away. Take plenty flags. Evvery man that can drag a seal, get ready! Evvery man out o' them castles. Get on, me darlin' b'ys!"

A gala air swept the *Terra Nova*. Master watches came tumbling up; and with them, from forward, gathered their crews. The men needed no urging. Keen as whippets for a race, already they were lining the barricade and rails, whetting knives, brandishing red-pointed gaffs, buckling on belts, casting blood-stiffened ropes over the shoulders of their crimsoned jackets.

From the bridge I watched it all. Already I could see the outscouts of the herd. The ice world extended gray under immense striations of storm and wind clouds; and all across that mighty, frozen breast of ocean, the herd lay sown. In a bay of water, near at hand, a few dogs and bitches were "braychin'," but nobody now gave them any heed. They were blowing bubbles, tossing their tails, playing with no heed whatever of the ship. They flung up sheaves of foam that flashed in scattered rays of sunshine, sea diamonds all asparkle—swift, joyous forms that plunged, rolled, and dived in dashing froth; Nature's supreme last word in vital force and loveliness and grace.

As we drew near the resting herd, boxes of ugly, soft-nosed dumdums—vicious things that would blow a seal's head to ribbons—were tossed up from the lazarette and broken open in the runway at the top of the cabin-companion stair. The riflemen fetched out their precious guns from bunks and corners; each man with the rifle he knew and loved better perhaps than he had ever known or loved a woman. They jacked in cartridges, jostling for ammunition as Billy Richards, Mike Donovan, and Uncle Edgar served it out, filling their magazines. The dogs (gunners' attendants) were meanwhile getting gaffs, belts, knives, and canvas nunch bags. In those bags, along with the cartridges, they stowed hard-bread; for who could tell what swift blizzard might cut off hunters miles from the ship? And in case of having to spend a night on ice, such bread helps out a meal of fipper cooked over a fire of gaff-stick shavings and strips of fat. The master watches also made sure they had their compasses.

The dogs took very good care not to sling their bags of ammunition over their shoulders, but to hold them in their hands. And there was a very good reason for that. Two hundred and fifty cartridges form a considerable weight.

"An' wid a bag o' cattridges fast to y'r shoulder, me son," a gunner explained to me, "if ye fell troo a rifter ye'd make a pierhead jump fer de bottom, an' ye'd bide dere, too. But wid de bag in y'r hand, ye can layve un go, an' crawl out on ice. An' nodder t'ing, it ain't healthy to drap one o' dem bags. A dog done dat last spring, an' de cattridges went off, an' 'twas a bloody miracle nobody didn't get shot!"

The companion alley was all a noisy seethe of men. From the cabin, below, sounded a rattle of dishes and kettles as the gunners mugged up for the hunt.

Voices jumbled:

"I'll go dog to ye, Skipper!"—"Want to go dog to me, eh? Well, look alive, den!" "I got a gert gun, b'ys! She'll reeve a bullet troo vifty swiles!"—"We'm on to a hundurd t'ousand, I'm bettin'!"—"Get y'r dogs ready, dere!"—"Prime-cut harps, dem is, an' wonnerful fine!"— "De nothren patch, I'm sayin'!"—"We'm goin' into de blood of 'em, now!"

All were inflamed with glorious anticipation as they gathered in the ship's waist, with rifles, bags, knives, and gaffs. Here, there, the *snick-snick-snick* of steel marked where some zealous hunter was putting a finer edge to his weapon. Voices only murmured, for at the Cap'n's command, none now spoke loud or shouted. Muffled now the scunner's steering directions drifted down from the barrel; and quietly the bridge master transmitted them to the wheel. Hardly an echo wafted back, in place of the usual lusty roars. Few sounds arose from deck or barricade.

The *Terra Nova* was running free, pursued by the *Ranger*, coasting along.

A fierce wind whipped my face, but what mattered wind or cold? Nothing mattered now but the kill. The whole ship quivered for that—the berserker rage of shooting, flailing, ripping, cutting, flinging carcasses and blood about—the glory of dominance over brute creation.

"Run down the steam!" ordered the Cap'n. The funnel must not smoke, now; that might alarm the herd. "Master watches, get ahl y'r men on ice. Take plenty flags an' tarchlights. Ahl the crowds get with their master watches, now!"

Bosun Mike served out torches. Tremendous was the enthusiasm. With luck, here was the loading of twenty ships, let alone one! From Cap'n down to lowliest stowaway, all were now co-equal in the thrill of conquest. Some of the soberer-minded put on ice-goggles or gave a final look at gaffs or guns. A few belated ones were swallowing the last of their mug-up.

"Now den, me sons," directed the Cap'n, "let's see how quick ye can get a bumper trip o' fat! Dis may be an ahl-day rally. We'll putt tarchlights on 'em. A full ship an' ahl flagged out, that's my motto! Evvery man in their carcass get out. They're ahl round, to nard. Go get evveryt'ing with hair on it. My, my, my, I wish I had an old-time tearin' crowd o' men!" Excitedly he waved his fur-clad arms over the weather-cloth. "I've a mind to putt on skin boots meself an' try me luck. *I'd* show ye some gunmanship! We're on 'em again!"

Vast was the good Cap'n's agitation, for one good day's butchery would cram the ship—hold, decks, even cabin space. Yes, given the fat, the *Terra Nova* would stow it, "till ye could lay on y'r stummick an' wash y'r hands"; stow it, even though every bunk had to be ripped out and all hands sleep on putrefying sculps.

"De gunners is gettin' ready, an' de dogs is gettin' aeir tails curled up over deir backs!" rejoiced Joe Stirge. "Dis is as good as arr nickel!"

The Cap'n invited me up on the bridge to get a view of the herd. My binoculars revealed in a broad bay thousands, beyond counting, of old seals splashing.

These were the fringes of the monster herd encamped on ice beyond. The ocean boiled with them in broad patches, but no one gave them any heed. Farther the quarry lay.

And what a quarry! The world's greatest hunt, indeed!

"I told ye," smiled the Cap'n, as if he owned the herd, "told ye you'd see somethin' few Americans has ever seen. Ain't that fair wonnerful now, an' beyond ahl?"

Like "the cattle upon a thousand hills" they lay resting, heaving slowly in the long swell. Under the white, streaking, staring arctic light they lay in scattered groups and patches. Some were slowly moving, their raised heads and tails making them look like fantastic, enormous birds. Some were sprawled out on mottled sides. Here, there, one hunched itself to a more comfortable resting place. Some kept lifting their noses into the wind, as if sniffing. Their labours for the year all done, now they were in the midst of their ice riding, their "enj'yin' time." All they asked was to be let alone.

All at once, overcome by excitement, one gunner on the barricade fired at a seal that had surged out on a pan near by.

"You, there!" the Cap'n shouted, "stop that! If you can't use that gun right, it'll be taken away from you! An' you that's hammerin' up there, stop it, too! No nonsense now, me sons, an' no unnecessary noise. We got great goin', now. Evvery shot has got to get a seal!"

The batsman who had been pounding a nail into the spun-yarn seizing of his gaff stopped. Even that noise might alarm the herd; and again, betimes, nothing could frighten it. Seals are temperamental. Now they flee at a breath of disturbance. Again, you can drive a ship within fifty feet of them or less, and shower them with lumps of coal, and they will not budge. I have seen the *Terra Nova* crush the very ice on which they rested, yet unable to make them take to the water.

Chances were, however, that silence would now prove golden. This was to be a stalking expedition, the quieter the better. An hour's killing might load the ship.

"Stop ahl noise, now, or I'll stop *you!*" the Old Man threatened. "There's two or three hundred thousand seals out there. Evveryt'ing is lovely and the goose hangs high!"

"Dey must be wantin' to ride de ice wonnerful bad," judged bridge master Hillier, "when dem bides up a cold day like dat. Dem tired, I 'spects, makin' fifteen or twenty mile a day down narth, swimmin' ahl night. No wonder dem wants to rest."

"I only hopes they *stays* tired," the Cap'n growled, "till we cleans 'em up!"

With the decks a bristle of gaffs and flags, and in as near silence as the engine permitted, the *Terra Nova* rapidly bore down on the herd. The seals lay roughly east and west, now about two miles off. Cap'n Kean swung the ship parallel to the skein and worked westward.

"Take y'r gangs, now, an' go away!" he ordered. "John Domeney, you go first. Get away, an' God bless ye, me son!"

All day the kill lasted. Despite the fact that most of the seals took to water, an enormous lot were butchered. The sun looked on red work, that day, as it glowed through a shining mist that blued the pinnacles with evanescent marvels of colour, and as the sun died, it gave up its ghost in a miracle of beauty that took a form not known to us of warmer seas. "Sun hounds," the sealers call such spectacles. Sinking through mists, the sun projected itself gradually in duplicated spheres. Down from its flattened disk, and up and sideways, it flung rosy bands, so that a flaming cross glowed against the west.

The central sun was incandescent gold, fading to brass. On the up-shooting band another sun—fainter but still marvellously bright—burned redly. This sun, too, shot out streamers; and these streamers bore faint blurs of mock suns, drowned in Hesperian vapours. Once and once only on the whole journey did I see that extraordinary phenomenon.

Then night blanked out the wonder and the glory of it, closing down cruelly with many of the crew still on ice. In masts and cordage a keen wind whistled, now or then shrieking like maniacs gone free. Sudden snow flurries blanched the tremulous rawness on deck. Under the urge of mysterious currents, the vast field began to shift, grind, buckle. Still the old ship fought on, smashing along to pick up pans where torchlights wavered.

Night brought news of the final scene in the crippled *Diana's* career, a message that her crew had "manused" in good earnest, had abandoned her in a sinking condition, and burned her with all her thousands of sculps still aboard.

CHAPTER XXIV

NEWFOUNDLAND CONTRASTS

THUS the *Diana* "perished," as our men expressed it. "Dey had a fair manus, a rig'lar mutiny, aburd, an' sunk 'er in de hice!" The word manus, by the way, may have come from "menace," but when the Newfoundlander "is in fer" that sort of thing, it usually goes far beyond menacing and comes to stern work.

The official account of this event, as given by Levi G. Chafe in his invaluable "Report of the Newfoundland Steam Sealing Fleet" for 1922, is brief:

The *Diana* killed and panned 7,000, and on the 16th of March, the ship being jammed all day and while endeavouring to get clear, lost her tail shaft. She was abandoned on March 27th, about 100 miles S. E. of Cape Bonavista. The crew of 125 men was taken off her by the S.S. *Sagona*, Captain Job Knee, and landed at Old Perlican.

To my surprise, since for the most part these people seem so meekly law-abiding, news of the mutiny excited no adverse comment. The hunters expressed neither blame nor praise; just accepted it as a fact and let it go. Talk wandered to other manuses, to strikes and fights and "rough shacks" of other days.

Under sufficient provocation, these simple and kindly men will run suddenly amuck and do deeds of extraordinary wildness. Their violence, on occasion, knows few bounds. Little as they understand modern labour conditions and much as they denounce strikes, they can, if put to it, strike with zeal and vigour. Not so many years ago—in 1902, for exactness' sake—three thousand sealers struck for a minimum of $5 a quintal for their fat, the abolition of $3 charge per man for berthing and coal, the abatement of a 33 per cent. increase in the cost of their supplies, and the guarantee of free food. With great gusto Joe Stirge told how a mob of them once rove a cable to a sealing steamer and held her from sailing. They probably would have pulled that ship right up into St. John's, if her captain hadn't cut the cable and let it escape.

Said Joe:

"'Twas no use tryin' to quash de men in dem ole days, when dey get deir minds med up. You couldn't putt 'em back, whatever. An' dey'd call dem cap'ns evveryt'ing. Dey took deir gaves [gaffs] one time in de *Ranger*, an' paraded in St. John's, an' de Cap'n took gunners an' dogs an' got after 'em. But dey had to kipp cl'ar o' de strikers or de strikers would slay 'em. De strikers got cropped [supplied] an' jumped out of 'er in de deed hour o' de night. Dey 'auled de cable up in de street an' it begin to grind round de bitts, too. Dere was seven hundurd men on to it. De Cap'n, he kipp a haxe ready, an' tuck it an' cut de cable an' got 'er cl'ar. Oh, what a muckery on de w'arf! De fisses [fists] was flyin', my dear man! Nobody didn't know de Cap'n, dat time.

"An' I was on a ship as mutinized at de hice, too," he added, puffing away at the blackest of cutty pipes. "Dat was de spring de *Roarer* had new barrels in 'er, an' wonnerful wedder it was, too, cold as de deed o' winter."

Just in passing, many of the sealers reckon time not by dates, as with us, but by reference to certain springs. "De disaster spring," for example, refers to 1914 when the *Newfoundland* suffered such tragedy and the *Southern*

Cross went down. "De spring o' de Wadhams" means a certain year when seals were very plentiful off the Wadham Islands. The men even understand references such as: "De spring dat So-and-so went first [chief engineer] in de *Kite*," or "De head [first] spring Such-a-one had de *Osprey*." Better than any baseball fan with us knows batting records, the sealers are versed in the history of their calling. They speak of "me t'irty-t'ree springs" as we might of so many years. Everything seems to be reckoned by springs. Sometimes for short periods, however, they count by "*Bruces*"; *i. e.* by trips of the steamship *Bruce*, running from Cape Breton to Newfoundland. As for example: "I come over six *Bruces* ago."

But to resume Joe's account of the manus he was in:

"It was 'gard o' stayin' out to de ice too lang. Dey got rampin' mad an' tole de Cap'n to bore up, an' he wouldn't. He was into good fat an' wouldn't liff it. We called our watches up an' ondly t'irteen went aft. De mutineers took up de side-sticks." This is always a formal declaration of mutiny, meaning that no more work will be done. "Dey stowed 'em in de scoppers, an' when de Cap'n asked wadn't 'em goin' to resume duty, dey'd ahl sing out: 'No!' You'd hear it ringin' in de hair.

"'You might find dat a harse of anodder colour, afore you'm troo up wid it,' said de Ole Man, but dey ondly laughed. Dey spilled [brought] deir gaves an' ropes alang, an' it was ahl shoutin' an' fightin'. Sheet knives was drawed, an' men was knocked down, but dey picked deirselves up an' took to 't agin. Some down in de hold had de pickle, de pork liquor, fired down on 'em.

"You didn't know *what* time you goin' to get it. One son of a scaldy grab me, an' I t'ought 'twas a dog had me hold, he hung on so tight, but I knocked un out. My darlin' man, such a muckery! *Flaus*, evveryt'ing was goin'. Dem sons o' ones was goin' to carry deir p'int, b'ys. De Ole Man said he'd go see de Gover'mint when he bored up, an' dey tole un to go see hell's flames. If he didn't give in, I don't know *what'd* 'appen to he!"

Joe relighted his pipe, pondered a smoky minute, and concluded:

"Dere was narr bit fau't to be found into de way he give up. He had to or get killed. Dey said dey'd shoot de next son of a dog as crossed 'em. Dey tored up evvery t'ing in a few minutes. An' dere was no one you could come on fer a look-after [damages]. So he had to pa-tienate, an' bear it. De law couldn't come on de men, by dis reason, dat he kipp 'em out too lang.

"'Cap'n,' dey'd say, 'my name's John Smit', an' I signed till de first o' May, an' it'm damn quare you kippin' me out langer. If you want trouble, 'ere 'e come, hellety-up!' So dey beat un an' got deir p'int. But 'twas an awful time, my sweet man!"

Joe's reminiscences elicited others.

Uncle Edgar added his bit:

"Dey gives t'ree cheers when dey gains deir p'int, an' gets merry as crickets. In dem ole days, a man 'ardly ever got killed, but I seen 'em broke up, wonnerful. Used to be men stabbed, when de Dundee swilers come out. Scatterin' men got stabbed. Dem Scotchmen 'd walk round in full rig [best clothes], an' de Newf'un'-landers 'd come on to 'em wid guns. 'Twas de divil's hole, dem days, St. John's was. De baymen an' de townies 'd fight, an' you couldn't stop it no ways. I've seen stick-up fellers an' sports [men without tickets for berths] try to get aburd, in boats, an' capsize, an' some-times dem'd get aburd an' call de Cap'n evveryt'ing."

"Ye mind de time," asked another, "when dey'd farm a ring on deck an' fight? De second spring I come out dere was ten fights to one time. You could manage wid a man in liquor, dem days, better dan sober. Dem was de gert, enj'yin' times, dough. De swilin' racket gone back a lot, now! . . ."

Cap'n Kean's opinion seems to differ from all this. According to him, mutiny is now of commoner occurrence than formerly. In his little book we read:

The Captain is no longer master of the situation. The history of the seal fishery between masters and men up to a very recent date reflects the highest credit on our people. Although suffering hardships of the worst kind and many times on short rations, the crews have always shown respect to their officers.

In 1877 when the late Hon. S. Blandford was in charge of the S. S. *Iceland*, when ready to go on her second trip, some casting had to be made in her engine-room and she was anchored in . . . this Harbour for several days and was not ready to sail . . . until the 3d of May. Such was the loyalty of her crew . . . that when she was ready to sail, not one of her crew failed to turn up.

Underlying all the outport men's submissiveness and piety lurks a fighting streak, and a broad one.

At outport dances, I have heard that strangers trying to be gallant to local lassies often face a fight that usually ends in a knockout. One Newfoundlander told me of having been thrown out bodily through the side of a dance hall by a gang of jealous swains and chased for a long distance by one of them, the others, six of them, tagging on behind.

"'Hell's fire an' flames!' says I," he narrated, "'I'm going' no furder!' I was bet-out wid runnin', you see.

"'But be glory, ye're goin' to hell, de day!' says de feller as chased me, comin' up. De cockabaloo o' de whole settlement, he was. Well, we fought, an' tore de clothes off each odder till we was in our naked buff, me son. *I* didn't know he was talkin' to [courting] de girl I danced wid. Jakers, no! An' I licked un an' knocked un cold; an' den up come de odders an' I had to take to 't agin an' run.

"I run in a house, an' hapsed de door, an' dey broke in an' took after me. I jumped out a hupstairs winder, an' run to de bay, an' out over de ice; an' anodder feller come up on me an' I licked *him*. It took de odder five to down me, an' I had wonnerful gert lumps on me 'eed, an' de blood was runnin' out o' me like a spern wheel [sperm whale] spoutin'. I never wants to geeze at narr nudder judy I don't know, ner have no more bird dances ner Cat Harbour reels wid 'em. No, sir!"

When I got back to St. John's, I had an hour's personal interview with one of the *Diana's* officers. Here is his story, much condensed:

"We broke our shaft in clear water. Then the ice nipped, pretty soon, an' we laid there about twelve days. We had a bunch o' World War veterans aburd as liked a fight. All they wanted was someone to make the balls, an' they'd fire 'em. They had five rifles forrard. The rest was aft.

"Well, a delegation o' forty men come aft an' got ugly. Said they'd bust up the Marconi house an' throw the Cap'n an' the Marconi operator overboard if they didn't send an S O S. I rigged a hose to give 'em a shot o' steam. The mutineers was led by a master watch. We was only leakin' six inches in four hours an' could of kept afloat easy. But anyhow, after a while the Cap'n give in to 'em.

"When he did, I'd be damned if I'd furnish steam to hoist out the seals. It was only three mile to the blue drop, an' we could of got clear. Anyhow, our wireless man sent the message, an' relief was headed for us. The sealers took out the powder an' provisions. Even then I didn't hardly think they'd quit. I was standin' by the ship, all right.

"But when I went on deck, one time, I found she was all afire, forrard. It was a bloody crime, the way she was burned, her an' all them thousands o' sculps. The last I seen o' her, as we was goin' away on the *Sagona*, she was still burnin' but not yet sunk. She sunk later, o' course. Yes, sir, a bloody crime!"

The sealers' temper, when it shows, seems like the tantrums of a usually placid child. The Germans found that out to their cost, in the war. The "Blue Putties," as the Newfoundland regiment was called, raised particular hob with the Boche. That regiment included many young sealers.

Ten thousand Newfoundlanders enlisted in army and navy, and some six thousand went overseas. They fought at the Dardanelles, Gallipoli, Suvla Bay, the Somme, Monchy-le-Preux, Guidecourt, at Passchendaele, Cambrai, Polygon Wood, Ypres. So daredevil was their bravery that the regiment as a whole was decorated by the King and given the title of "Royal." They served in the North Sea, on perilous mine-sweeping work, and were generally shoved forward into the most exposed and dangerous positions.

Conscription was passed, but not needed in Newfoundland; no conscripts went overseas. Right nobly the volunteers wore the "cracky" as some of the sealers call khaki. From 1,500 settlements of Newfoundland and the Labrador they came. Even a few Esquimaux enlisted; and one of these, a young rifleman named Siwaw, achieved fame as a sniper. Many Nova Scotia and Canadian regiments were full of Newfoundlanders, too.

St. John's alone sent a thousand men. Eight hundred

and fifty went into action, and some four hundred were killed and as many wounded. I have heard that only forty-three of that St. John's contingent returned unscathed. In all Newfoundland, 1,750 were killed and 4,000 wounded; and this in a country of only about 250,000 population. Had the United States suffered in like proportion its casualties would have totalled some 2,300,000! A thousand Newfoundlanders went into the battle of the Somme and only about a hundred came out. The Island now—and no wonder—keeps July 1st as "Commemoration Day."

Only seventeen V.C.'s were bestowed at all, in the war; and of these, one went to Thomas Ricketts, a Newfoundlander. Four D.S.O. and thirty-two D.C.M. decorations went to Newfoundlanders; and of all classes, two hundred decorations were given. "Caribou Hill," at Gallipoli, was named thus in honour of the Blue Putties. As part of the Anzacs, the Newfoundland Regiment shared in the General Staff's recommendation that no names be sent in for distinction, as "where every man was so wonderfully brave, no distinctions should be made"; and the Regiment —what was left of it—finished the Gallipoli campaign "acclaimed as heroes of the Victoria Cross class."[1]

As might be expected with a race brave, laborious, hardy and for ever poor, considerable shrewd native wisdom has developed among the Newfoundlanders. After the manner of the Spaniards, they are rather prone to interlard their remarks with proverbs; and many of these reveal their quaint yet truly sagacious points of view.

A proverb was never made by an unthinking mind [says T. J. Murphy, one of Newfoundland's greatest authorities on folklore and history], nor did it ever gain currency among an unthinking people. A flash of almost the lustre of genius gives it birth. It was never,

[1]*Newfoundland Quarterly*, April, 1916.

either in its general or local adaptability, accepted by an unobservant
people. They must see as the seer saw, to adapt it as a wise and
compactly uttered observation upon a general environment. . . .
There are many short and pithy sentences used by Newfoundlanders.

I can do no better than cite a few examples as recorded
by this enthusiastic student:

"Empty craft always loom high."

"A warm smoke is better than a cold fog."

"To plough and reap, but never sow."   (Fishermen's
work.)

"An empty stage, an empty stomach."

"In a leaky punt with a broken oar, it's always best to
hug the shore."

"The more fog, the more fish."

"The more rain, the more rest."

"Slave in the summer, sleep in the winter."

"A fisherman is one rogue, a merchant is many."

"The older the crab, the tougher his claws."

"If you can't bend your sails, you must bend your
back."

"Before you leave the sealer's side, the ice or slob must
first be tried."

"Out dogs and in dieters."   (When the fishermen return, the dogs are ousted from the houses.)

"The planter's eye spreads the water horse."   (The
boss of a fish room gets the fish quickly spread.)

"A fish in a punt is worth two in the water."

"No cod, no cash."

"Fish in the punt, pork in the pot."

"Up sail and down bakepot."   (The women feast
after the men have sailed away.)

"Spare the salt and spoil the scrod."

"When the rum's in the kag, the tongue doesn't wag."

"The best line is not the best liar, nor is the best gaff the best gabbler."

"The biggest fish was lost at the gunwale."

"Out of the fog and into the fat."

"Moonlight dries no mittens."

"There's no splicing splinters."

"With God on the lookout, it's easy to steer."

"It's by fishing, not by wishing."

"Cape St. Mary's will pay for all." (Cape St. Mary's is a splendid fishing ground.)

"Baccy and rum make things hum."

"The ice eats up the wind, the land eats up the fog."

"Nofty was forty when he lost the pork." (Never be sure of anything.)

"If you squeeze the sculpin, you'll find his thorns."

"A full cupboard warms the winter."

"When the weather is fair, your oil jacket bear."

"The craft flies and the breeze follows." (Pure luck.)

"The tow of an iceberg is better than none."

"The tiller stick forward and the grapnel aft." (Extreme confusion.)

"When the fish eat, we all eat."

"When the wind is inshore, don't go out any more." (A lazy fellow.)

"When you haul a squid in, look out for your chin. (To avoid being squirted with ink; *i. e.*, don't argue with a blackguard.)

"The sea is made of mothers' tears."

Through all these proverbs runs a thread of poverty, thrift, saving; a canny and profound wisdom born of long, hard battles for life, with a pitiless environment. For pitiless it is, and when added to the merchants' and the employers' exploitation, it becomes well-nigh insufferable.

Whether sealing or codding, the livyeres are usually paid on some kind of share system that always gives the toilers "de little end o' de stick." The curse of these men is the credit system, whereby thousands of them lie always in the merchants' debt. Many are illiterate and cannot figure; the merchants, if so disposed, have everything all their own way. Once the men "fall back," they are sometimes never again able to "put up money" or to "straighten up," *i. e.*, pay their bills.

"I niver expects to get cl'ar," one old fellow told me, "not till I goes acrost where de sweet oranges grow." A man of good Christian faith, he, as a tattooed cross and bleeding heart of Jesus on his toil-worn hand attested "De owners bears down wonnerful hard on some o' we simple folk. An' I know one cap'n, too, as runs a store; an' one year when de men was paid off de swiler, he took a canvas bag an' stood on de w'arf, an' as de men come off, he collected ahl as was owed him. Yes, he had de right to, but a lot of 'em went home bare. An' dat was crool hard, me son. But, well—six feet o' yearth makes ahl men de same size, in de end.

"'Tis a wonnerful hard take, sometimes, on de swilin' rackets. 'Tis bad to work ahl day on de ice, an' den back to de ship late after dark, widout narr hot drap in our insides ahl day lang. An' a man got more space to be buried in dan a swiler has to sleep in aburd o' doze! An' swaller y'r grub down holus-bolus. Why a dog wouldn't live so! Sometimes I t'ink a man's foolish to go to de ice—'most as foolish as Sal Glover, what got out o' bed one cold night to cover up her feet."

Dejectedly he shook his head. I offered tobacco. To my surprise he declined.

"De more I tried to use un," he explained, "de bigger turn I got agin un. It'd make me hayve me stummick, sarnly, if I was to smoke or chaw. No, I ain't got no use fer baccy; but women, now, I allus loved 'em, in evvery shape an' farm."

"What *you* know 'gard o' women?" interrupted another, a mocking young fellow.

"Gi' lang wid ye!" the old man retorted. "Ye lang, slinky cod hauler, wid legs crooked as a rainbow an' I dare say webbed feet on ye. I don't make no wonder de ondly engagement ye iver had was a washout. De judies ain't blind!"

"When y'r hat covers y'r fambly, ye got no worry."

Two or three others drifted up, laughing. One remarked:

"Some good, dough, in not bein' married, b'y. When ye got a loose leg an' y'r hat covers all y'r fambly, ye got narr pick o' worry!"

"My woman," the old man proudly added, "her'm a gert armful. I first runned up agin she in a vog an' niver let she see me in de light at ahl. Dat'm how I winned my woman! At first I couldn't get a'eed none whatsomever. Ah," with a sigh, "her was sarnly a fine-looking woman. An' couldn't her split fish, dough? When her'd skin up her sleeve, her arm look like de mainmast o' dis one. Man, dear!"

"I'm kind o' knocked out about women, meself," volunteered another. "De man as 'duced me to me wife done me a proper good turn. I t'ought I'd niver get dat woman, but one summer I med a good ketch o' fish, an' her said yes. 'If de fish don't come in in de summer, de bells won't ring out in de fall,' ye know. Ah, dat was a fine, logy [hot] summer, last summer twelvemonth. When I was lovemakin', wadn't dat de enj'yin' time, dough? I was rate full o' sediment [sentiment], I was!"

"I been married twenty-one year gone," said still another. "If me woman gone evveryt'ing gone fer me!"

Thus, out there in that frozen ocean thoughts were going back to the outports in the "nothren" bays, to the women and little ones in the box-like little houses perched high on stilts far up some black and craggy cove, tickle, or fjord—going home.

CHAPTER XXV

A NEWFOUNDLAND OUTPORT

A GLANCE or two at the home life of the men may not come amiss after having seen so much of their life in the icefields. The typical Newfoundland outport is fringed with fish flakes, in summer snowy with split and drying salt cod. Fish illimitable.

"I shouldn't think anybody would ever have to starve around here," I once said to the owner of a fish room. "What's to hinder a hungry man coming at night and taking a fish or two?"

"Nothin' in de world, me darlin' man," he answered, lighting his pipe as he sat there on a leaky drum of gasoline. "An' us don't mind dat. What *do* chafe we, dough, is when some angyshore [worthless fellow] carries off a putt o' fish at night an' den in de marn come round an' sell 'em to we agin!"

Which gives some measure of the livyere. Generous to a fault, simple yet shrewd, and for the most part impeccably honest, now and again a rogue exists among them. But most of them are first-class men. Only such can drag a living from the cod banks and the icefields. I have seen some families existing in a manner apparently impossible. Their whole property was a hand-rowed dory, a windlass to drag it up with, a tub of trawl, a tilt in some wildly barren cleft, and a tiny flake where in a whole summer they might possibly cure a few quintals, if they had luck.

Life for many is just one long, heartbreaking struggle to

get white flour, tea, pork, and molasses wherewith to vary the diet of fish and brewis. Lassy loaf and "gandies" (pancakes made with pork fat and molasses) are about the farthest limits of gastronomic revelry they can "reach to." Tea is their bane. Even the children drink far too much of it, strong and boiled over. Newfoundland needs schools above all else; and next to those, instruction in dietetics, for the salvation of the people's vitality.

And yet an incredibly hardy race grows up. Perhaps, as in ancient Sparta, only the toughest survive, to fish on the Banks, go "down Narth" in summer, and to the ice in spring. Thousands of outport men migrate almost as regularly as the seals themselves. With small, home-built schooners—this ingenious people can turn their hands to making almost everything they need—they take up the sea trek every summer and go down the Labrador. If they pick some berth and settle down, they're called "stationers," "squatters," or "roomers." If they keep on the move, they're "floaters."

Whole families go—women, children, and all. And everybody works. Even the girls must take a hand. It is an immense seasonal shift of population, like our own wheat-belt work. While the fish are running, twenty hours of labour on end are not uncommon. There is little sleep, either on the Banks or down North, when King Cod summons. The men catch, the women dress the fish. If you still believe women are the weaker sex, visit the fisheries. No wonder the rosy-cheeked lassies soon fade. No wonder that at thirty they're half gone; at forty, old. And that's a pity, too; for types more freshly blooming than some of the children you can hardly find.

Perils are their daily fare; fog and tempest their arch enemies. Perhaps they dread fog even more than storm, if they dread anything. Sinister, unrelenting, it takes steady and heavy toll. In the fog, schooners are crashed down by liners; dories go adrift and are lost. Newfoundlanders have been picked up after having spent a fortnight on the open Atlantic in small boats. One dory crew a few years ago rowed nearly two hundred miles to land. Innumerable families mourn fathers and brothers who, fog-lost, have never returned. The Atlantic, nurse and feeder of Newfoundland, is also its devourer.

Sometimes these Vikings work all night, fishing, with flares. Days and nights on end they're never dry. In ugly weather they snatch one-tub sets between squalls, fairly pulling the whiskers of death.

One who knows how poor their food resources are at home and during the cod fishery can perhaps understand why the "swilin' racket" attracts so many. For once aboard a sealing steamer they can always get enough to fill their bellies, no matter how poorly. And that, to many, is sheer luxury.

Dotted along the stark Newfoundland coasts—especially in the northern bays—perched high on bald headlands or jammed into the bottom of stark fjords, ravines and clefts in the wild black palisades for ever collared with froth, lie the outports where dwell this rugged breed of men. The scenery overawes, it exalts the heart. Indescribably majestic is its magnitude of cliffs that affront the moon, its bellowing sea caves and leaping surf, its crags and islets mazed in swarms of screaming sea fowl.

The Vikings, however, care little for scenery. They are looking for safe harbours; so they often stick their villages miles up cracks in the sea wall where in foggy weather steamers can navigate by echo, and where you can almost toss a hard-tack into the shouting surf on either hand. Miracles of seamanship, to navigate such ocean gorges!

See one outport, and you more or less see all. Invariably you find a huddle of tiny toy houses built of wood and, when painted at all, gaily coloured. Sometimes, however, you can't be sure that a house which seems blue is really painted. That colour may be only flies. Where the cod is, there will the flies be also, as you very presently learn when you go ashore from the "stage" where the whole population foregathers to see the semi-occasional steamer come in. The church dominates everything. Often there are two or three rival churches in tiny settlements, all competing. Many of the buildings are perched precariously on stilts to keep them level amid the jagged rocks. They seem to be striding up the cliffs.

Motor cars languish and die in such a land, without roads. Even if the livyeres could afford them, there's nowhere to drive. Nearly all communication is by sea. When the Atlantic so wills, some of the outports are completely isolated. The thoroughfares are mazes of crooked lanes, edged in with fences of wattle or of spruce poles over which hang well-scrubbed hooked rugs, family washings, and brown nets.

Buoys, "old grannies" (kellock anchors), and all manner of strange gear, for every tiniest bit of which a name exists, lie scattered everywhere. The fences are maintained to keep vagrant goats and sheep—the sheep marked with red paint to identify them as So-and-so's property—from ravaging the meagre gardens. These animals often wear yokes; so too, the hens. A yoke on a hen is something of a novelty. At first I could not understand why so many of the domestic fowl had sticks lashed horizontally under their wings. But the explanation: "Green stuff be's so wonnerful 'ard to raise 'ere, sir," soon made all clear.

Few of the houses boast shutters, for sunshine is always

welcome. Nearly all carry ladders on their roofs, because there are no fire departments.

"If a 'ouse gets on fire, me dear man," an ancient told me, "dem 'most allus burns up, annyhow, 'fore us gets dere, an' dat save we de trouble. Sometimes in winter de serf bate in, rate to de 'ouses, an' us got to board up de winders to save 'em. An' one time us 'ad a livin' starm blowed so 'ard, us ahl 'ad to bide in our 'ouse to kipp un from blowin' away, an' dat'm as true as de light!"

No painter could be in an outport five minutes without wanting to set up his easel and get to work. He might see a lighthouse stayed with wire cables to keep it from being blown off the cliffs; or a group of big-booted, canvas-jacketed men "barking" a sail—which is to say, boiling it with spruce in a huge kettle. He might behold a woman fetching in a backload of firewood; a little lass "spillin' in a yaffle o' crunnocks" (bringing in an armful of kindling); an old man carrying water in two buckets with an archaic English neck yoke; a ruined whale factory; a fox farm with furtive, cod-fed silvers; a jaunty constable talking with a shovel-hatted Church of England parson; two oldsters toiling up a lane with a hand barrow of rocks; a grandame making soap from "de hile off de livers, sir, an' de loy of ashes."

Perhaps he might have the good fortune to find a wedding in progress, with "joy guns" being fired and fiddling and dancing under way. If instrumental music lacked, some old livyere might hold quid in hand and furnish "cheek music" with a lively refrain of "Tra-la-la, Toora-loo!" or of "Ty-de-lit-lit-de! Do-de-do! Tiddle-do-do-dum!" while others patted time to encourage him and shouted: "Kape 'er rollin', brud! Long life to ye!"

A group of the seal fishers at home, trying to spell out the news in the cable dispatch book at the post office—

their only newspaper—might make a capital painting. So too would a group of the tousle-headed children playing in dories, pretending to fish and to cure the cod. Little men and women they are, rather than children. They make believe to paddle boats; they drag bundles of rags, for dolls, in boxes up and down the rocky lanes; they keep imaginary fish rooms and markets. Give them a big Newfoundland penny and their fortunes are made.

Beautiful children, of pure Nordic stock, most of these. Get them away from the fried food, the tea more bitter than sin, the bread that could easily be used for anchors; and give them good diet, schools, a chance in life, and what a race they would develop! Doctor Grenfell can tell you more of this.

Some of the little outports and coves whence come the sort of men who go sealing bear names that cry aloud to be worked into fiction. Could anything be more inviting to a writer than Deadman's Cove, Pushthrough, Famish, or Hooping Harbour? Then there is Seldom-come-by, Happy Adventure, Bareneed, and Gallows Cove; Breakheart, Little Cat Arm, Hauling Point, Great Harbour Deep, Confusion Bay, Grappling Point, Winter House, and Rattling Brook. Other names of romantic connotation are: Wild Bight, Sunday Cove, Leading Tickle, Great Triton, Noggin's Cove, Joe Batt's Arm, Offer Wadhams, The Bat, Squib Tickle, Oarblade, Doughfig, Horse Chops, Hanging Hill, Bowline, Bay Bulls, Butterpot, Mistaken Point, Come-by-chance, Famine, Pistolet Bay, Steering Island, Peter Snout, Jack-of-clubs, Nameless Cove and no end of others equally thought-inspiring.

Many outport names bear traces of the early French occupation; but Newfoundland has done some desperate deeds to French names! La Manche, Lapoile, Aux Morts, Fermeuse, Denier, and Cinque would hardly know themselves as now pronounced. Grand Bruit has become "Grand Brit"; L'Anse au Loup and L'Anse à l'Eau are "Lansy Loo" and "Lansy Lo"; Rencontre is "Round-counter"; Tasse de l'Argent has been metamorphosed to "Tossolo John"; and L'Anse au Diable has altered to "Nancy Jawble!" La Baie d'Espoir has completely reversed its meaning as "Bay of Despair"; Trépassé is now "Trepassey"; Rose au Rue has metamorphosed to "Rosie Roo." Cino Cerf has a Frenchy look, but what it originally meant I cannot guess. Baccalieu is obviously the Spanish "Bacalao," or cod. So runs the world of names away.

Over the outport world hangs a tenuous fog much of the time; and through this fog loom ghostly sails, while the *putt-putt-putt* of motorboats is always chattering. Here are seines hauled up on rocks, there a wreck that went ashore because the vessel's crew could not furl her frozen sails—dumb witness to winter's rigour. At wharves, schooners from Cape Breton or Spain are discharging coal or salt with a roar and rattle of gasoline winches. Barrels of well-ripened cod-liver oil mingle their perfume with smells of molasses, tar, and spruce boughs piled up for dunnage. Then, too, you can scent tubs of bait, including "mushels," "wrinkles" (periwinkles), and "cock an' 'ens," another kind of shellfish. Herring, capelin, and squid, of course, are the commonest baits; and these add their own aroma to the zephyrs. Huge fellows are rolling drums of gasoline. Others are counting the fish, sorting, classifying, packing, loading it.

You will look far or ever you find a scene more needful to be painted than a crew of the lusty, hip-booted Vikings rowing their catch in from a schooner to the beach and forking it into enormous boxes right in the surf. There others stand and wash the cod with rough-mittened hands, then throw it up the beach into waiting, two-wheeled carts pulled by small stocky horses with straw collars. Sea air rings with laughter and song as the washers roll out some chantey such as:

> "We'll sell our salt cod fer 'lassy an' rum,
>   Oh, you Rio!
> An' get back 'fore Thanksgivin's come,
>   We're bound fer de Rio Grande!
> We'll call at de Funks, an' full 'er wid eggs,
>   Oh, you Rio!
> Den de skipper'll broach one o' dem little kegs,
>   Fer we're bound fer de Rio Grande!
>   An' away, you Rio,
>   Ho, you Rio!
>   We're bound fer de Rio Grande!"

It's a long, tedious job to cure the cod, needing from three months to three and a half.

Much of the outport work is done by girls and women. Morning after morning you will see them, and hear them, too, with their rough shoes clacking down the stony lanes littered with seine-cork fragments, their sunbonnets neatly tied, streaming to the flakes. There they labour all day, making up the fish, carrying it on dredge barrows, spreading and turning it; while along the stages "headers" and "splitters" are busily at work with "heading palms" on hands, with keen knives never still.

The usual burden for a couple of these Vikings' wives is a quintal of fish—112 pounds. Two men ordinarily carry twice that; "barrow" it, as they say. All day long, men and women toil, walking with complete nonchalance over the dried fish. At night they stack up the fish, if rain threatens, and tarpaulin the piles.

Large areas of the Vikings' land, amid pale horizons under gray skies, are just rocks, skinned over with a spongy tundra of moss where only partridge berries and baked-apple berries grow, where only caribou and ptarmigan thrive. The forests lie far inland, away from the littoral that contains most of the inhabitants. Corn and grain will not ripen; cattle are few; fruits are practically non-existent. Only root crops mature, and even these very scantily. Newfoundland must live by the Atlantic, by cod and seal, or perish.

In many outports there isn't enough earth for even a cemetery. The coffins have to be laid on the rocks and covered with earth brought in boats from some more fortunate place that can spare a little. I have been told that at some outports, like Cape La Hune, it is quite the thing to fetch a basket of earth to a funeral, just as we send flowers.

"An' in Placentia Bay," a Viking informed me, "de graveyard 'm part unner water at high tide, so dey has deir funerals at low tide."

Gravestones soon sag and fall. I have seen many prone. And that's a pity, because the outport stones are often rather elaborate, with gilt letters, lots of home-made poetry, and the stonecutter's name always added by way of advertisement.

One will often see clothes poles set up by being thrust into a barrel full of rocks. Cellars are non-diggable in that stony environment. Such cellars as exist, to store potatoes, are built on the surface; made of stone, like little houses, sodded over and furnished with a stove and chimney. On these cellars the best grass grows, and vagrant goats graze aloft. Everything seems topsy-turvy in those latitudes. You shall even behold Vikings frequenting offshore islands to make hay. A dory motor-load of hay scooting up a fjord arouses the most jaded outlander's interest.

Vikings of the North—that is how I think of the liv-yeres. Newfoundland has its rich folk and its cultured ones aplenty. With them I am not concerned. I am thinking, writing only of the types who catch the cod and hunt the seal; the obscure, patient, tireless ones who live and labour by the chill and fog-bound northern waters; the poverty-bitten, humble, heroic, cheerful, truly pious, and indomitable men who gamble with death, and who all too often lose.

CHAPTER XXVI

TRAILING THE HERD

NOW that we had picked up the spoor of the migration, northward the hunt must hold its way.
Fifteen, twenty miles a day the ship must win,
every day if possible hitting the herd, hoping always for
luck that would bring wind, weather, ice, and seals all
into such happy accord as would fill the ship and turn
her, richly laden, southward once again to port.

Morning dawned with stars paling through an amber
radiance that presently glowed to a furnace. Lakes
began to blaze, ice to reveal broad traces of yesterday's
butchery. Early as I was on deck—well before five—
gangs were already out killing and hauling, while the
barrelman from aloft directed the chase. We moved on,
throbbing and grinding, under a flood of gold, our shadow
striding blue.

From the barricade I admired the incredible surefooted-
ness of those amphibious men as one by one the gunners
went away, each with his dog and batsmen.

"Get away on the lee bow!" shouted the Cap'n from the
bridge, massive in fur cap and coat, "Get alang, an'
God bless you!"

They climbed the rail, slid down the ropes and leaped
for the tip-tilting, boiling ice. At a round pace they
strode, streaming out into a line across the immense
sheet. Sometimes they ran and leaped. The batsmen's
gaff points snicked little pieces from the heaving pans.
At rifters, the men jumped like athletes. I leaned

against the icy gusts that blustered, that stung like knouts, and saw them dwindle in distances. Such agility! They became marionettes. The arctic light possessed a quality that annihilated all detail in the figures, sank them to one flat dimension. Their bodies, all absolutely alike, became jetty silhouettes against the dazzle. Soon they looked like ants crawling over frosted cake. From this they dwindled to mere moving dots among the hummocks.

Master-watch Killoway, hardiest of all.

The ship was thrusting onward, grinding through heavy ice, and every quarter mile or so the Old Man ordered a gang out; and all these gangs trailed away toward the herd, advancing like troops *en échelon*.

Sometimes the men would stop, test the ice or slush with their gaffs, then make wild leaps and land safely. They seemed to have a kind of super-skill in gauging slob or even sish.

As the gangs went away the parties split up and began stalking their game, creeping up behind ridges and clumpers. Guns began to whack once more, their reports muffled by the frozen air that absorbed sound as blotting paper sucks up ink. I could see the huge seals—all old bedlamers and saddlers—beginning to wallow off the ice. But some went trailing blood and others lay still, to move no more. All along the line rifle fire was leaping. Faster, ever faster the herd was dipping, scuttling to the sea, with derisive waves of the flippers. Roundly Tom Fillyards cursed the seals and the ill-luck that refused us warm weather so that they would bide on ice.

"If us could ondly hit de patch wid a hot sun, de swiles 'd stay up an' us could almost bat a load, to say nothin' of shootin' one!"

Luck proved bad, indeed, but despite all this, the ship made fair hunting, and ere night some hundreds more of sculps were tallied down in underhold and 'tweendecks. Unable to kill thousands, with hundreds we had perforce to be content.

Next morning the Cap'n bade me hasten to the bridge "to see a fair wonderful sight, me son!"

It proved all of that and more. Uncounted thousands of seals were "braychin'" in bays close at hand, or resting with their heads up, peering at us. The whole ocean boiled with foam and froth. A goodly number also lay on ice, refusing to be driven down even when the ship drew near. The Cap'n deplored the cloudy day. With sun, hundreds of thousands would have lain on ice and we could have loaded at once. But the mass of them stayed in the water. All we could do was stop now and again to "clap a lickin'" to some scattered spots.

We kept running through small "sculls" of old fat, and picking up odd lots of a few. Cries rang from the barricade: "Dere's one on de port bow! One on de broadside!" Out leaped hunters across drifting pans. They made their kill, sculped and towed in to the ship, reaching it ere it passed. Marvellous work, that!

One seal, a huge fellow, almost escaped. A wild race was staged between it and the hunter, with long rows of men yelling at the rail. The hunter caught his seal just at the edge of a bay. One second more and that seal would have been safe. But the idiot had to show fight.

It swung, snarled, flashed two rows of gleaming white teeth and snapped at the hunter with a savage *arrrrrrh!* Whack! It was dragged in; and in two minutes its pelt was smoking with the others.

An old dog was butchered right under our bows, so that the ship nearly ran down both slain and slayer. The exploit raised a tumult of plaudits. As in a theatre gallery, masses of men clung to vantage points to watch every episode, every turn of technique. Talk about your Spanish bullfights! How tame by contrast with this! One man plunged into open water and turned back to the ship. His comrades unmercifully railed at him with jeers and hoots. Shamed, he dashed on again. Wild yells of approval pursued him as he ran harder than ever, water flying from every rag he wore. He landed his seal, and immediately went out again from the moving, crashing ship, not even waiting to change his clothes. Ere he got back again, his clothes were frozen stiff as boards.

Miles on we pressed, a noisy impertinence ringed by vast white silences of majesty and beauty. Onward we killed, our crimson trail zigzagging through the ice. Intermittently carcasses were hurled over the rail, flopping into water that they reddened, or landing on ice with a sickening *squush*. The sky veiled itself with freezing clouds. Came flurries of snow and hail.

Two men, miscalculating, found themselves caught on a pan in wide waters. Away they floated across a bay. Wild hilarity burst from rail and barricade:

"Layve me y'r cap, uncle?"

"Gi' me y'r chist an' clothes, ole friend!"

"If y'r makin' y'r will, b'y, I want dem cats ye stole from me!"

"Any last questions ye'd like to ask, me sons?"

They shouted back rough banter; and all at once a

string of ice floated along. Taking desperate chance they leaped for it, landed, "copied" from cake to rocking cake. By incredible skill, agility, and speed they reached the ship and scrambled aboard without her having slacked for them.

At last, swinging a tremendous circle, we hove in sight of some gunners we had put down that morning—long lines and groups of black figures. We bore down on them with mutual shouts. Straps were flung even before the ship had stopped at the first pan. Eager hands hauled the wire out a hundred yards or more. A great mass of skins was yanked over wide ice, then through bloody foaming water and aboard. Shouting gangs escaladed our flanks and rushed to the galley for a gorge, and away the ship pounded again.

No moon, no star—a ghostly night, tempestuous enough for all the witches and warlocks of Newfoundland to ride abroad. The ship fought on and on. Every few minutes we had to reverse—"*reculer pour mieux sauter*"—and charge the crashing floes. No lively shouts that night sounded from the wheel. The desolate wildness of the elements contrasted strongly with the cabin where the old clock went tac-tic-tacking away as if in some farmhouse kitchen.

I, happening to be out of range of the clock, asked one of the men what time it was. His ingenuity in evading an admission that he couldn't tell time was worth recording.

"Dat clock, now, I niver trusts dat clock, whatever. Somet'ing always floggin' dat clock a'eed or astarn. I tries to get a cross-bearin' on 'er, an' give 'er a quarter hour one way or de odder. Dat'm as nigh an' handy as I can navigate to 'er. Somet'ing radical wrong wid dat clock, sure!"

Vastly content with the day's work, the Old Man was devouring fipper, " 'lassy loaf," and tea. His meal ended, he commanded Gearge: "Clear away this, b'y!" and sat down to the sport he liked best of all, like a miser counting gold—his nightly pleasure of reckoning seals killed.

"How many you get, John Domeney?—An' you, an' you?—An' how many you 'low there was on deck, to-day?—How's she lookin' now, b'ys?—In the marnin', quick as first mess over, get on 'em again! Whip it, me sons!—While there's fat, gather it; that's my motto!"

"She's lookin' lovely now," optimized Joe Stirge. "I was on ice, an' she look lovely comin' up toweard me. She look lang, sir—look big agin as arr one in de water!" By which he meant sunk deep, heavily freighted.

The Old Man smiled and nodded as he gave directions:

"Go ahead an' finish the pound o' coal, an' take in some ice for the cooks. What's the other pound take? Two or three tallies, eh? Good enough! Have you got 'em properly covered up, Skipper Ed? Don't let the men trample on 'em, anyway. A good rally, to-day. Good lively work. Lots o' turrs an' ice gulls to-day. That mean plenty seals."

"Them swiles is feedin' heavy, too," reported Arthur Roberts. "Full o' swile bait. One I cut open had buckets o' whitefish in 'er."

A few minutes later Skipper Nat came down to an-nounce that the *Nipshun*, *Haygle*, and *T'etis* were lying near us, and, various men going up to have a look at them, the conference ended. Soon after, we burned down for the night.

"See arr sign? Is there arr good string of ice out to east-nordeast?" was the first question I heard from the bridge very early next morning. The ship was drifting in loose ice under a gray sky. Busy labours had long since begun, despite gale and snow. Men were out, running through drifts after a few scattered seals. Some of these I noticed they only half skinned on ice, passing their towropes between the sculps and the vertebræ. Once aboard, they finished the job and then had the carcasses for the grisly barrels of meat.

Cries of "Spare road!" sounded, as some carried the dangling, dripping carcasses forward, to chop them apart on planks laid across barrels. The steps to the barricade reeked crimson; the warm, sickly stench of blood drifted everywhere. Out of his galley issued the baker with three pans of loaves. He pushed aft, over undulating piles of fat, then slopped through runnels of redness. I should be hungry indeed or ever I would eat seal carcass—horrid-looking objects, with protuberant eyeballs. After all, I had not then become fully case-hardened.

The ship heaved ahead, leaving men far behind in scudding mists of snow. With her she carried a quite incredible ugliness.

"Ain't narr slaughter house can tetch doze," Tom Fillyards volunteered, as I reported for the potato squad. "I'm gettin' enough. If us ain't in by anodder week, it'll be shockin' fer baccy. A wonnerful tarmentin' t'ing, me darlin' man!"

I enjoyed working in the galley, dissecting spuds and turnips. It was always warm in there and reasonably clean. Blood, carcasses, entrails were excluded. Nothing more sealish entered than mere fipper. A relief!

A miserable, eternally long day of snow and gale and frost; seals scattered and prospects disheartening. The hunt had resolved itself into a tremendous game of patience, with the prize always sardonically fleeing. One never realizes how vast the ocean really is, till one tries to find something on it. My rage against the seals kept steadily mounting. Selfish brutes, to keep us so long at sea! Come, all ye herds, and liberate us from bondage to ice, from dirt, solitude, and peril!

Night ushered in the usual shoptalk and rivalry about one ship's hail and another's turnout. The consensus of opinion was that we were "kippin' up our end o' the plank." Gunners occupied themselves with oiling and cleaning their precious rifles, pulling the rags through with their teeth. Skipper Abe polished the lenses of the "long gun." This master telescope, by the way, was always an object of vast solicitude; the old *Bloodhound's* glass, it formed one of the *Terra Nova's* chief treasures.

That picture faded. All of life there was constantly dissolving from one scene to another. The Old Man summoned his grandson Cyril and gave him a lesson on the compass. White-bearded, hierophantic under the dim lamp shine, the Cap'n adjusted his nose glasses and bade Cyril attend his words of wisdom.

Cyril, ruddy and black-haired, with sparkling eyes, watched the brassbound compass on the table, while carefully the grandfather boxed it for him.

"Nord! Nor'-be-east. Nor'-nordeast. Nordeast-be-nord. Nordeast. Nordeast-be-east. East-nordeast. East-be-nord. East!" And so, and so on, all the way around.

Eager to learn, the boy was flattered by this attention. More eager to teach, even more flattered by exhibition of superior knowledge, the Old Man.

Came at last the final scene of one more day—God knows how long!—with decks all sheeted in heavy snow, rails hooded, tophamper inky against the gray-looming heavens.

By torchlight the poor devils were still slaving. My very bones ached for them.

The aspect of the snowbound decks, early next arctic morning, and of the barometer—now down to 29.05—looked none too reassuring. All hands claim our only chance for seals is fine weather; naturally we have foul!

But the threatened tempest failed to develop, or else we ran away from it, for at midmorning the flying snow scuds gradually thinned and before noon the last squalls had given way to a wan and frozen sun. Concomitantly an arresting piece of news ran through the ship—a report that only one week's "fire" was left.

By this the hunters meant that only cartridges enough remained for a week more of shooting. One week more was enough for me!

"Dey been wastin' de fire," claimed Bosun Mike, "an' when de cattidges away, you'm done!"

"Them cartridges has been shoved out among ahl hands," the Cap'n complained, "an' at this rate, in no time you won't have one to bless you!"

If true, this meant we would have very proximately to "bore up" for St. John's. I commenced to view life with equanimity.

Under a sun rapidly growing more amicable, we flogged along. In open bays floated numbers of exquisite jelly-fish; mere cloudy forms trailing skeins of delicate threads among which wavered vivid crimson streamers. No one paid any attention to them. The men whetted their sheath knives, dissected dangling carcasses, and quarrelled about ownership of this repellent flesh. Odd how savage they got about those carcasses when the supply seemed inexhaustible! I heard that one ship nearly had a "manus" because some of the men went out carcass hunting when they had no right to.

"Pretty soon, dough," John Kelloway told me, "dey get deir barrels full, an' den nobody want to go. My sweet man"—and he leaned anxiously over the rail—"but I'd like to get a rally at de beddamers wid de gun!"

Aft to the galley came a black-faced galliard with:

"Oh, cook, 'ave ye got a spurt o' water?" He had ice in his tea kettle, and what he wanted was hot water to melt it. Tom Fillyards gave him boiling water from the range, and away he went, singing at the top of his voice. But when another, out of favour, arrived:

"No, me son!" Tom denied him. "Me tank's b'iled dry an' rusty as a bloody hyland!" Happy the man who stood well with Tom!

The Old Man claims: "It's a very anxious time, b'ys; a beautiful day like this, an' no seals." Beautiful weather, indeed, with a brilliant sun gleaming on the floes. Marvellous tawny hues shade the ice, where seals have died. Fairy greens and blues mingle with spreading rose-red patches. Fantastic grottoes gleam, laced with icicles of purest azure; and here or there blue-burnished lakes, liquid steel, rock in long slants as the ocean breathes.

The men continue to jump out at scattered seals, taking some desperate chances. Their eagerness for approval is almost pitiable; so is their fear of blame.

A desolating monotony weighs on my heart. Shall I ever forget these interminable days of blood and ice? The last night of March brings a high north wind, far gray loom of ice, and drifts of slaty cloud. Only two timid stars peep out but soon draw timorous veils over their faces. Black lifeboats creak on davits; vague figures pace the bridge; torches flare in the waist. How inexpressibly dreary a prospect, lying amid the ruins of ice cities, a lost ship in an ocean of stupendous dreams!

April Fool's Day was ushered in by my taking stock of my tobacco. Something seemed to tell me I should very presently stop smoking. For some time a frantic borrowing, begging, even stealing had been going on; and now all over the ship crumbs were being scraped from the bottoms of pockets, old pipes being reamed out, used-up butts sought and revived. Such conspiring, planning, importuning, such scheming, promising, gambling, complaining, never was!

The day, too, brought rough skylarking, false alarms that the Marconi aërials had broken, that Tom Fillyards had killed a rat in the galley; that the order had come for us to "bore up"; that a man had fallen overboard into a bay. Some were bedevilled by such canards, but not I. Never should these hardy Newfoundlanders guffaw at my expense. Therefore, when one came, exhorting me to go swiftly on deck and behold the finest "town of hoods" yet sighted, I coldly refused.

Shots presently echoed on deck; and going up in a casual manner, not at all looking for hoods, I discovered that some of the largest and finest specimens of the spring had just been captured. They already lay on deck. Word as to how I had fooled myself by missing the hoods passed round; and all I could do was hold a discreet silence.

CHAPTER XXVII

AND STILL WE SLAUGHTER

A FEW days later we saw a new feature of the hunt—going out in a boat after pelts. The ice grew so loose that the men could no longer get about on it. So they put down a lifeboat and three or four hunters tumbled down into it, and shoved away into the fog. One stood up to row, pushing the oars from him in characteristic Newfoundland fashion, while another sculled at the stern. Away to pans of skins they went, on loose ice; loaded their boat; brought it back. Noisily the winch snaked the fat on board. Then the hunters tailed on to a line over the stern, and towed through open water. The boat shot wildly and rather perilously from side to side, with a gang of hunters guying the occupants from the quarter. Men in the lifeboat stood at its bows with gaffs, to stave off dangerous ice cakes; a hunter at the stern, with a long oar, steered as best he might. How picturesque a scene!

At last the ship reversed and some of the hunters clambered aboard, grabbing tackles and rail with their all-useful gaffs.

"'And over 'and, now, me lucky b'ys!" ordered Skipper Nat, directing the work of hoisting the boat aboard. "*H'ist*, b'ys! Now, just a little better—shake 'er up!" Two men remained in the boat, holding the falls and steadying them. "There she go! Make ahl fast! That's well enough!"

The last two scrambled over the rail; and one more new thing could never again be new for me.

The fog closed in again thicker than ever, like dirty gray smoke, and our world dimmed to nothing. The long monotony was broken by our chancing on a huge pan of sculps with a Job Brothers flag on it. These skins had been lost by ice going abroad, and had been drifting on the ocean since about the 15th of March. Now they were free for all. The men needed no orders to go get them. They swarmed overside, laughing and shouting, with incredible zeal; prized up the frozen skins and loaded them. If they had found a million dollars they couldn't have been happier.

Later in the day we made a kill; and after it the men vaulted the now low rail, some climbing up while the ship was still under way, taking fearful chances. All was frenzied activity, excitement, uproar. One or two of the men had froth frozen down their chins. Shouting, laughing, they hooked gaffs on ropes and rail, and stormed the *Terra Nova*. Some carried "cats," swinging like pendulums from gaff points. Their hands and boots and clothes reeked with to-day's fat and yesterday's blood; they were crusted, stiff.

They ran, leaped, waded through the piles of fat, and besieged the forward galley. Some grabbed dirty tin cups in their foul hands and crowded aft to the top tanks whence they could draw off the rusty water made of melted ice. Others dipped up dirty water from the bottom of a lifeboat on top of a coal pound. No matter what the water was like, everything went.

The morale of the ship seems going back as the filth increases; and an air of general discontent is making itself felt. So long as the men have plenty of slaughter, they are happy, gay; but when that slackens, enervation sets in. I find any occupation is welcome; even helping

Jardine rivet an ash bucket is a treat. Men stand about in the fog, smoking, and murmur disconsolately together. Nothing is visible but the vast swell.

I am, forsooth, a gummed, foul, repellent object, hardly of human guise, looking like an irreclaimable lost soul, "not worth saving." I am dirty, sick, and worn; nearly at the bottom of the pit, which however—paradoxically—seems to have no bottom.

That night—a cloudy, misty-gray night, with the ship painfully craunching ahead and torchlights blazing—the Old Man shot a wireless message to St. John's for more ammunition. My irritation was so keen that I pitched in and beat him at checkers; one of the only four games I managed to win that whole voyage.

"I've lost the pass," he admitted. "I surrender all!" But his spirits remained high, and he whistled gaily; for with the arrival of more cartridges he could still hang to his bulldog determination to fill the ship.

His decision caused general discontent. To stay out more weeks, with no tobacco, was more than even those hardy heroes could face with equanimity. Morning brought some complaints; but the Cap'n remained adamantine and diverted the cabin by telling tales of discouragement swiftly metamorphosed to radiant fortune.

"I mind one time Cap'n Harry Daw was goin' home in despair, empty, when at night they spied a patch, an' Daw ordered his men out, an' some went in their shirts an' drawers. Them as was part undressed, he didn't even give 'em time enough to putt on their pants an' jackets." (It sounded apocryphal, but all hands believed it.) "They bat a load in two hours. An' one time Willum Barbour bat his whole load after dark.

"I, meself," he went on, "one time sighted a patch at night, from the barr'l, an' went out on ice nine miles with me men. We started at 2:30 in the mornin', an' never got there till 10. Tight ice. Seals ahl quiet. I had me men take off their clothes, ahl but their pants an' shirts, an' I told 'em to get in a circle, an' when I'd putt me cap up on a gaff, they was to rush in. Well, I rose me cap, an' we bat evvery single one. Some o' me men worked so hard they got winded, an' dropped. You could hear the whackin' o' them gaffs, evverywhere, an' wasn't that the enj'yin time! Sometimes a bunch o' seals caught that way 'll come ahl together an' break through the ice, but that time we got 'em all—more 'an two thousand. Not one escaped!"

April 5th ushered in a cloudy, windy day, with the glass cynically marking: "Fine." I pretty well decided that morning to stop smoking. Many others had already sworn off. Such a begging, borrowing, whispering, plotting, such conferences, hidings-away, gamblings, never were!

Joe exhibited the workings of a master mind. Not so foolish, he, as to conceal his supply in his bunk or ditty bag. No; he tied it all up in a paper and summoned me when nobody else was around.

"Dere," said he, in strictest confidence, "I got ahl me baccy in dat bundle, cl'ar of a little in me pocket. Now, me son, will ye write somet'ing on dat bundle, fer me?"

"Of course, Joe. What shall I write?"

"Well, b'y, putt down 'Epsom Salts,' an' make un good an' plain, like. So dat evverybody as can read at ahl, can read un." When this was done: "I'm wonnerful grateful, me son. Now, den, I'll putt de package rate yere, an' dat'll be safe as if in God's pocket."

He hung the tobacco up by a string, over the mirror in the hellhole, and there indeed it remained safe. Once in a while he secretly abstracted a bit of the precious weed, but nobody else ever knew where he kept his store.

We have another sick man on board, now; and that there's only one is "a bloody marvel." The poor chap lies in the so-called hospital, with nothing much done for him; shut up in a stinking hole, its air rendered stifling by an oilstove that smokes. This would about kill a healthy man, let alone a sick one. No-body seems to pay him any attention. He certainly attracts far less attention than a seal. Whether he lives or dies is all his own business. Another man is hurt. "He got his foot twist, got a wrinch to it, 'ove un rate round, dere." But no one "middles" much with any lame duck. Men must get well or per-

Our "lame duck."

ish, as heaven sees fit. The Lord, of course, is looking out for it, and to go against divine judgments were little short of blasphemous.

Many rumours ran, that day: we were going to "bore up fer sugar"; we had only 6,000 cartridges left, or two days' shooting; we were "a sick vessel" for coal and must head south; the *Thetis* was going home and only three or four ships were now out; we were starting for St. John's at once; we were "goin' to carry de kay [key]," which means, be the last ship in the ice. One fact outstood: if the *Ranger* brought us no ammunition, we would have to quit the chase. And Uncle Edgar declared:

"De *Ranger* do a strange t'ing if she come out agin. She'm a mystery if she do. If she don't, us got a good look-up to see de Notch wonnerful soon, now."

Opinion was divided. Some clamoured to stay, others murmured: "Bore up!" To neither faction did the Old Man pay any slightest heed. A law unto himself, he held his own counsel.

A violent argument developed as to when Easter came—

as if it mattered, out there in the ice! Little enough I cared.

That afternoon, at sunset, luck favoured us and the spymaster sighted an incredible multitude of seals. Excitement gripped the crew.

"Handy to half a million prime-cut harps in that spot!" rejoiced the Old Man. "We're goin' to have another smack at 'em, again!"

How many seals comprised that army, who could guess? Hundreds of thousands they must have been; a vast string that swept from horizon to horizon, dead ahead.

Joe exulted, seizing his Winchester. "Me naze pains me pretty well ahl de time, an' sometimes dey'm courageous, but I'm goin', jus' same. We'll give 'em a bloody perishin'!"

The Old Man reported this the best spot of the spring, and gave excited commands as to which gunners must go first—"an' no noise, no hollerin' or runnin', an' don't try to cut one 'nother off. Fine seals, them. Five hundred are the weight of a t'ousand ornery seals. We're chasin' the same herd rate down to the Labrador, an' they're gettin' tamer ahl the time!"

However that might have been, it was obvious that on fine and warm days the seals were easier to come at than on raw, cold ones.

The "bloody perishin'" predicted by Joe did not materialize, and despite the Old Man's enthusiasm, we cleaned up only moderately well. The weather was so keen that the herd proved restive. Still, our decks were loaded with heaps of red rawness, by the time Skipper Abe reported: "Dey're ahl in now, sir, de last strap's comin' in." And I had a goodly lot of tails to count—another job of mine. I totalled them on the washstand in the hellhole by a dim seep of light from the frosted porthole, with the engine grinding mightily, while the black-faced gunners watched.

Late that night, Marky picked up a sorry piece of news: that the *Ranger* had decided to make a second trip and to come out with ammunition for us. Thus, on the very eve of "boring up," all was indefinitely postponed. The Old Man was determined never to quit so long as a single seal remained in sight or a plank of ship to carry him.

CHAPTER XXVIII

TAILS AND TOBACCO

BOSUN MIKE next morning informed the Cap'n that we still had 5,000 cartridges left—enough to keep us busy till the *Ranger* should arrive. A sober, serious-minded man is the bosun; wears a sou'wester, a stiff canvas jacket that has gradually changed from white to black; is belted with a knife, and has vast canvas trousers over enormous sea boots. He toes in; has a slow and simple manner of speech; wears a wrinkled brow and an air of intense preoccupation.

A pious man, they say; goes every night to his own locker, forward, to his prayers. He is always busy on tasks of his own, with canvas, spun yarn, and tools; is always carrying torchlights and clumping about with candles for some mysterious purposes of his own. He and his mate occasionally sweep the decks with footy little willow brooms—as if anything short of total destruction could clean them!

"A shockin' man fer scrubblin'," Uncle Edgar calls him. He leads an unfathomable life and sleeps under a piece of sailcloth in the hellhole, never minding the leaks. Silent, reserved, anxious, and worried-looking, a man of mystery is he. For twenty years he has been sealing; and in all that time has been, I was told, reprimanded only once. Excellent Bosun Mike!

The ice that morning presented some peculiarly lovely aspects of blue-fringed icicles in delicate lacery; of dark olive shadows; of quicksilvered leads afar, under the

344

slanting arrows of a sun shooting down through gray cloud banks. Dazzling white slashes of sunlight cut distant floes; and farther still, misty bergs faded into dream horizons.

"All gunners out! Take lots of ammunition!"

That order broke into the ship's routine; into the icing-down of seals, the wading of men through mucky masses with teakettles and bread, the dumping of ashes, the dragging of skins with grab hooks. It even broke up the efforts of a stowaway at the galley door to sell a mess of fipper for a bit of tobacco.

The sick man was better and came to the cabin table. He was pale, silent, lonely; a most unhappy-looking creature. But all the others were cheerful enough. A general feeling seemed to prevail that the end was nigh. A great deal of talk about home was beginning to develop, with yearnings for wives and children; and interminable were the speculations whether or no the *Ranger* would come out. Though most of the men gave lip service to the hope that she would, I needed not much shrewdness to see that if she failed to reach us, the majority would not greatly mourn. Even Newfoundlanders have limits, and most of our crew had pretty well reached theirs.

As the gunners came aboard, the Old Man ordered me below to count tails. Lo, without volition of mine own, but solely because I could write swiftly and make some sort of stagger at a column of figures, I had been elected tail enumerator! Many a time and oft I served as such. Let one description serve for all.

Down into the smoky, stuffy cabin, its white paint long since smudged with gore, the gunners and dogs clumped to receive their meed of praise or blame. Each dog bore his bloodstained canvas bag drooping beneath the weight of the cut-off tails. The Old Man came below and pre-

pared to receive the figures. Exultant, he, with a:
"Well, me sons, we got 'em beat to a frazzle! A very
good spill, to-day. How many old ones did we get
aburd?"

He sat down and produced his notebook and pencil, all
anticipation. Gearge poked the fire and brought him
bread and butter, also the inevitable tea. The Old Man
stroked his beard, sipped tea, nibbled bread, hummed
"After the Ball," lighted a cigarette, grew expansive. A
great occasion for him this tail counting was, every time.

The cabin fairly reeked of heat, smoke, stenches, and
was brimmed with babels. Master watches crowded in,
tired but vociferous and greedily attacking the pantry.
While they stuffed, while knives and forks rattled together
with cups and spoons, and while all the talk was what they
had and hadn't done, and why and wherefore, I under-
took my usual task.

Tails of shot seals have to be counted, you must understand, because, as the Cap'n himself explained, "We
don't want to lose time lookin' for seals the gunners
claimed they shot but didn't. If we knows the number
o' tails, we can tell how many we got to pick up an' not
leave any on ice. It's me own invention," he boasted,
"an' now ahl the other cap'ns is doin' it too, copyin' my
methods. Sometimes, at first, some o' the gunners used
to try an' fool me with the ends o' scutters to make me
think they done better 'an they did. But I was too smart
for that, me son. Because, y' see, there's a bone rate
down to the end o' the tail, an' in the scutters there ain't.
Oh, ain't narr gunner can haul the cod off *me!*"

The dogs dredged the tails from their bags and dumped
them on the oilcloth or into a soup plate—a plate from
which we should later eat our scouse. Each dog finished
his work and each gunner's lot was counted before the

next began. Plate or oilcloth soon became all smeared
with fat and blood. Anxiously the gunners crowded; the
dogs no less anxiously, for they too shared their gunners'
encomium or rebuke. To be "high-liner" for the day's
shooting was an object almost pitiably striven for; to come
in "low-liner" seemed to them little short of catastrophic.

The tails were small and triangular. Only a bit of the
tip was brought in. Each was fat, and fringed with silky
fur. Begrimed, red-handed, the men eagerly watched
me under the gleaming old brass lamp, as I fingered the
tails toward me and enumerated them like a bank teller
counting bills. Had they been bills indeed, I doubt if
the men could have hung more eagerly on my results.
The dogs seemed a trifle overawed by the cabin's splendour, into which they were at no other time allowed to
penetrate.

A brief dispute arose about some tails that the Old
Man claimed were only scutters. The Cap'n won his
point. Rosy-faced, flushed with power, and perhaps
with a tot or two of sugared ale, he laughed, rubbed his
hands together, and exulted: "Well, b'ys, ye can't fool
me!" He seemed as proud of his knowledge of the difference between a tail and a scutter as, say, Edison of his
many inventions. Prouder, perhaps.

I entered each man's name on a page of my notebook
and carefully set down the number of tails his dog had
brought in. Then I copied the enumeration down on a
near-clean piece of paper, for the Cap'n's august inspec-
tion. My hands grew mucky with grease and blood.
No matter how one tries, aboard a sealer one can't keep
out of the general welter.

"Yere'm 'nudder one!" exclaimed a gunner, fishing up
a tail from his pocket. "How many do dat make, I got?
Fifty-t'ree? Gentle Moses, I know I shot more 'an dat.

Why, one time dere, I was shootin' so fast de rifle got hot an' I had to hold un down in de snow to cold un!"

"It ain't the number o' guns ye shoots, me son," the Old Man chid. "It's the number o' hits as counts. Ye lost the pass, me b'y." The abashed gunner stammered and shuffled. "I'm fair surprised with ye. Do a job good or don't try it at ahl; that's my motto. Here's another man brought in a hundred an' seventy-two!"

The gunner mentioned inflated with importance.

"I got five more to me 'and," announced another, a very giant of a man, cut on massive planes. Despite an

"Yere'm 'nudder one, Cap'n!"

incongruous and infantile "cowlick" on top of his close-cropped bullet head of enormous size, he looked a formidable object with bristling beard and moustache; vast shoulders almost bursting through a blackened sweater; mighty, blue-tattooed hands and wrists; crimson face blood-spattered. This giant's dog had just discovered a few more of the silky, triangular tails in a fold at the bottom of his nunch bag. These he tossed on to the gunner's pile. "Sure ye ain't got narr 'nudder one?" anxiously demanded the giant, his solicitude pathetically keen.

The doctor got up an impromptu "sweep" on the number of tails the day's work would total. The gambling spirit waxed strong; it made men risk even part of their precious tobacco. Cannily the Old Man refused to bet.

Tails lay in blood-smeared heaps on the oilcloth and in soup plates. Eagerly the men, with inflamed eyes and frost-burned faces, watched the counting and recording. Now and then, as I finished with a lot, Gearge scooped them up and flung them into the roaring bogey which smoked and roared the louder and diffused a violent stench of seal fat through the cabin. A racket of broken talk blent with the roar of the stove and the grind and shatter of the floes.

"In an hour an' a half, by de Law Harry, I killed a hundurd an' t'irty-seven wid one gun."

"De first little wad went off, but de rest bid up. A big spot of 'em."

"*I* got a wonnerful whack after sunset, b'ys. De sun, he was gone afore I fired arr shot!"

"How many flags did ye stay up, Tom? Siventeen, eh? I branched off to west'ards, but I seen ye workin' like a flyin' scaldy, I did."

What a scene! I wondered if perhaps in the true old Viking days, banquet halls of ancient northlands after battle might not have been quite like that? Those black-faced men with blood and grease-stained jackets, with bristle-bearded jowls and crimsoned hands, seemed transmuted to ancient Norse heroes; that bogey became for me the Eorl's blazing and huge-mawed fireplace; that table a sea rovers' board; those fippers and toast, wild boar's head; that tea, flagons of mead. Ice enough was there, and violence of elements, for any feast of Thanes; and the same northern stars looked down and wondered as in the days of Ralf the Rover or of Beowulf!

My totalling finished, I passed it over to the doctor for him to verify. He added it with a murmured:

"Five, an' a hought, an' a seven, an' a nine, an' a height, an' heleven——"

Joe Stirge meanwhile was telling how he had that day cut the tail off a seal supposed to be dead, which seal had revived and escaped; so perhaps another year some other gunner might be surprised at killing a tailless seal. Joe brought in all his tails himself in a black kerchief and dumped them unceremoniously on the table. He had apparently had no dog to serve him but had gone out lone-hand, as best suited him.

The "low-line" gunner consoled himself by remarking: "Well, by tapers, I got more 'n Bill Harvey done, de time he brung in two an' a half swiles!"

"Two an' a half!" exclaimed Tom Fillyards, who sat there leaning bare and very hirsute arms on the table. The cook's dark face, saturnine eyes and black mustachios formed a virile portrait. "Two an' a half. Dat'm unpossible!"

"Not-at-ahl!" the gunner retorted. "A bear bit one in two, an' Bill got half de swile away from un!" Laughter roared at this tradition; and the abashed gunner recovered a certain prestige.

"Well done," the Old Man concluded. He reviewed the totals, glasses far down on nose. "Very good, indeed. I've seen better, but we 'ad a rally, anyhow. We got on track of 'em, again." He beamed at his sons. "We'll give 'em a punchin', yet." To the "high-liner": "Me an' you has got to drink a bottle o' lemonade together!" but immediately forgot all about it and no lemonade appeared.

Though most of the seals that day had gone off, many hundred had been killed in a short time. Even the stokers had got about twenty. Everybody was exultant, especially the Cap'n; and all laid plans for the morrow's work.

"How d'ye like that after-sunset job?" he laughed, as if he had given them a rare treat—which indeed he had. He fired the last shot of the party by having Gearge open a bottle of beer for him, wherein he invited none to join. Thus he celebrated. "It must," I thought, "be awful to stand alone on such an apex of import, of authority and glory, as does the captain of a superannuated gurry-bucket sealer in the ice!"

Just as the cabin was quieting down, came a timid knock at the door, and one entered, timid but determined.

"Well, me son, what ye want?" demanded the Old Man.

He from the fo'c's'le in a meek voice begged a rifle.

"I'd like to go out on de ice, sir, shootin' swiles, if ye don't mind."

"Can ye shoot?"

"I was in de war." (He made it rhyme with "far.") "I was a sniper, sir, an' I killed dey Germans, a wonnerful lot." He turned his cap nervously. His hands trembled. He who had faced the Boche without a quiver now stood abashed in the Old Man's presence. "If ye'll layve me have a gun, sir, I'll do me best."

"Well, well, well," nodded the Cap'n, patronizingly. "I'll see. Gi's y'r name, an' if there's any guns to spare mebbe I'll gi' ye one!"

"Thankee kindly, sir!" And the World War veteran humbly withdrew. Incidentally, he never got his rifle. Supreme favours like a gun wherewith to run over open ice and risk one's life shooting seals are not in any such haphazard manner doled out to mere heroes.

Morning brought a report from the barrel that the spy-master could "rise de smoke o' de *Nipshun* on de 'orizon," storming after us to catch our own private string o' swiles. This stirred all our patriotism, and when presently the call drifted down: "T'ousands a'eed!" joyful was the rally.

But now an ominous worry obtruded—the lack of cart-ridges. Joe and Uncle Edgar reported that there were "wonnerful few."

"Well," gloomed the Old Man, "we shan't get the

352

rights o' this thing till we get the bosun!" Bosun Mike therefore meekly arrived. "Now, then, how many more cartridges we got, me son?"

"There's a couple more boxes in de lazareet, sir."

"Go down an' see, again, will you?"

Bosun Mike went down and Fate hung by an eyelash.

"Tell ahl the gunners to bring alang their loose cartridges," the Cap'n ordered, "an' we'll count 'em an' get a proper tally, an' from now on I can only send out choice gunners. Go tell the top'us fellers, too!"

A messenger departed. Uncle Edgar and the bosun brought up every cartridge they could find below. Uncle reported:

"Dere's one 'ole box, sir, an' one box got 600 into 'er, an' 1,600 on de .44's. We ondly got cattidges fer a couple o' days more—ondly 2,200 in ahl."

They gathered all the loose "fire," and worried, and counted, and fretted like bankers going to the wall, and tried to make the most of every scrap of ammunition. In the midst of this prospective penury, the tantalizing cry of: "Big spot o' fat!" rang down; and once more the slaughter began.

The day ended with a goodly lot of skins aboard, but our cartridges down almost to the vanishing point. Should the *Ranger* fail to locate us, we must "bore up" almost at once.

We jammed that night, but blasted clear, and by morning the north wind had given us our liberty again.

That afternoon we sighted the enormous herd once more, but the *Eagle* edged us away from it and came in for some virulent malediction. The hunters made a rally, but the seals were wild and ducked to the water. Our whole day's hunt netted us only a few score.

All night long the ship rolled heavily, and groaned as if

giving up the ghost, with the ice hammers battering her ribs. This rolling, by next day, had ground up the fat so thoroughly that our starboard quarter pound began to "run to ile" very badly, and an overpowering stench invaded the cabin. "Gurry," they call such seal oil, and the name fits. Thick, pungent, stifling, the fetor almost stuns you; it is quite unlike anything else in the world.

Presently we got "on top o' de swiles agin," but a dense fog kept us from more than desultory killing. Thus we spent the fifth Saturday of the infernal "racket." Men kept going away, being swallowed up in the gray mystery of the fog. They had to use caution or they might have shot one another, out there. How they ventured to leave the ship and lose themselves on that broken-up ice, in mists impenetrable, passed my comprehension. Some, aboard, were toiling to carry casks of ice with ropes slung over a long pole. They worked like Chinese, only harder. What men! Some of them were now reduced to smoking molasses and tea, if you can imagine *that*.

The stench below was getting so fearful that I spent most of the day on deck, watching the wondrous effect of the ice swell rolling in and in beneath the fog, like long hills walking by. Onward our grim ship heaved through a silent, mystic immensity of vapours shrouding the rocked and riven ice.

And of a sudden, out of the viewless stupendousness, news drifted from the *Ranger* that she was caught in heavy ice and that the shaft of her wireless dynamo was broken.

"Ondly juice enough in her batt'ries to send four or five more messages, dat's ahl she've got," Uncle Edgar informed me. "She'm a good bit from we, too; she'll never face troo de jam."

Despite the superstition that shaving might bring bad

luck about getting any more seals, nearly everybody forward had a clean-up that night. Peter John Killoway borrowed my talcum powder and my strop, too, and carried them off forward, whither I no longer cared to follow them.

CHAPTER XXIX

HOMEWARD BOUND

BY half-past one of the morning of April 10th —a zero hour of desolating cold—the *Ranger* had won up to us and all hands were tumbling out to welcome her. I tumbled with the rest.

The *Ranger* came to a stop and put down men on a pan, then began winching out our supplies. Our own ship hauled up and many of our men leaped out, running away to the other vessel with wild wavings of gaffs, with crisp *crk-crk-crks* of sparables. Away over ice our men rushed like mad creatures, fairly panting for tobacco. Alas, save such as they could wheedle from the crew, man-to-man, none was yet to be had. All our tobacco lay in boxes on the Ranger, not yet available.

I slid down one of the greasy ropes, leaped to the heaving ice and, gaff in hand, followed toward the other ship.

I reached it safely enough, though not a little disconcerted (which is a polite way of saying scared) by grindings, boomings, thunderings in the ice under my very feet. Before I could clamber aboard the *Ranger* she moved off, and a number of us tried to return to the *Terra Nova*. But now she lay unapproachable, in open water, and we found ourselves marooned on a pan in the blue drop. I have known more agreeable moments than that during my somewhat feverish career.

We waited, the men talking among themselves, and I wondering what condition my life-insurance policies might be in, just supposing our pan should happen to break.

Thus for a while we stood and floated, wallowing in the ocean swell, while all about us ice growled and quarrelled.

At last the *Terra Nova* swung down on us and shoved our pan, with acres more of ice, so that it all closed up and we were able to get back to the supply pan. After another shivering wait, I made shift to scramble back aboard; and glad enough I was to be there!

Men are streaming back and forth between the two ships, hoping no doubt to get a sly drink or two. The quest for rum is unending. Cap'n Wes, of the *Ranger*, comes aboard in his leathern jacket—a squat, capable-looking man. Mails are brought over to us and distributed. I get nothing. Imagine being cut off from the world for all these weeks on end!

Our Old Man eventually gives the order to "scun her up into the narwest" and settles down with his son for a confab that lasts till nigh morning. Away we go, the *Ranger* in our wake. I turn in and for a little while am wrapped in oblivion.

Early as I was once more afoot, the boxes of tobacco had already been broken out and the doctor deputed to sell it in his hospital. It proved the most popular medicine he had ever dispensed, barring rum. The business, however, could not be run on a cash basis, as none of the men seemed to have any cash. So he was constrained to take down the names of all applicants, as they stood in a long queue up the companion stairway, and give each man four sticks—two light, two dark.

While this was going on forward, serious trouble had developed aft. Through some mistake, the owners had sent us many thousands of cartridges a size too big for our rifles. Well, now, there *was* a situation!

But Newfoundlanders are nothing if not ingenious and resourceful, and in no time the aft gang was at work reducing the ammunition to proper diameter.

Uncle Edgar cut grooves in several boards, each groove

just large enough to hold a cartridge. Then he routed out all the files on board and everybody set to with a will. I bore a hand, too, though filing a dumdum cartridge in the midst of a lot of other men doing the same by no means disposes one to tranquillity. Joe, however, assured us all that so long as we didn't overheat the cartridges or hit a percussion cap, probably none of the ammunition would explode.

We filed thousands of cartridges. The rasp and *zee-zee-zee* of our labour filled the cabin and hellhole. On table, bunks, and knees we toiled. As each man finished a cartridge, he handed it to Joe, who tested it in a rifle. If it fitted, he laid it in a box. If not, he handed it back with:

"Jus' de laysses' little pat wid de vile, b'y, an' she'll do!"

Any accident might have made some of us candidates for being iced-down and stowed in a pound-board coffin on the Marconi house; but nothing exploded; and gradually, working in relays, we reduced all the cartridges to usable size.

Away we went on what was really our second trip, away off to northeast, beyond which lay Greenland, bearing the distinction of having been the only sealing ship ever thus to have been re-supplied at sea. News went round that only a fortnight's "steamin'" remained; but on a pinch no doubt the Cap'n could arrange to have coal sent out, too. Some, however, said that if he did, ways and means might be devised to lose that coal under layers of ashes in the buckets.

Another ship now set itself to tagging us. All day it kept close, and when at nightfall we burned down, mooring to a pan surmounted by huge clumpers, the rival ship also burned down, determined to keep a sharp eye on us.

Next morning loud complaints arose against the other ship's captain. The hunters claimed that he was "dravin' down our swiles," and anger waxed hot. "He'm a barbarous man," they cried. "He'd take our swiles rate at the end of our guns." But someone pointed out that the other ship was "heavy in number one," that is to say, in her forward pound, so that she was "by de 'eed," and hopes were expressed that she might "full an' sink."

The men spoke of fights between ships caused by such interfering; of side-sticks and ropes of rival ships being cut; even of ships being boarded, and skins—alleged to have been stolen—heaved overboard.

"I once helped board a ship an' hayve over eight hundurd skins," affirmed Joe. "It nigh come to murderin'!"

The Cap'n added:

"That other one, out there, he's a cowardly man. Our gunners would have had five hundred seals by now, today, but for him. My, my, my, he come up on us like lightnin'. You'd swear there wasn't another seal on the ocean. He's tryin' to spile us. What we got to do is spile *him*. My, my, my, he's the childishest man out here!"

In the middle of the indignation meeting, *Bang!* went a crashing shock, and everything flew. One man catapulted over the red-hot bogey, knocking off kettles with Uncle Absalom's precious hot water. Men sprawled all ends up, over benches and in corners, on the floor all awash, with steaming, scalding swirls. Lamp chimneys clattered off and smashed. "Evveryt'ing's goin' alee!" was the cry. Loud-voiced excitement raged.

"Wonnerful gert hoi pinnacle, us must of struck!" shouted one.

"Might of drave our sides in, like dat!" another.

Others rushed on deck to see what had happened.

Our Chief went below to his engine room, plainly worried.

What had happened was this: a growler, which we had ventured too near, had rolled over, had come up under our "tuck," or counter, and delivered a blow that would have smashed in any steel ship afloat and probably have sent it to the bottom. Only our huge greenheart beams had saved us.

Chief McGettigan—a braw and jovial Scot, ruddy and ever cheerful—made a survey. He reported that one of the bunkers had been shifted, and that some minor breakage and loss had resulted, but that we were "tight as a bag, me sons; tight as a bottle."

That day I came down with the grippe and suffered more than any man reasonably should. Grippe is an affliction anywhere and at all times; but on a sealer in the ice, it becomes what Josh Billings calls "2 mutch." Nevertheless, I kept on at work, with sweat pouring at every exertion. I spent the afternoon—an afternoon that, all unsuspected to me, was destined to be my last complete one aboard the *Terra Nova*—filing cartridges. We of the rasping squad had to toil fast to keep pace with our gunners' demands, for big gangs were out on very loose ice, hunting innumerable thousands of "de rale ole smallagins, now"—that is to say, very large seals.

Rolling heavily, we pushed on through much open water all a-glister in the sun. Good shooting the men made, for the seals, too, enjoyed that sun, and could hardly be chased down. Some, near the ship, refused to leave their pans even when we came crashing down upon them and when men along the rails hit them with lumps of coal or ballast. Constantly, men were jumping over to gather in such oddments of the herd. One hooked a seal through the back with his gaff. The seal dragged him fairly to the edge of a pan, and it was pull dog, pull devil, with vociferous cheers from aboard. It looked as if the panting hunter would have to let go his gaff or else take a chilly bath; but at the critical moment the gaff hook tore through the seal's fat and hide, and away his sealship surged with a mighty splash, leaving the man empty handed and agape.

Some of the rival ship's men presently came working in among our own. Altercations threatened. Points of ownership were not drawn any too fine. "I don't care *oose* de swile is, bring un in!" seemed the motto.

April 12th, my last morning on the *Terra Nova*, dawned immense and gray, with all available hands at the files. My own were sore and blistered, to add to the delights of grippe, but never mind.

Already the ammunition brought out by the *Ranger* had begun to run short.

"But," a master watch encouraged me, "wid ondly one gun left, de Cap'n 'll bide out yere an' chase everlastin'. If us gets a good rally to-day, it'll use ahl de cattidges, cl'ar of enough fer t'ree guns. We'm pretty well up troo, now, I'm t'inkin'."

At 5:30 of that aching afternoon, the Old Man sent down word to me, filing and sweating away, that the *Eagle* was hauling up on us. He added that, should I so wish, and if I looked alive, I might transfer over the ice to her and go in with Cap'n Edward Bishop, now homebound.

My answer was to drop everything, hustle into my great-coat and furs, and make "a pierhead jump" for the other ship. I left everything and departed; stood not upon the order of my going but went at once.

In five minutes I had concluded a deal with Uncle Edgar, selling him my binoculars for his sealing equipment; had put most of my duffle, including my two cat skins, in his keeping; had thrust my camera upon the doctor, with a plea to take all the pictures possible for me; had jammed a few things into my ditty bag; had called out good-bye to everybody below; and had run up on deck with such extreme alacrity that no doubt the Old Man took it for a deadly insult.

Him I sought on the bridge, and with a hearty handshake assured of my gratitude, enjoyment, and appreciation. Then, with a general farewell to all, dizzy and sick, I escaladed the rail for the last time.

The *Eagle* had come up to within a quarter mile or so and lay waiting, her rails—like our own—lined with men curious to see the doings of "dat quare fish, de 'Merikin." A few of our own chaps, good-hearted to the last, volunteered to serve as my escort. Down and away we went, with a chorus of: "Good-bye, me son! Good luck to ye, b'y!" They shouted and waved their caps and bade me be sure to send them photographs. I waved a last grippy farewell to all hands. Such was my exit from the *Terra Nova.*[1]

Aboard the *Eagle*, I was kindly greeted by Cap'n Bishop whom I had already met in St. John's. A splendid type of master, staunch as oak, hardy, fearless. He made me quite at home; and it was Yo-ho-ho and a bottle of ginger pop as we got under way.

Of the homebound journey I shall write little. I found that life aboard the *Eagle* was essentially like that on the *Terra Nova* except that we had sardines with our night mug-up at 9:30. Rain, wind, and fog companioned us

---

[1]She reached St. John's on April 20th with 23,157 seals, "high-liner" for the year. Her hunters each received $74.90.

all the way, as we made our southing. They bothered me not at all. Somewhere beyond them, I knew, the sun was surely waiting to welcome me—the sun of spring!

It is now just past midnight, the morning of Friday, April 14th, and all chances are that we shall reach port before night. I feel no inclination to sleep; am too glad for that; don't care if I never sleep again.

Out on deck, somewhat later, I find *no ice!* We are speeding southwest, and now out in the blue drop. One never realizes the consummate beauty of open ocean until one has been for long weeks ramming through ice. It gives one an intoxicating sense of liberty, almost of flying.

Have a very early mug-up in the cabin, which the steward is scrubbing down with soft soap. The Cap'n's hand on a freshly washed panel leaves a huge stain. Everybody and everything is indescribably dirty, but some futile efforts are under way to clean up a little. I forego the useless attempt. After all, what matter?

On Good Friday Cap'n Bishop announced that land was visible. We were now "nearly chock to Sugarloaf"—

Cap'n Bishop, staunch as oak.

which meant almost within sight of a landfall—a mountain by that name close to St. John's; but as yet I could see nothing on account of a dense fog. The Cap'n by no means reduced speed because of that, even though the danger of running slam into a growler and sinking with all hands was imminent. On, on we rushed, cleaving fog and sea. No chance existed to take a sun sight. I suppose the Cap'n was smelling his way in. Never having taken an observation since she left the icefields, yet square to the Notch the *Eagle* sped.

From miles at sea, gulls began trailing us in with plaintive cries. No doubt they scented our cargo. Eagerly I watched the dim, black iron cliffs, now beginning to trickle with rivulets of spring, here or there touched with a breath of verdure amid still-clinging patches of snow. I saw Cabot Tower, the Sugarloaf heights, and knew it was but a question of minutes now till I should once more tread solid earth.

We drew up swiftly on the land, up toward St. John's, where soon the sealers, having unloaded the fat, would be carrying off their sea chests on little two-wheeled carts, going aboard schooners bound to their northern outports, or taking train for far places whence they could tramp home again; St. John's, where boxes and barrels of flippers and carcasses would soon be seen, together with shaggy hunters trailing "gads o' fippers" from black hands; St. John's, where so ragged, greasy, and bewhiskered was I that at first my acquaintances knew me not and mistook me for a tramp. A tousle-haired and particularly degraded-looking specimen of tramp, at that!

In through the Narrows we swept, with people shouting, waving at us from dour heights. Our siren yelled, flushing up coveys of echoes from cliffs. The *Cambrian*, a British man-o'-war lying immensely grim amid a ruck of harbour craft, lowered her ensign to us. We dipped our colours in reply as we slowed to a South Side wharf.

All seemed confused to me—a shouting and a running, with unintelligible greetings hurled back and forth. Ropes sprangled; men on the wharf dragged a splashing hawser, made it fast. A winch began to bucket and chatter.

I seized my ditty bag, slung it over my shoulder, and as the *Eagle* touched her berth, made a jump for it. With a glad shock my feet thudded to a grease-soaked wharf. Oh, wonderful and never to be forgotten contact!

My voyage with the Vikings of the Ice was over, finished and done with, for ever and a day!

And now, with some verses that I wrote aboard the *Terra Nova* one night of ravening blizzard, I shall for all time say farewell to

THE SEALERS OF NEWFOUNDLAND

Ho! We be the Sealers of Newfoundland!
We clear from a snowy shore,
Out into the gale with our steam and sail,
Where tempest and tumult roar.
We battle the floe as we northward go,
North, from a frozen strand!
Through lead, through bay, we fight our way,
We Sealers of Newfoundland!

Yea, we be the Sealers of Newfoundland!
We laugh at the blinding dark;
We mock the wind as we fling behind
The wilderness hoar and stark.
We jest at death, at the icy breath
Of the Pole, by the north lights spanned.
In a wild death dance we dice with chance,
We Sealers of Newfoundland!

Sealers, ho! Sealers of Newfoundland,
With engines begrimed and racked,
With groaning beams where the blue ice gleams,
We push through the growlers packed.
With rifle, with knife we press our strife;
What lubber shall understand
The war we fight in the ghostly night?
Aye, Sealers of Newfoundland!

The ice glows red where our skin boots tread,
And crimson the grinding floes.
From mast we scun till our race be run,
Where the Labrador current goes.

From ship we spring to the pans that swing;
By stalwarts our deck is manned.
O'er the blood-red road the sculps are towed
By the Sealers of Newfoundland.

Oh, some may sail with a southern gale;
Some may fare east or west.
The North is ours, where the white storm lowers,
Wild North that we love the best!
O North, we ken that ye make us men;
Your glory our eyes have scanned.
Hard men, we be, of the Frozen Sea,
We Sealers of Newfoundland!

Bitterly bold through the stinging cold
We vanquish the naked North.
We make our kill with an iron will,
Where the great white frost stalks forth.
"Onward!" we cry, where the bare bergs lie,
Dauntless our course is planned.
With blood, with sweat, scant bread we get,
We Sealers of Newfoundland!

"Starb'rd!" and "Steady!" and "Port!" we steer;
Press on through the grinding pan!
We labour and muck for a fling at luck,
Each man of us, God! a man!
We cheer at the bawl of the whitecoats all,
We labour with knife and hand,
With rope and gaff. At the North we laugh,
We Sealers of Newfoundland!

Where the old dog hood and the old harps' brood
Lie out on the raftered pack,
We tally our prey. Then away and away,
Men, ho! for the homeward track!
Till the day dawns near when a rousing cheer
Shall greet us, as red we stand
On the decks that come to our Island home,
We Sealers of Newfoundland!

THE END

GLOSSARY OF COMMONLY USED
NEWFOUNDLAND WORDS AND PHRASES

GLOSSARY OF COMMONLY USED
NEWFOUNDLAND WORDS AND PHRASES

A-be. Be.
Abroad. Scattered; dispersed.
Aburd. Aboard; sometimes means the cabin.
A-dere. There.
Adurt. Across.
A'eed. Ahead.
Affliction case. Sad case.
Age. Edge.
Ahl. All.
Ahl of a slam. Violently.
Ahltogedder. Altogether.
Ahl to pieces. Thoroughly (I knows un a. t. p.).
Airsome. Cold; stormy.
Alang. Along; aboard.
Alee (Goin' a.). Breaking loose.
Andramartens. Pranks.
'Andy to a man. Vexing him.
Angyshore. A worthless fellow.
'Ape. Heap.
'Ar. Hair.
'Arn. To earn; a herring.
Arr. Any.
Arr'ntall. Any one at all.
Ash cat. One of ash gang.
Ashore. Aboard.
'Atch. (To draw or pull de 'a. over). To duck under water.
Ate. Eat.
'Ate. Heat.
Av'lidge. Average.
'Azy. Easy.

Babtize. Baptize.
Back weight. Weight subtracted from sculps for adherent flesh.
Bad word (To have the b. w.). To talk in a pessimistic manner.
Bake. A meddlesome busybody.
Baked-apple berry. A small edible berry: the *rubus chamaemorus*.
Ballycatters. Heavy shore ice.
Banished. Exterminated.
Barbarous. Bad.
Bare. "Broke"; without money. **(B. water.** Open water.)

Bark (To b. a sail or cordage). To boil these with hemlock bark.
Barn. Born.
Barrelman. Man who spies for seals.
Barrycatters. *Cf.* ballycatters.
Barrow. To carry on a barrow.
Bart. Brought.
Batch. A fall of snow.
Bate. Beat or beaten.
Bater. A beating seal; young migrating seal.
Battycatters. *Cf.* ballycatters.
Baulk. A sea fowl; otherwise the haigdown.
Bay-noddies. Outport men.
Bay tilt. Rough hovel in isolated place.
Beater. *Cf.* bater.
Beddamer. A third-year harp; also a second-year hood.
Bedflies. Bedbugs; lice.
Bedlamer. Bellamer; *cf.* beddamer.
Belly an' back. Odd ones; not a pair.
Bend round. To dissipate.
Bet. Beaten.
Bet out. Exhausted.
Bibber. To shiver.
Bid. Stayed.
Bill. Earnings; a bell.
Binnacy. Cross; ill-tempered.
Bitch. A female seal.
Bitch and dogbody. Cakes made of flour, pork fat, and molasses.
Bite. Share of money.
Bizun. A broom.
Black. Sunburned.
Black-backs. Fourth-year harp seals.
Blank (To make a b.). Get no seals.
Blasses. Blasts.
Blay. Brown.
Bloody pinnacles. Ice pinnacles marked with blood or entrails.
Blow de roast. Tell.
Blow up. Fatten.
Bluchers. Old-fashioned matches.
Blue drop. Open water.
Body-bulk. Main weight.

Boil at. Keep at (as *e. g.*, a bottle).

Bore up. Bear up for home.

Bosthoon. Fool.

Bote. Both.

Bottled. Jammed in the ice.

Bow together. Said of two ships approaching at an angle.

Braffus. Breakfast.

Braychey. Brackish.

Braychin'. Jumping (said of seals in water).

Breeze. Gale; breed.

Brewis. Boiled hard-tack.

Bridgemaster. Officer who transmits orders from scunner to wheel.

Brile. Confusion; mess.

Brin bag. Gunnysack.

Bring-up. End.

Bruck. Broken.

Brud. Brother.

Brudge. Bridge; porch of a house.

Buff (In de naked b.). Stripped.

Bull. Bulwarks; rails.

Bumper trip. Big load.

Bun o' bread. Loaf.

Burn. A blister; scar.

Burned. Frozen.

Burned down. Stopped for the night.

Burned out. All coal exhausted.

Butter-bitch. Man in charge of the butter.

B'y. Boy.

By de 'eed. Sinking at bows.

By dis reason. On this account.

Cad o' baccy. Box of tobacco.

Calibogus. Liquor made of spruce beer, rum, and molasses.

Call (A good bit o' c.). Considerable business.

Can. A boiler.

Cannonball. Old duff.

Capelin. A small fish often employed for cod bait.

'Cardin to. On account of.

Carey. Queer.

Carner. Corner.

Carner boys. City youths or men.

Carry de kay. Carry the key; *i. e.*, be last ship to enter port.

Cat. A stillborn seal.

Catamaran. A large sled.

Catty. Active, energetic.

'Cay. To decay.

Codology. Fooling; "jollying."

Chair. Cheer; to be "up in chair" is to be cheerful.

Chaw-round. A discussion.

Chew de fat. To talk.

Chickers. Checkers.

Chin-waggin'. Talking.

Chip. To peel potatoes or cut tobacco.

Chisel. A boot nail, worn to keep from slipping on ice.

Chisel bar. Iron bar to chop ice.

Chock. Nearly up to, or in sight of; to change about (The wind **chocked**).

Chafe. Vexation; to bother.

Choil. Child.

Chop. *Cf.* chock; 2d definition.

Civil. Good, as applied to weather, seasons, etc.

Clane. Clean.

Cl'ar. Clear.

Cl'ar drop. Open water.

Clever cat. A good stillborn seal.

Click. The ship is going fast (A good c. on 'er).

Close aburd to dat. Nearly that.

Clumper. A heaved-up formation of ice.

Coaleys. Playing cards.

Coady-duff. Duff with boiled molasses.

Coalies. *Cf.* coadies.

Coarse. Bad (as applied to wind, weather, etc.).

Coat a ship ahl over. Put her deep in the water.

Cobbin' (Give 'em a good c.). To beat; to slaughter.

Cockabaloo. A bully; boss.

Cock an' 'ens. A kind of shellfish.

Cod. This word is applied in many senses, all meaning to fool, deceive, or "jolly." 'Aul de c. off a man; codology; de law's a c.; a c. of a feller; to c.; these are some of the many applications of the word. The general meaning is derogatory.

Cod 'auler. A derogatory name for a Newfoundlander.

Coffer. A lie; tall story.

Cold. To cool.

Cold smack. A hard blow.

Come agin. To offset or overbalance.

Come back on. *Cf.* come agin.

Complaint. A disease, often tuberculosis.

Complete 'and. A good worker; clever; efficient.

Conkerbills. Icicles, usually on eaves.

Copy. To jump on loose ice.

Cornder. Corner.

Corn (Ain't got a c.). Has no sense.

'Count. Consideration; liking. (Take wonnerful 'c. o'. To like; esteem.)

Courageous. Painful, hard (Me naze is c.)
Court work. Legal proceedings.
Covey fellers. Outport men.
Cowed out. Tired out.
Cowly. Hard, severe.
Cozy. Fast; energetic.
Cracker. A large seal (Rig'lar ole c.)
Cracky. Khaki; also a small dog.
Cr'ased. Creased.
Crawley's curse. The six of hearts.
Cribbage. To steal.
Cristle. Gristle.
Crool. Cruel.
Crop. Outfit.
Cropped. Outfitted for cruise.
Cross-handed. Alone. (Work c. Work alone.)
Crunnocks. Small pieces of wood.
Crust. Crusted.
Cuff. A mitten with all fingers together.
Cuffer. Cf. Coffer.
Curanteen. Quarantine.
Currier. A third-year hood seal.
Curvey. A quilt.
Cut. A slaughter; a direction; a reduction in pay.
Cuttin'. A slaughter; a reduction in pay.

Dark cake. Strong, heavy tobacco.
Darn. Dawn; a drink (A d. o' rum).
Dart (A hard d.). A hard time.
Dat. This.
Daughter. The dotard seal.
Day. The day's quota, or work.
Dead spot. A big spot of seals.
Deck-rowters., Second master watches.
Deed. Dead.
Desp'rit. Very.
Devil's bulk. Major portion.
Dimmyjohn. Demijohn.
Dinamore. Dynamo.
Dip. Said of young seals taking to the water.
Dippin'-time. Time at which young seals dip.
Disaster spring. 1914.
Disgusted. Sorry.
Dob (To take a d.). Go.
Dod (A straight d.). A direct course.
Dog. Gunner's assistant; a male seal.
Dog. To follow.
Dog wedder. Bad weather.
Donkey. Winch.
Donkey man. Fourth engineer, or oiler.
Doss-down. A nap; sleep.

Douse. To fool.
'Dout. Without; unless.
Doze. These; these ships.
Doze days. Now.
Draf. Load; rubbish.
Drave. To drive; have driven.
Dreshed. Dressed.
Driet. Quality of drying (No d. in de wedder).
Drill. Work; to work.
Drinch. To drench.
Dror de vog. To draw the fog; i. e., smoke tobacco.
Drung. A patch of woods.
Duckish. Dusk; twilight.
Duff bag. Canvas bag in which puddings are boiled.
Dunch. Heavy; soggy (as of bread).
Dungeon. The under forecastle.
Dwoy. A sudden shower.
Dyin' about. Very fond of.

'Eed. Head; ahead; first (De 'e. Spring).
Ellery. Elderly.
'Ellety-up. Very fast.
'Ellum. Helm.
Engreaved. Engraved.
Even so. Common for "Yes."
Every. Very.
Evvery. Every.
Evveryt'ing. All to pieces (Me gaff went e.).

Fadom out. To explain.
Fair. Very.
Fairity. Rather well or good; fairish.
Faith. To fade.
Faitour. A lazy fellow.
Fall back. To go in debt.
Farden. Farthing.
Farm. Form.
Farmer. A poor sailor.
Fat. Seals; sculps.
Fat pig's back, on the. Prosperous.
Fausty. Mouldy.
Faychure. Feature; to resemble.
Fear. Fair.
'Feared. Afraid.
Feller. Son.
'Fin. To offend.
Find. To feel.
Fipper. Flipper.
Fire. Cartridges. (To make f. To quarrel or fight. To f. a pipe. To light it.)
Fire spanels. Sparks.
Fishes' faces. Cod heads.

Fish room. A cod-curing establishment.

Fisses. Fists.

Fit. To fill and prepare torchlights.

Fit-out. Outfit.

Flagged off. Decorated with flags (said of a ship).

Flags (Putt de f. on). Decorate, in sign of success.

Flake. Fish-drying ground or staging.

Flakes o' money. Lots of money.

Flankers. Large sparks.

Flaus! Exclamation denoting violent or sudden action.

Flaus down. To go down or sink suddenly.

Flip. Going fast (A good f. on 'er starn) (said of a ship).

Floaters. Labrador codders who move during the summer.

Flog de time a'eed. Set it forward.

Flop. To faint.

Flute. Mouth.

Flyin' light. Without much ballast, coal, or cargo.

Flyin' ship. A fine, smart ship.

Fooley. A fool.

Foreright. Careless.

Foxy. Red-haired.

Fray. Free.

Froster. A boot nail worn to prevent slipping on ice.

Fruz. Confusion; turmoil; to frizz.

Fudge (An awful f.). Great confusion or trouble.

Full. To fill.

Full rig. Best clothes.

Full-sledged. Full-fledged.

Fuss (A 'ard f.). Trouble, difficulty.

Gad. A string (of fish or flippers).

Gadderin'. A collection; a boil or swelling.

Gallus. Suspenders.

Gandies. Pancakes made with pork fat and molasses.

Gansey. A jersey.

Garagee. A free-for-all fight.

'Gard of. On account of.

Garmaphone. Phonograph.

Garricky. Trouble; confusion.

Gaves. Gaffs.

Gaze. A shelter for shooting birds; aim.

Geel. Gale.

Geeze. Cf. gaze. Also, a spymaster.

Gert. Great.

Gert-time wedder. Good weather.

Get it out on one. Get even with one.

Givin' out produce. Giving credit.

Glin. Dazzle of the ice.

Glitter. Frozen mist on rig; ice on rig.

Glutch. To swallow; a swallow.

Go. A gang; to defy.

Go away. Leave ship.

Goat's house. The quarter hatch.

Gob. Mouth.

Gobbet. A morsel.

Gob stick. Stick for prizing-up and carrying sculps.

Gommel. A fool.

Gozaroo. Fellow.

Grase. Grease.

Grayback. A louse.

Greasy-jackets. Sealers.

Grog bag. Toper.

Gross. Large.

Guffy. A fool.

Gulch. Hollow of waves.

Gumbean. A small lump of tobacco.

Gurdy. A winch.

Gurry. Seal oil, ground out by ship rolling.

Habbage. A savage.

Haigdown. A kind of sea bird.

Hail. Estimated number of seals. (To h. for. To report estimate, as "She hails fer 25,000").

H'agle. The Eagle.

Hand. A flipper.

Hapse. To hasp.

Ha'r. Hair.

Hard as de hobs o' hell. Very hard.

Harness cask. Locked barrel for food-stuffs.

Harse. Horse.

H'ater fashion. Shaped like a flatiron (said of ice).

Hatchet. An axe.

Haul de cod off a man. To "jolly" him; fool him.

Haype. A heap, a lot.

Hayve. To heave.

Hayve down. To quit.

Hayve one's stummick. To vomit.

Hayve up de cruise. Stop the cruise.

Head. First. Cf. 'eed.

Header. One who cuts heads off fish.

Heading palm. Kind of mitten for heading fish.

Hearty. Strong; rough.

Heel (On de h. of it). As a result of it.

Hell's alley. Very far; nowhere.

Hell's flames. Adjective used in many ways (A h.-f. smart man).

Helt too hard. Overworked.

Hicky. A drink.

Higgy. Cf. hicky.

High-liner. Leading ship or man, in number of seals or fish taken.

H'ile. Oil.

Hippers. Nails to attach trousers to suspenders.

Hocks. Boots.

Hoffy. Foolish; crazy.

Hoi. High.

Hold out. Persevere.

Hold up de harm. Acknowledge the blame.

Holus-bolus. Hastily.

Honest-up? Really?

Hoppers. Spyglasses.

Hot. To heat; used also as past tense of "to hit."

Hot seals. Freshly killed seals.

Hoven. Hove; heaved.

Humgumption. Sense.

Humours. Traces.

Hungry-lookin' ice. Lacking in seals.

Hunt a man. To "jolly" him.

Huv. Hove; heaved.

Huv it down. Stopped it.

Hyse. To hoist.

Hyssen. *Cf.* hyse.

Ice candle. Icicle.

Ice claw. Kind of anchor to hold ship in ice.

'Id. Head.

In it. The way to do it (That ain't i.i.).

Infectious. Harmful.

Inside. At St. John's.

Inside water. Water between ice and land.

Intrude on. To bother.

In 'gard of. On account of.

In bunk. Sick.

Jack-a-tar. A west-coast Newfoundlander of French extraction.

Jacket-warmer. A warm place.

Jade. To vex; annoy.

Jag. A lot ("A big j. o' fat").

Jake. All right.

Jakers! Common ejaculation.

Jam. To bother; puzzle; outwit; defeat.

Jammed up fer. Lacking.

Jammer. A jammed condition. (A pure j. on de land." A condition where ice is hard on the land.)

Jib. The nose.

Jife. A direction.

Jig. Scales or stillyards.

Jink. To "hoodoo." ("To make a j. of it." To fail.)

Jinker. A "Jonah."

Joggle. A piece cut out of anything.

Jonnick. I swear, or affirm.

Jowler. Lucky or successful person.

Joy-guns. Guns fired at festivities.

Judy. A girl; woman (rather disparaging).

Kay. Key.

Keecorn. The Adam's apple.

Kenat. Fool.

Kindim. Condemn.

Kinductor. Conductor.

Kink (Putt a k. in 'er). Labour hard at wheel or elsewhere.

Kipp. Keep.

Kipp against. Offset.

Kitch. Catch.

Knobbly. Rough.

Knocked out about. Worried.

Knot. A hard ice formation.

Knotty wedder. Stormy.

Knowledgeable. Intelligent; learned.

Laid down. Said of a seal brought in without being completely sculped.

Landwash. Shore.

Lane. Lean.

Lang. Long (L. in de water. Sunk deep—said of a ship).

Larry string. A small string of seals.

'Lassy loaf. Bread and molasses.

Lay. A chance.

Lay back. To loaf.

Layde. To lead; a lead; or open stretch of water.

Laysses'. Least.

Layve. Leave.

Leper. The *Leopard.*

Level. Sunk deep in the water.

'Levener. An eleven-o'clock lunch.

Lewardly. *Cf.* looardly.

Lickshur. Lecture.

Lie-down. A nap; sleep.

Liff. Leave; left.

Light. To lighten; said of weight, clothing, or fog.

Light cake. Light, mild tobacco.

Line off. To sketch.

Litted. Lighted.

Live 'ard aginst. To bear a grudge; to blame.

Live swiles. Freshly killed seals.

Liverish. Sickly.

Livin' squads. Large quantities.

Livyere. A native of Newfoundland; usually an outport man.

Loaf. Soft bread.

Lobby. The quarter hatch.

Lobscolla-meed an' waggle-me-jaw-water-talk. Nonsense.

Lobscouse. A kind of stew.

Log-loaded. Fully loaded.
Logger load. A full load.
Logy. Hot.
Long gun. Large telescope.
Long-tripper. A captain who makes long voyages.
Looard. Come to; get into trouble.
Looardly. Clumsy or stupid; unlucky.
Look-after. Damages.
Look-up. Prospect.
Loose leg (Have a l. l.). Be free.
Lost. Loss.
Lousy. Said of whitecoats beginning to lose their first pelt and turn "scruffy," or brown.
Low-line (To be on de l.-l.). To have the fewest fish or seals.
Low-liner. Man or ship which has fewest, as above.
Loy. Lye.
Lug. An ear.
Lun. The lee of anything.
'Luninum. Aluminum.

Maggoty. Drunk.
Male. Meal.
Man Above. God.
Man down. To take off opponent's pieces at checkers.
Manus. A mutiny; to mutiny.
Mark out. To sketch.
Marn. Morning.
Martal. Mortal.
Mashy. Soft.
Massarge. Trouble. (I putt de m. to 'em. I troubled or vexed them.)
Mawzy. Dull or close (said of weather).
Med. Made.
Merry-me-got. A bastard.
Middle. To meddle.
Midnight glory. A heavy quilt.
Mind. To remember.
Mired. Tired out.
Mitt. A kind of mitten with separate place for forefinger.
Moider. To vex; annoy; trouble; overwork.
Moil, or moild. A mild, warm spell.
Monch. To play truant, loaf.
Mope. A foolish fellow.
Muckered. Tired out.
Muckery. Trouble; confusion.
Muckle up. Haul up.
Mug-up. A "feed"; to eat; often in the sense of a lunch, rather than a heavy "scoff," or regular meal.
Mushels. Mussels.

Nade. Need.
Nailers. Busy as n.; very busy.

Nard. North.
Narr. No, none.
Nars'ls. Nostrils.
Narth. North.
Naze. Knees.
Nickel. A motion-picture show.
Niggin'. Annoying; hitting at.
Nippin' (To cut one bloody n.). Cut one short.
Nipshun. The Neptune.
Nit. A net.
No'd. North.
Noddy water. Rough water.
Nogg-head. Motherless young seal.
Nonplush. Nonplus (Dat ketched me too much on a n.).
Nonsinse (Don't be n.). Don't talk or act foolishly.
Nook of a pan. A small pan of ice.
Norrid. North.
Notch. Entrance to St. John's harbour.
Nothren. Northern.
Nudge. To urge; bother.
Nunch bag. Small canvas bag for use on ice.
Nurr. Another.

Odd days. Some o' doze; sometime.
Offer. A chance.
Offshoot. To offset.
Ole B'y. The devil.
Ole granny. A kellock anchor (made of sticks and stones lashed together).
Ole man's ice. Smooth ice.
Omadaun. A fool.
Omaloor. Cf. omadaun.
On de savin' hand. Economical.
Ondly. Only.
Onshook. Cf. omadaun.
Or. Are.
Oppers. Cf. hoppers.
Orvis. Harvest.
Oxter. Arm-pit.

Paddle. Oar.
Pan. A cake of ice; a heap or pile of skins; to gather skins into pans.
Pant. To heave (said of the ocean).
Parlour. Barrel on mast.
Patch. A spot of seals.
Patienate. To be patient.
Patrick's brush. Storm on or about March 17th.
'Pend. Depend.
'Pendex. Appendix.
Perish. To die; rot; suffer.
Perishin'. A killing; abuse.
Pew. Berth; one-tined fork for pitching fish.

Pick. A bit. (Narr p. None. Me stummick's beginnin' to p. To be hungry.)

Pick pans. To gather heaps of skins.

Pierhead jump. A quick start.

Pinnacle. A raised ice formation.

Pinnacle tanks. Tanks on ship to melt ice.

Pinnacle tea. Water from melted ice.

Pinnackly. In a "raftered-up" or elevated condition (said of ice).

Pint and peas. Low rations.

Piper. A kettle.

Pipper. To pepper.

Pitch. To go down, settle down, as of birds.

Pliny. Plenty.

Plumper. A full load.

Pool. To pull.

Poor. Adj. usually prefixed to name of all deceased persons.

Pound. A storage enclosure for coal or skins.

Powder-devil. A rag enclosing charge of powder.

'Preciate. To like.

Predujiced. Prejudiced.

Prent. Print.

Primin' (De first p.). The first catch or lot of seals.

Prosperous. Lucky at seal hunting.

Proud. Glad.

Pry. A stick for prizing up and carrying skins.

Puckaloon. A fool.

Puckerin'. Sickly; sick.

Puddick. Paunch; spirits.

Pummely. Soft; loose.

Pummy. Soft, ground-up ice or fat (To go to pummy. To become like this).

Punch (A 'ard p.). A hard time.

Punchin'. Attack; slaughter.

Punishment. Embarrassment.

Punt. A lifeboat; sometimes a two-masted vessel.

Pure drop. Open water.

Putt. A small quantity.

Putt in fires. Build fires.

Putt up money. To save.

Quananteen. Quarantine.

Quare. Queer.

Quash. To put down.

Quate. Quiet.

Quieten down, or out. To make quiet.

Rack. A comb.

Racket. A hunt, a " time."

Rackly. Directly; immediately.

Rafter up. To rise (said of dice, rising as result of pressure).

Ragged-jacket. Young seal beginning to change coat.

Raisin' fer. Very eager for.

Ral. A mild term of reproach.

Rale. Real.

Rally. A sortie after seals.

Rate. Right; exactly; very.

Rattlin' it (Dat's r. i.). Good work or hunting.

Ravinis. Ravenous.

Raw. A rough, hard fellow.

Rayche. To reach. (Rayche to. To afford.)

Reach to. Cf. rayche to.

Reeve. To drive or carry.

Rent. A space of open water.

Ride. To "jolly." (To take out fer a r. The same.)

Rifter. A space of open water among ice floes.

Rightify. Rectify.

Rig-out. Outfit.

Ringbolt to. Steady or attentive to.

Rint. Cf. rent.

Rise. To raise; to promote. (To r. de smoke of a steamer. To sight the smoke).

Ritch. Reach; give.

Roarer. The Aurora.

Rockery-ware. Crockery.

Rookery. Fight; confusion; turmoil.

Room bert'. A berth given on a sealer by a sealing firm.

Roomers. Cf. stationers.

Root. Trouble; a drink; damage. (To take r. To run away.)

Rosen. Rose.

Rot hole. A soft place in the ice.

Rote. The sound of the sea, or breakers.

Round-seal. A seal killed and ripped but not sculped.

Rowt, a 'ard. A hard time, or labour.

Rudder. Rather.

Rudge. A ridge or hill.

Run to h'ile. Said of skins grinding or melting down to oil; in general, spoil, ruin.

Rusties. Second-year harps.

Rusty-jackets. Cf. rusties.

Rusty rangers. Second-year harps with rounded spots that have not yet opened to harp-shape.

Saddle with. To agree.

Saddleback. A fourth-year harp; a louse.

Saddler. *Cf.* saddleback; first definition.

Salmon pip. Salmon guts.

Salt, fresh. Ice.

Salt down. To ice.

Sample. Example.

Sarnly. Certainly.

Sayzin'. A bandage.

Scad of snow. A flurry; light fall.

Scaldy. Epithet of abuse. (Son of a scaldy. The same.)

Scarrited. Scared.

Scat. *Cf.* scad.

Scatter. A few.

Scheme. Mischief.

Scoff. To eat heartily; a hearty meal.

Sconch lamp. A lamp to hang on a wall.

Scoppers. Scuppers. (Scoppers-in. Deeply loaded.)

Scote. To drag or tow; a tow.

Scouse. Kind of stew.

Scrapple. A lot of seals.

Screecher. A sunburned seal; a nogghead, *q. v.*

Screechin' (To go s.). To get excited.

Scrob off. To rub or scrub off.

Scrubblin'. Scrubbing.

Scruffy. Said of seals when coat is partly shed.

Scuddy wedder. Windy weather.

Scudge o' snow. Flurry.

Scull. School of fish or seals.

Sculp. To skin a seal; the skin and fat of a seal.

Sculpin'-knife. Knife for sculping.

Scun. To direct ship's course from aloft.

Scunner. Man who scuns.

Scurwinks. Kind of sea fowl.

Scutters. Hind flippers of seal.

Seal dog. Iron hook for hauling seals aboard.

Seal finger. Infection caused by seal fat.

Sediment. Sentiment.

Selvage. Edge of the icefield.

Shack (A rough s.). Rough or hard time.

Shad of snow. Light fall.

Shade. To shed.

Sharooshed. Taken aback; surprised; disappointed.

Shayt' knife. Sheath knife.

Shayth knife. Shaythin' knife. *Cf.* shayt' knife.

Sheen. Shin.

Sheer. To share.

Sheet knife. *Cf.* shayt' knife.

Sheeve. To back water.

Sheila's brush. Storm about the 18th of March.

Shipped out. Troubled; distressed; afflicted by loss.

Shockin'. Very.

Shooler. Fellow. Usually in a pejorative sense, as in phrase: "sneaky shooler."

Shore. Shorn.

Shore-crew. Crew remaining on ship.

Shot (A grand s.). Good luck; speed.

Shove-off. A meal.

Shuck unner de pan. Slide under ice.

Shuff. Shove.

Sick vessel. One without coal.

Side sticks. Horizontal beams along outside of sealing ship.

Sidewalk (On de s.). In smooth water.

Sign. Indication of seals.

Sile. Seal.

Sill. To sell.

Silver glitter. Ice on rig.

Sish. New and very thin ice.

Skein of ice. String or lot of ice. (Skein of seals. Line or quantity of seals.)

Sketch off. To photograph.

Skiff. A schooner.

Skinnies. Skinny woppers, *q. v.*

Skinny, it's. It is bad, unfavourable, dangerous.

Skinny woppers. Esquimau skin boots.

Skip. Captain.

Skirr. Hurry.

Skungeon. A garbage bucket; dirty ship.

Slam, ahl of a. Violently; suddenly.

Slant. A chance.

Slap. To complain.

Slatchy water. Water with loose ice in it.

Sleeve vest. A reefer.

Slew (One s. o' y'r heye). One look.

Slindge. To loaf.

Slindger. A loafer.

Sling or slingo. Ejaculation denoting sudden motion, or noise, as *e. g.*, an explosion.

Slinky. Thin.

Slob. Thin, loose ice.

Slopped. Drunk.

Slovey. Soft.

Slup. Slipped.

Slut. A kind of kettle; broken hard-bread.

Slut lamp. A primitive form of lamp.

Smack. A while; hardship. (A 'ard s. A hard time.)

Smallagen. A large seal.

Smart. To suffer.
Smellers. Seals' whiskers.
Smutty bitch. A female seal that has never pupped.
Snap. To miss fire.
Snick. A "dud" cartridge.
Snifter. A drink.
Snog. To steal.
So. Such. (S. wonnerful chums. Such great friends.)
Softs. Bare feet.
Soggy. Deep in the water.
Soize. Size.
Sommons. Summons.
Sopped. Drunk.
Sove. Saved.
Sparable. A boot nail worn to prevent slipping.
Spare. Left over.
Spern wheel. A sperm whale.
Spike. A stick for handling sculps.
Spill. A time or while; a lot; a rest; to rest; to bring or carry.
Spilled. Scattered.
Spit (Deed s. on). To have accurate aim at.
Spittin' image. Exact likeness.
Splitter. One who splits cod.
Sport. A sealer who ships without a ticket.
Sportin' ship. A fine and smart ship.
Spot. A patch of seals.
Spottedy. Spotted.
Sprayed. Chapped.
Spun out. Exhausted.
Spurt. Activity or quantity. (A s. o' singin', o' water, etc.)
Squad. A quantity. (Livin' s. Large quantities.)
Square bender. A debauch.
Squat. To crush.
Squat 'atch. The quarter hatch.
Squatter. Labrador codder who settles down on shore for the summer.
Sringe. Syringe.
Stabber pole. Long ironshod pole to shove ice away from ship.
Stage. A wharf.
Stain o' rum. Drink or small quantity of rum.
Standin' ice. Heavy ice.
Starber pole. Cf. stabber pole.
Start. Point. (S. of a gaff. The point of it. S. of a berg. Part projecting under water.)
Stationers. Cf. squatters.
Steamin'. Coal for steaming.
Stick. Speed. (We got a good s. on us.)
Stick-up feller. Man without a ticket. Cf. sport.

Stigger. Full load.
Stim. Stem.
Sting-go. Strong liquor.
Stip. Step.
Stole away. Stowed away. (He s. a., stowed away.)
Straight. Deep in the water (said of a ship).
Straighten out. To pay debts.
Strap. Rope for fastening sculps for loading; a reckoning of ten skins.
Strick. To strike.
String. Cable.
Stritch. Stretch (said of ice "going abroad").
Studdy. To steady.
Stunned. Confused; intoxicated.
Stunt. Cf. stunned.
Suddren. Southern.
Suent. Bending pliant.
Summer. The cod-fishing season, or work.
Sunday side (To get on de s. s.). To get into one's good graces.
Sunday men. Men who refuse to work on Sunday.
Superstitious. Suspicious.
Surge o' fat. A large quantity.
Surger. Cf. surge o' fat.
Swag. To carry.
Swatch. Open water in ice; to shoot seals in swatches.
Swate. Sweet.
Sway. "Dash." (Cut a 'ill of a s. To show off; to cut a dash.)
Swear blind. Swear vehemently to the truth of a statement.
Sweep. A kind of lottery, based on estimated catch of seals.
Swile. Seal; to hunt seals.
Swile-bait. Seal food.
Swill. Swell in the ice.
Swim (Ahl in de s. o' de day's work). All in the job.
Swindge. To singe.
Swit. Sweat.
Switchel. Boiled-over tea.
Synagogue. Bunk or berth.

Tailed off. Chosen.
Take. To get angry; be sensitive; a sensitive person. ("Take it on." Assume the blame. "Take off." To make a certain speed, e. g., "De ship takes off eight knots." "A hard take." A hard time. "Take to." Begin, e. g., "He took to go." "Take-up." Loading.)
Talk to a girl. Court.
Tally down. To stow and record sculps.

Tally stick. Stick for recording sculps.
Tarch, or tarchlight. A lantern without globe, for use on ships or ice.
Tare. *Cf.* "back weight."
Tarmentin'. Tormenting.
Tarred up wid de lazy stick. Afflicted with laziness.
Tarry. To stay.
Tawnies (Black as t.) Very black.
Tearin' crowd. A gang of hard workers.
Teller. Tiller.
'Tempt on. To make an effort to get.
T'etis. The *Thetis.*
Teveen. A patch on a boot.
Tibb's Eve. Never.
T'ick. Thick or foggy.
Tickle. A narrow waterway.
Tight. Hard. (To work t. Work hard.)
Tilt. A small hut.
Tinted. Tainted.
Tizzer. Comparative of "'tis" (Dar 'tis, an' can't be no t.).
Toasses. Pieces of toast.
To'gal'n house. Forecastle.
Togged off. With all sails set.
Tolt. A sharp hill.
Tomahawk, tom'awk. A hatchet.
Tootootler. A teetotaler.
Top'us. *Cf.* to'gal'n house.
Top tanks. *Cf.* pinnacle tanks.
Tored. Tore.
Touched. Ice blind.
Tow. A quantity of skins laced for towing.
Toweard. Toward.
Towustin' round. Going around.
Trapline. Line of traps, on land.
Trash. Nonsense.
Travel. A trip from the vessel.
T'reaten. To promise.
Treckly. Immediately.
Trimly. Trembling.
Troo up wid. Through with.
Trot. To "jolly."
Tuck. Took; stern of a vessel.
T'um-up. A hatchet.
Turly. Thoroughly.
Turned over. Sick.
Turnout. Exact number of seals in cargo.
Turr. A kind of sea fowl.
Tyfoy. Typhoid fever.

Un. Him; it.
Unner. Under.
Unriggler. Irregular.
Urr. Other.

Vaddum. Fathom.
Vate. Vat.
Ven. Fin.
Venimis. Eager or anxious.
Vexed on. Angry at.
Viddum. *Cf.* vaddum.
Vifty. Fifty.
Vile. File.
Vir. Fir.
Vog. Fog.

Wad. A quantity (A w. of ice; a w. o' swiles).
Waddin'. Scarce; few seals.
Wadhams (Spring o' de W.) Spring when seals were plentiful at the Wadham Islands; 1852.
Wad'n'm? Wasn't it? Wasn't he?
Wag o' say. A bit of wave, or sea.
Wagon (Go wid de w.). Go with a tow of seals.
Wahrm. Warm; a warming up.
Wahrm flaw. A worthless fellow.
Wahrm swiles. Seals freshly killed.
Wake. Weak.
Wangles. Beams at bow, beneath bowsprit, for men to stand on when clearing away ice.
Washout. A failure.
Water bear. Polar bear.
Water-horse. Cod at a certain stage of preparation.
Water welps. Sores on hands or wrists caused by salt water.
Way off de line. Much mistaken.
Wayhead. Headway.
Wedder. Weather.
Wedder age. The weather edge or outside of the ice.
Wedderish. Threatening.
Weepin'. Leaking.
Welt. To drink hard.
Whack. A share; a hard time. (Dead w. Great difficulty.)
Wheel. Whale.
Whelpin' bag. Seals' afterbirth.
Whelpin' ice. Ice suitable for seals to pup on.
Whip it. Go fast.
Whipline. Rope used in loading sculps, to draw out the "wire" and hold sculps from dragging on ship's side.
White b'y. Fine fellow.
Whitecoat. A young harp seal.
Whitecoat cut. A slaughter of young harps.
Whitenose. Man spending first winter in Newfoundland.

Whiteycoat, whiteyjacket. *Cf.* white-
 coat.
Wind-rod. Head into the wind.
Wing pound. Compartment, below, for
 sculps or coal.
Wire. A wire hawser.
Wonnerful. Wonderful; very.
Wonnerful wheeler. A speedy ship.
Wop bag. *Cf.* whelpin' bag.
Wopped out. Flayed; whipped.
Word out a piece. To recite the words
 of it.
Workin' swiles. Killing and pan-
 ning.
Wrinch. Wrench.

Wrinkles. Periwinkles
W'rout. Worn out.

Yaffle. A bundle, bunch.
Yare. There.
Yary. Energetic, quick.
Year. Hear.
Yeard. Heard.
Y'earth. Earth.
Yere. Here.
Youmonia. Pneumonia.
Young fat. Whitecoats.
Youngster. A man on his first sealing
 trip.
Yurred. *Cf*, yeard.